Belleville Sons Honor Roll

Remembering the Men Who Paid for our Freedom

By Anthony Buccino

To Mike Granata!
Thanks for your support

11/2016
Anthony Buccino

BELLEVILLE SONS HONOR ROLL
Remembering the Men Who Paid For Our Freedom

Copyright © 2004, 2012, 2016 by Anthony Buccino and Andrea Buccino

V 3.16

Fourth edition published by

Cherry Blossom Press, PO Box 110252, Nutley NJ 07110

ISBN 978-1470036515

ISBN 1470036517

All rights reserved. No part of this book may be reproduced or transmitted in any form or by any means, electronic or mechanical, including photocopying, recording, or by any information storage and retrieval system, without permission in writing from the copyright holder.

DISCLAIMER: While every effort has been made to check and crosscheck references and sources, conflicts and omissions may occur. We welcome additions, corrections and supplemental information for inclusion in future editions

Photos where available:

Front Cover Photo: Normandy American Cemetery at St. Laurent-sur-Mer, France, Copyright © 2004-2009 by Robert Caruso, creator of VeronaHeroes.com, used with permission. All rights reserved.

Additional photos courtesy George Sbarra REMEMBRANCE collection.

State of New Jersey Dept. of State Div. of Archives & Records Management: World War I Casualties: Descriptive Cards and Photographs.

For more links, visit BellevilleSons.com

BELLEVILLE SONS HONOR ROLL

A Brief History 5

American Revolution 6

War of 1812 16

Civil War 29

Diary of James C. Taylor 33

World War I 49

World War II 57

Letters Home to Belleville 122

Korean War 147

Vietnam War 153

POW Martin S. Frank Returned Safely 167

Peacetime Casualties 173

Streets Named For Local Heroes 177

Names Added to Memorial 179

American Revolution Roll Call 181

Alphabetical by War 186

Chronology 194

Acknowledgements 197

About the Editors 207

Belleville Sons Honor Roll
Published on the 60th Anniversary of D-Day.

Remember these Belleville Sons who perished
in the Normandy invasion and Fortress Europe

Francis C. McEnery, William B. Jones, Ralph Ledogar, Patrick J. Barbone, Herman M. Doell, Albert Lariviere, Carmen Olivo, Lee White, Arthur Burke, Edward R. Henris, Ronald McCormack, Emil Ostrowski, Steveno Mosco, Victor R. Bruegman, John J. Daly, Angelo Guarino, Wallace Reed, Robert Stecker, John Verian, Joseph A. Masi, Patrick J. Hoey, William H. Deighan, Walter Antonik, John L. Smith, Frank Rankin, William Hamilton, George Malizia, William Thetford Jr., Walter A. Nusbaum, Wilfred Potis, John Brown, Frank H. Metzler, Leonard R. Willette, Ernest H. Alden

In Loving Memory of

Pfc. Angelo Mario Buccino

U.S. Army, Americal Division,

Guadalcanal & the South Pacific

Feb. 7, 1941 to Sept. 22, 1945

This book is dedicated to the Belleville sons

who paid for our freedom

with their youth, making the supreme sacrifice

and the high cause they served.

And to all our veterans,

Thank You

A Brief History

In the last century alone, 156 Belleville sons died while in service to their country.

World War II, by far, took the largest toll of 117 young men.

World War I took 20 young lives.

The Korean War took four lives.

The Vietnam War took 11 young lives.

Preserving the peace cost us three, and our most recent, Belleville Sons.

Many names of our fallen are recorded on the war memorial statue base set on a well-manicured strip of land on Union Avenue. Another monument in front of Town Hall lists our 20 fallen from World War I. Another is at St. Peter's Church Cemetery. And yet another plaque at School 7 honors Sgt. Rene Flory "and all other sons of Belleville who made the supreme sacrifice."

Beyond the names of our fallen are their stories.

The young men of Belleville, New Jersey, here listed paid with their lives to prove "freedom is not free."

Our intent is to honor their sacrifice.

Information about our Belleville sons, brothers, fathers, uncles and cousins has been gathered from those same monuments, plus The Belleville Times, and other published, private and government sources.

Additional background and confirmations have been found on reputable Internet sites.

We encourage families, descendants and friends of those listed here to search their attics and storage spaces for newspaper clippings and war era photos of these loved ones. There is still much more to learn about these men and their legacies.

The first edition of this book resulted in several town streets being named for our local heroes and the names of the fallen being etched into the war memorial on Union Avenue.

This second edition has added information and been arranged chronologically.

Please contact us to add content or suggest changes for future editions of this commemorative project.

American Revolution

The Retreat Across the Jerseys

It was the second year of the Revolution, and the Declaration of Independence was but a few months old. Washington's reverses in New York were disheartening. The battle of Long Island was lost on Aug. 27, 1776. Fort Washington fell Nov. 16 and Washington crossed to Fort Lee.

Cornwallis followed over the Hudson, and the Continental army was ordered to abandon Fort Lee and to retreat to the Delaware, "over the Essex Hills." Thus began the memorable "Retreat across the Jerseys" when the patriot army under General Washington and the pursuing British under General Lord Cornwallis marched through the region which we now call Nutley. Washington had hastened from Fort Lee to Hackensack. To reach Newark the Passaic River must be crossed. The only available bridge was at Acquackanonck (Passaic) and the village was rumored to be a "Tory hot-bed." A detachment was sent ahead to hold the bridge and to send on stores and ammunition to Morristown by way of Great Notch. Orders were given to destroy the bridge as soon as the army had crossed. The patriots approached with the British often so near that "the sound of their bugles was heard." Over the rude wooden bridge they tramped and that evening or the next day a force from the neighborhood destroyed the bridge with axes and saws and burned the approaches.

Washington spent one anxious night at Acquackanonck, Nov. 21, 1776. The next day, the 22nd, with 3,500 men he started for Newark along the River Road (along the Passaic River through Second River, now known as Belleville).

Near the northern limits of our area, his forces divided, one column to continue by the River Road, the other to go "over the hills" to Bloomfield. There one brigade remained for several days while another went on to Orange and thence to Newark. Washington spent six days in Newark and on Nov. 28th, proceeded to "Brunswic" (New Brunswick). His headquarters in Newark are uncertain.

Source: HISTORY OF NUTLEY, Elizabeth Stow Brown, 1907

Pursuit of the British

Cornwallis pursued in two divisions. One came from Hackensack to Rutherford, and crossed the Passaic at the ford where Delawanna now is, camping there for several days. The rest of the British army followed Washington through Lodi and Wallington to the bridge to find it destroyed and 3,000 men on guard. They turned and crossed above Passaic Falls. Cornwallis spent a week between Passaic and Newark, a week filled with carousals and revels and forages extending widely inland. He took the River Road to Newark.

"Their advance guards were entering the town by the time our rear got out," wrote Washington from "Brunswic."

Source: HISTORY OF NUTLEY, *Elizabeth Stow Brown, 1907*

Flight of the British in 1778

There was another flight of soldiery through this region in 1778, after the battle of Monmouth, when the British were running before the Americans to reach the Hudson. Skirmishes took place at Belleville and at the restored Acquackanonck Bridge, the red coats escaping across it in the darkness. (A marker at Mill Street in Belleville Park commemorates the skirmish in that area between Sept. 12 and 14, 1777.)

Source: HISTORY OF NUTLEY, *Elizabeth Stow Brown, 1907*

The Raiders and Refugees

While the British were in possession of New York and Staten Island, no part of Jersey suffered more from raids than the banks of the Passaic. Farms were stripped of crops, cattle and sheep were driven off, and the defenceless inhabitants on their scattered farms were wantonly murdered in defending their property. So great were the terror and sufferings of the people of this region that a guard of the State Militia was raised for the "Defense of the Frontiers." There was a guard house at Belleville and Captain Speer's company was stationed there. John Vreeland (grandfather of Mr. Warren Vreeland of Nutley) was a River Guard who rode up and down the river bank on the lookout for raiders, or "refugees" as they were also called, British, Hessian or Tory. He carried two huge brass-mounted pistols, one of which is now in Mr. Vreeland's possession, marked, "J. V. 1776." Though he often shot to frighten "raiders," only once did the young soldier actually kill an invader across the river.

Source: HISTORY OF NUTLEY, *Elizabeth Stow Brown, 1907*

Captain Abraham Speer

The most striking figure that we can summon from dim colonial times in this farm and woodland region is the young Dutchman Abram Speer. He was the eldest of five sons of John Speer of Second River, who owned a large estate in the center of that village and who was a descendant of John Hendrick Speer, an original grantee near Hackensak and also one of the Acquackanonck patentees. Abram (or Abraham) came over Third River seeking a wife. He found her in the daughter of one Wouterse or Wouters who had a blacksmith shop at Povershon. He was commissioned Captain in the Second Essex Regiment on May 28, 1777, and stationed at Belleville with this company to "guard the river."

It was his father who from the church steeple shot the "refugee" across the Passaic.

Source: HISTORY OF NUTLEY, Elizabeth Stow Brown, 1907

Skirmish of Second River

In September of 1777 there was an engagement which is most frequently referred to as the "Battle of Second River". It is for this engagement that a memorial plaque has been erected in the park. The British intended to expand their invasion with a larger force in central Jersey. But first, they had to pass through Second River and beneath the old church tower.

Eyes in the tower saw the advance and sounded the alarm. Under the direction of Captains Hornblower, Joralemon, Rutgers and Rutan, a defense was prepared. Skirmishes went on for two days. It began with an artillery barrage of our town followed by musket and cannon battles in the streets.

Sending for reinforcements, the American troops valiantly held their ground and managed to damage British General. Sir Henry Clinton's hilltop headquarters with a direct hit from a cannonball, which happened to be on what is now Franklin Ave. September 14th turned into an all-day pitched battle.

With patriot reinforcements pouring in from neighboring communities, front lines eventually took shape near to Mill Street and Union Avenue. The British forces, overwhelming in numbers, eventually broke through. But once again, the local militia had succeeded in delaying the advance and weakening the invading army.

A skirmish was recorded on Jan. 27, 1777, between British foraging party and large body of rebels, according to Battles and Skirmishes in New Jersey. That source says that on June 1, 1779, the militia captured a Tory named Lawrence as he enlists men for the British Army.

A large boulder also rests at the fork in the road between Union and Franklin Avenues on Mill Street as a landmark to mark the spot where the final shots of the Battle of the Second River were fired. A bronze plaque was placed on the rock in 1932

Sources: Norman Price, Village of Second River author; Michael Perrone, Dave Hinrichs, The Belleville Times. David C. Munn, Battles and Skirmishes of the American Revolution in New Jersey.

Dutch Reformed Church

Belleville, the old Village of Second River, was a hot-bed of patriot activity, not to mention the processing center for the Schuyler copper mine, then the largest copper supply in the country. In addition, Main Street was a major thoroughfare for troop movements going south to Monmouth, Princeton or Trenton, which must pass below the old Dutch church tower. We were high on the British "watch list". Much attention was focused on our activities.

In our defense, the Second Essex Regiment, mainly men of the village, was charged with the task of defending the road, the river, the village and the tunnel to the mine. No easy chore was that. British troops were stationed across the river in Arlington watching the mine entrance. Homes along the river were within musket-shot range of British patrols along the Passaic. Going to the barn to milk a cow or fetching water from the well were life-threatening activities for local citizens. But watchmen and snipers stood guard in the old church tower and the guardhouse at the church had "minute-men" at-the-ready.

The old church tower served the patriot's cause on numerous occasions. Several clashes of troupes occurred within sight of the tower, including the Battle of Second River. History tends to blur these various military actions into a single "Battle of Second River", but it appears that there were several.

After the battle at Fort Lee, General Washington was in full retreat, trying to save what was left of his army. British General Howe was in hot pursuit, intent upon Washington's capture and ending the Revolutionary War right here. But the militia men of Second River, together with the Second Essex Regiment and rear-guard detachments from Washington's army were not going to let the war end in defeat here on our turf.

Source: Norman Price, Village of Second River author.

Philip Van Courtlandt

A hero of the Battle of Saratoga, Van Courtlandt served in Poor's Brigade as Colonel of the 2nd and Lieutenant Colonel of the 4th New York Regiments. He was promoted to Brigadier General in 1783. The son of Pierre Van Courtlandt of Courtlandt Manor in New York, and the husband of Catherine Ogden, whom he wed in 1762. The long-lived officer's name was inadvertently omitted from the church plaque honoring the Revolutionary War veterans interred in Belleville's Dutch Reformed Church Yard because he did not serve in a local regiment.

Birth: Unknown - d. November 5, 1831; American General, Revolutionary War.

Burial: Belleville Dutch Reformed Churchyard, Belleville, N.J. Plot: Van Courtlandt Crypt.

Source: Find A Grave; Bio by: Nikita Barlow.

Cadmus Plot

Second River had its own female heroine in the wife of Peter Cadmus. A party of redcoats approached her homestead. She saw them coming so hid her two children in a large oven built in the side of the fireplace – admonishing them to keep very quiet. When she refused to give the British any food and wouldn't tell them where the men were, the angry officer plunged his sword in her side. When the Cadmus brothers came home they found her bleeding heavily. The children heard their voices and came out of hiding. Mrs. Cadmus eventually recovered.

Source: Belleville Historical Society

Hornblower Plot

Josiah Hornblower at the time of the Revolution had acquired considerable property, was the father of a large family and had become a justice of the peace. He was an ardent patriot, and though too old to carry arms himself, he served the Revolutionary cause with advice, financial aid an as a member of the Provincial Assembly. He brought the first steam engine over to America in 1753 to pump the water out of Scuyler Mine.

The British regarded Hornblower as a very dangerous man, and several times he barely escaped arrest. It was small wonder that he watched prudently from his porch as a rather large party of men was being ferried across the Passaic River by Robert Kip, his son-in-law. At first the score of strangers seemed inoffensive enough of Kip. They were dressed as farm laborers, and had a plausible reason for crossing. But in the middle of the stream they pulled pistols from under their greatcoats, primed them and got ready for action. Kip kept his peace until the ferry was near enough to the shore so that Hornblower, still seated on the porch, would hear his call. Then he dropped his oars overboard, rose to his feet, and shouted, "Father, the British!"

History holds no record of what the British did to Kip. Hornblower had flown and his daughter, Kip's wife, had been able to hide the family silver. The enemy searched and set fire to the house, but rain and neighbors extinguished the blaze before much damage was done.

Source: Belleville Historical Society

James Kidney Plot

Captain James Kidney, Captain Henry Joralemon, Halmark Joralemon and Jacob Garland on a dark and winter night caught the British relaxing at a school house dance in Bergen Heights. They selected the highest ranking officer and a loyalist refugee and bundled them off to a waiting sleigh and brought them back to Second River (Belleville). For several generations the Joralemons proudly exhibited the silver-belted sword of the captured officer. Richard Kidney's home near Smallwood Avenue for years had holes in his front door made by British bullets.

Source: Belleville Historical Society

Rutgers Plot

Anthony Rutgers was an artillery captain. He had six children and his eldest son Anthony constructed the first bridge over the Passaic River. Gerard and Robert Rutgers were both colonels. Col. Henry Rutgers, after whom Rutgers University was named, was a colonel and fought in the battle of Long Island. Harmon Rutgers was killed in the battle of Long Island on Aug. 27, 1776.

Source: Belleville Historical Society

Speer Plot

Captain Abraham Speer commanded the Second Essex Regiment that was stationed here at Second River. John Speer, the captain's brother, was a lookout in the Reformed Church belfry when he spied a British officer across the river. He shot him and kept his watch and the brass buttons from his coat. On an occasion Captain Speer was informed just before daybreak five horses had been driven off by a party of refugee Tories. Speer, with two Vreelands and several other men, followed the tracks to the Hackensack. While considering whether they should continue into enemy territory, they spotted a rider farther upstream. One of the Vreelands fired and dropped the man, whereupon several other men, who had been hiding on the opposite bank, broke shelter and fled. The riderless horses neighed loudly and were answered from a thicket where the Second River men found the other horses.

Source: Belleville Historical Society

Van Cortlandt Plot

Stephen Van Cortlandt spied a British patrol coming across the Passaic River on the ice. He rounded up the half a dozen militiamen that were in the village at that time. They hid among the thick cedars near the river bank and made such a din that the invaders thought there was a whole army after them and retreated to the other side of the river. It is said that the Van Cortlandts could not draw water from their well without being shot at by the British on the other side of the river.

Source: Belleville Historical Society

Van Riper Plot

Cornelius Van Riper was a blacksmith whose shop was the place where slugs of iron were prepared in the absence of ball, having exhausted his supply of iron suited to this kind of shooting, he surrendered to the gunners first his hammer and then his sledge to be used in place of ball. The British discovering the kind of shot used, were heard to call out loudly to their comrades, "Get out of the way for God's sake, before they send us the anvil."

Source: Belleville Historical Society

American Revolution Soldiers Buried In Belleville

Sixty-five American Revolution veterans are interred in Belleville. It could be that no other town in the United States can make such a claim. The Rutgers buried here are related to Col. Henry Rutgers, whom Rutgers University is named after. George Washington's army passed through Second River on its retreat from New York on November 22, 1776.

Soldiers of the New Jersey Second Essex regiments were posted here during the Revolution to watch for an English invasion from New York. Skirmishes occurred in 1779 and another in 1780. The American detachment that guarded Belleville or Second River was part of Jersey Militia raised for the "defense of the frontiers". Its commander was Abraham Speer, a native of Second River who was commissioned Captain in the Second Essex Regiment on May 28, 1777. Speer's guardhouse was near the ferry across the Passaic. Here was the spot most in need of defense against a possible surprise attack on Second River. Washington's army retreating from Fort Lee crossed the Passaic River at Passaic and then proceeded down the west coast of the Passaic, knowing that the Americans at Second River would protect him.

He spent the night of Nov. 22, 1775, in Second River (Belleville) and then proceeded to Newark and points south.

The British, under the leadership of General Cornwallis, was forced to stay on the east side of the Passaic and never did catch Washington. A watch was maintained in the belfry of the Dutch Reformed Church.

At the first sign of the enemy's approach, an old mortar would be fired to rally the residents against attack. Watchfulness had to be doubled in winter due to the river freezing and they could walk across.

Colonel Philip Van Cortlandt commanded a New Jersey regiment in the Revolution. Minard Coeyman served under him.

Sources: Norman Price, Village of Second River author; Michael Perrone, Belleville Historical Society.

John Bayley
Henry Brown
Isaac Brown
John Brown
Henry Cadmus
Isaac Cadmus
John P. Cadmus
John H. Cadmus
Peter Cadmus
Lt. Col. Thomas Cadmus
James Campbell
Minard Curen
Capt. Amos Dodd
Thomas Doremus
Anthony Francisco
John Francisco
Jacob Freeland
John Garland
Garrabrant Garrabrants
John Gilliland
John Harrison
James Hornblower
Josiah Hornblower
James Jacobus
John Jacobus
Henry Jacobus
Richard Jacobus
Capt. Henry Joralemon

Helmich Joralemon
Lt. Capt. James Joralemon
Capt. John Kidney
Abram King
Aurey King
William King
John King
Isaac Kingsland
John Kingsland
John Luker
Joseph Miller
William Nixon
Ensign John Peer
Jacob Pier
Jacob Riker
Daniel Rutan
Capt. Robert Rutgers
Capt. Gerard Rutgers
Capt. Thomas Seigler
Capt. Abraham Speer
Capt. Cornelius Speer
Capt. Henry Speer
Francis Speer
Lt. Herman Speer
James Speer
John Speer
John Spier
Lt. John Spier Jr.
Christian Stimets
Daniel Teurs
Col. Van Courtland

Thomas Van Riper
Simeon Van Winkle
Michael Vreeland
Capt. Ezekial Wade
Samuel Ward
John Winne

American Revolution War memorial at Dutch Reformed Church cemetery.

War of 1812

General Alexander Macomb Jr.

The General Alexander Macomb House at 125 Main Street, Belleville, N.J. was erected circa 1784-1797, frame addition to south end and all windows replaced about 1870. This was originally the home of Sarah Macomb, a widow who lived here with her young daughter. Around 1799 she took in her 17 year old nephew, Alexander Macomb, (1782-1841) who lived with her while he attended Newark Academy. In 1803 he married his cousin Catharine and they continued to live here while he pursued his Military career. He became most famous as the Commanding Officer of a series of stunning U.S. victories during the war of 1812. Major General Alexander Macomb Jr., 1782-1841, Senior Officer and Commanding General of the U.S. Army from 1828 to 1841.

Married: Maj. Gen. Alexander Macomb of the U.S. Army and Mrs. Harriet B. Wilson Balch, daughter of the Rev. Dr. Balch, Pastor of the Presbyterian Church of Georgetown, May 2, 1826, by the Rev. Mr. McCormick.

National Intelligencer, May 25, 1841 (Norfolk, May 20)

Major General Scott and Colonel Bankhead arrived here in the steamboat from Richmond yesterday afternoon, and we learn that Major General Macomb, Commander-in-chief of the Army, is expected this morning by the steamboat from Baltimore. The subject of the visit of these distinguished officers, it is understood, is to inspect the military works at Fort Monroe and the Rip Raps. -- Herald.

National Intelligencer, Saturday, June 26, 1841

We regret to announce the death of General Alexander Macomb, the General-in-Chief of the United States Army which occurred at half past 2 o'clock yesterday. His funeral will take place on Monday next at 10 o'clock a.m.

National Intelligencer, Monday, June 28, 1841

The Late Major Gen. Macomb

We have a melancholy pleasure in transferring to our columns the following Biography of Major General Macomb, whose Funeral is this day to be solemnized, in whose death this city has to mourn the decease of a virtuous and beloved fellow-citizen, and in whom the Nation laments the loss of the distinguished and gallant Commander of its Military forces.

Major General Alexander Macomb was born at Detroit, April 3, 1782. The city of Detroit, at that time, was a garrison town, and among the first images that struck his eyes were those of the circumstances of war. These early impressions often fix the character of the man.

His father was a fur merchant, respectably descended and connected. He removed to the city of New York while Alexander was yet an infant.

When he was eight years of age, he placed him at school at Newark, in New Jersey, under the charge of the Reverend Doctor Ogden, who was a man of mind, belonging to a family distinguished for talents.

In 1798, while Macomb was quite a youth, he was elected into a select company, which was called, "The New York Rangers." The name was taken from that Spartan band of rangers selected from the provincials who, from 1755 to 1763, were the elite of every British commander on Lake George and the borders of Canada.

At the time he entered the corps of New York Rangers, Congress had passed a law receiving volunteers for the defense of the country, as invasion by a French army was soon expected. This patriotic band volunteered their services to Government, which were accepted, but he soon left this corps, and obtained a cornetcy at the close of the year 1798, and was commissioned in January, 1799.

General North, then adjutant general of the Northern army, soon saw the merits of the youthful soldier, and took him into his staff, as deputy adjutant general.

Under such a master as the intelligent and accomplished North, Macomb made great progress in his profession, and in the affections of his brother officers of the army.

The young officer that Hamilton noticed and North instructed, would not fail to be ambitious of distinction. He visited Montreal in order to observe the discipline and tactics of the veteran corps kept at that important military post, and did not neglect his opportunities. The thick and dark cloud that hung over the country passed away--a great part of the troops were disbanded, and a set of the officers and men returned to private life; a few only retained; among them was Macomb, who was commissioned as a second lieutenant of dragoons, and sent forthwith on the recruiting service, but it was not then necessary to push the business; and as he was stationed in Philadelphia, he had fine opportunities to associate with the best informed men of the city, and found easy access to the Franklin and other extensive libraries, of which advantages he did not fail to improve.

When his body of recruits was formed, he marched with it to the Western frontiers to join Gen. Wilkinson, an officer who had been left in service from the Revolutionary war.

In the company of Wilkinson, and of Col. Williams, the engineer, he must have gathered a mass of materials for future use. With him he went into the Cherokee country to aid in making a treaty with that nation. He was on this mission nearly a year, and kept a journal of every thing he saw or heard. This was good school for one whose duty it might hereafter be to fight these very aborigines, and, in fact, these lessons of the wilderness are not lost on any one of mind and observation.

The corps to which he belonged was disbanded, and a corps of engineers formed; to this he was attached as first lieutenant. He was now sent to West Point, where he was, by the code there established, a pupil as well as an officer. Being examined and declared competent, he was appointed an adjutant of the corps at that post, and discharged his duty with so much spirit and intelligence, that when the first court martial, after his examination, was convened, he was appointed judge advocate.

This court was ordered for the trial of a distinguished officer for disobeying an arbitrary order for cutting off the hair. Peter the Great could not carry such an order into execution, but our Republican country did; and the veteran Col. Butler was reprimanded for not throwing his white locks to the wind when ordered to do so by his superior.

The talents and arguments exhibited by Macomb, as judge advocate on this court martial, brought him into very great notice as a man of exalted intellect as well as a fine soldier.

He was now called upon to compile a treatise upon martial law and the practice of courts martial, which, in a future day of leisure, he effected, and his book is now the standard work upon courts martial for the Army of the United States.

In 1805 Macomb was promoted to the rank of captain in the corps of engineers, and sent to the sea-board to superintend the fortifications which had been ordered by an act of Congress.

By this service he became known to the first men in the country, and his merits were duly appreciated from New Hampshire to the Floridas.

In 1808 he was promoted to the rank of major, and acted as superintendent of fortifications until just before the war, when he was advanced to a lieutenant colonelcy.

He was again detailed to act as judge advocate on a court martial for the trial of Gen. Wilkinson, who had called the court on C.J. Butler. He added to his reputation in this case. Wilkinson was his friend, but Macomb discharged his duty with military exactness.

At the breaking out of the war of 1812, he left the seat of Government, where he had discharged an arduous duty, in assisting to give form and regularity to the army then just raised by order of Congress.

All sorts of confusion had prevailed, from the want of a uniform system of military tactics: he was fortunate in his exertions. When there was honorable war, he could not be satisfied to remain, as it were, a cabinet officer, and wear a sword only to advise what should be done, which seemed to be the regulations of the Army in respect to engineers; he therefore solicited a command in the corps of artillery that was to be raised, and was gratified by a commission as colonel of the third regiment, dated July 6, 1812.

The regiment was to consist of twenty companies of one hundred and eighteen each. It was, in fact, the command of a division, except in rank. His reputation assisted in raising the body of men, and in November of that year he marched to the frontiers with his command. Macomb and his troops spent the winter at Sackett's Harbor.

He contemplated an attack upon Kingston, but was defeated in his plan by the fears of some and the jealousies of others; but he soon distinguished himself at Niagara and Fort George; at the same time Commodore Chauncey was endeavoring to bring the enemy's fleet to battle on Lake Ontario.

The next service performed by Col. Macomb was under Gen. Wilkinson, and if the campaign was not successful, Macomb was not chargeable with any portion of the failure.

Source: The National Intelligencer, Monday, June 28, 1841

The Funeral of General Macomb

Which is to take place from his late residence today, at 10 o'clock, will be an interesting spectacle as well as an honorable tribute to the station, the services, and the personal character of the late Commander of the Army.

The Orders from the Departments, directing Funeral Honors to the deceased, will be found in our columns to-day.

The Company of U.S. Light Infantry on duty at Fort McHenry arrived here yesterday for the purpose of attending the Funeral.

It is probable, we understand, that a number of Volunteer Military Companies also will arrive in this city from Baltimore this morning for the same purpose.

Little did we expect, when we attended the Funeral of Gen. Harrison, on which occasion Gen. Macomb commanded the Military escort, that we should so soon have to follow the remains of the living General to the tomb.

The National Intelligencer, Tuesday, June 29, 1841

The Funeral of General Macomb, Commander of the Army took place yesterday, agreeably in the order of arrangements officially announced, and was attended by the President, and all the Officers of the Government, both Houses of Congress, the Diplomatic Corps, Military and Naval Officers, etc.

The solemn military and civic array which filled the broad avenue through the city presented an imposing spectacle, in keeping with, and appropriately closed by, the impressive ceremonies at the tomb.

The Evening Star, Saturday, March 16, 1901

Brave Gen. Macomb Proposed Monument to Commemorate His Services
American Hero of the War of 1812

Once the Commander of the United States Army

Distinguished Career

The erection of a monument commemorative of the service of Major General Alexander Macomb at Detroit, Mich., his birthplace, sixty years after his death in this city, when in command of the United States army, is a matter of interest not only in military circles, but to many of the older families of the District, as well as many of his relatives resident among us.

The latter third of his three score years of life was passed in this city, and such was his intercourse with the people that, upon the announcement of his death here June 25, 1841, the press spoke of him as "the brave soldier of forty years, the useful citizen, the philanthropist and poor man's friend."

His remains were followed to the grave by thousands of people--the funeral being one of the largest and most imposing, being attended by the President, cabinet, diplomatic corps, both houses of Congress, the corporate authorities of the three District cities--Alexandria not having been retroceded – and civic associations.

The military escort was composed of Major Ringgold's light battery of artillery, from Fort McHenry; a battalion of marines, under Major Tyler; the Washington Light Infantry, National Blues, Mechanical Riflemen, the Georgetown Grays and other volunteer companies of the District. The Baltimore military organizations were deterred from paying tribute to General Macomb, as they were the same day escorting the remains of General Harrison through Baltimore.

A handsome marble monument was erected over the remains of General Macomb in the family lot in which are also the remains of some of his family.

There survive him quite a number of descendants to the third and fourth generations, a number of them residents of the District.

The services of General Macomb to the country were of inestimable value, but the crowning glory of career was his success in defending Plattsburg and defeating a British force six times as large as his own, saving the upper part of the state of New York to the country. The design for the Detroit monument represents him at this battle standing on the ramparts of one of his forts, field glass in hand.

While the place of his birth, the town of Plattsburg, where he obtained a phenomenal victory, and West Point Academy, where he organized the corps of cadets, are all suitable places for a monument to commemorate his services, it would appear that besides the modest family monument over his remains at the Congressional cemetery, there should be one erected in one of Washington's parks.

Indeed outside of army circles, he having served from 1821 as chief of the engineer corps, and from 1828 to his death, in 1841, as commanding general, there are hundreds of older Washingtonians in every walk of life who can recite pleasant reminiscences of the general.

These would warmly appreciate the placing of a statue in his memory at some point in the nation's capital city.

Of Irish and French Descent

Descended from Irish-French stock and born in Detroit in 1782, when that place was a trading station, and being sent to school at Newark, N.J., he there showed his proclivity for a military life.

When sixteen years old he joined the New York Rangers, and volunteered his services to the government. He soon after became a cornet of light dragoons, and next as assistant under Adjutant General North.

When the war scare was over, in 1799, he went to Canada, but soon returned, and became a second lieutenant of dragoons. He saw service as such on the Ohio, and with a commission, making treaties with the Indians.

He was then but a boy. When the army was reduced the dragoons were disbanded and an engineer corps, with one major, two captains, four lieutenants, and ten cadets were provided for. These, with artillery, were located at West Point and formed the nucleus of the Military Academy.

Young Macomb was retained in service as a lieutenant of infantry, and applied for and obtained a transfer to the engineers in 1802. Taking the course with the lieutenants and cadets, he was the first to graduate. He was made adjutant of the post, and as such organized the corps of cadets and became the head of the academy, being promoted to the rank of lieutenant colonel in 1811. In the following year, while performing the duties at the head of the academy, which had become a separate post, the duties of chief of engineers, the head being old and infirm, he also filled the position of adjutant general of the army.

The formation of two new regiments of artillery being authorized by Congress on the eve of the war of 1812, Macomb asked for and was given the colonelcy of one of them.

This was the regiment, recruited in the neighborhood of New York, and he marched with it to the defense of the northern frontier.

The British designed to capture and occupy the upper portion of New York state, and a naval force, under Capt. Downie, was sent against McDonough's fleet, while from Canada Sir George Prevost came down on the Americans, with 16,000 well-disciplined troops, to exterminate or capture Macomb and the few thousands with him.

The larger portion of the invaders were veterans who had served under Wellington, and Macomb had but few regulars which, with militia and volunteers, aggregated less than 3,000 men.

Macomb prepared for the attack by building forts to defend the town, and it is related that Gen. J.G. Totten, then a major and afterward the head of the engineer bureau and resident of Washington, was in charge of the work as the engineer officer. The attack came and the foe was vanquished on land and water. Macomb, with a loss of less than a hundred, defeated Sir George, inflicting a loss in killed, wounded and prisoners of 2,500.

McDonough sunk the British fleet. In an old song 'tis said:

"Sir George Prevost, with all his host/Marched forth from Montreal, sir./
Both he and they as blythe and gay/As going to a ball, sir."

After describing the battle and the astonishment of Sir George, the song ends:

"The rout began, Sir George led on,/His men ran helter skelter;
Each tried his best to outrun the rest/To gain a place of shelter.
To hide their fear they gave a cheer/And thought it mighty cunning--
He'll fight, say they, another day/Who save himself by running."

Electrifying Victories

These victories electrified the nation, the news reaching Washington shortly after the defeat of the British at Baltimore September 12.

General Macomb received the thanks of the legislatures of several states, the freedom of New York city tendered in a gold box, a gold medal and sword from Congress and the brevet of major general.

At the close of the War of 1812, in March, 1815, the army was reduced to a peace footing, with two major generals and four brigadier generals, and Macomb was retained in the latter rank in charge of the fifth military division, with headquarters at Detroit.

Under his administration of military affairs much was done in opening up the country, and he had so won the affections of the people that when, with his family, he left Detroit for Washington in 1821 the peopled crowded the wharves to bid him good-bye.

Having been appointed to the head of the engineer corps, he arrived at the capital in June, 1821, and took up his residence in Georgetown, his family consisting of his wife and nine children. Ere a year had passed, and before Mrs. Macomb became acquainted with the capital, the general was left a widower.

Five years afterward, in May, 1826, he married Miss Harriet B. Wilson, the daughter of a Presbyterian minister of Georgetown, and subsequently the family moved to the fine old brick residence at the northwest corner of 17th and I streets, erected about 1826 by Mr. William Williamson, who was long the navy agent here.

This became the scene of many brilliant society functions, General and Mrs. Macomb and the grown children being most genial as hosts; and though the parties were often magnificent, with a military air about them, the plain citizen was made to feel at home. In compliance with the teachings of her youth, Mrs. Macomb drew the line on dancing.

Though filling the requirements of their station in society, the members of the family found time and inclination for a work by which they won the respect of the community in relieving the poor and needy, and the alleviation of suffering in an unostentatious manner.

The general was the author of a number of military works and possessed some literary ambition. A drama of frontier life from his pen found its way to the stage, and met with some success. One of the adjuncts to his home, purchased in 1831, was a fine garden extending to K street. A fine tenpin alley near the house was an attraction for many of his friends, military and civilian.

In 1828, on the death of Major General Jacob Brown, the command of the army was given to General Macomb, and he retained the position until his death. General Macomb was a prominent figure at the inauguration of General Harrison, and so youthful looking was he that the populace could not believe that he was a hero of the war of 1812, much less the commanding general of the army.

A month afterward he commanded the escort at the funeral of President Harrison, whose remains were placed in the tomb at Congressional cemetery.

Less than three months afterward the body of the general was borne over the same route to the same cemetery, just after the remains of General Harrison had been forwarded to Cincinnati. The same minister, Rev. Dr. Hawley of St. John's Church officiated, and the same battery, Ringgold's, fired the salute. Many of the same troops and organizations participated, and, as stated before, almost the entire population of the District paid a tribute to him, thousands following the remains to the cemetery.

There survived the general two sons and five daughters, and the family is yet represented in the army. (Gen. Macomb's daughter Czarina died in Detroit April 24, 1846)

(Gen. Macomb authorized Joseph Nicollet's expedition to map Minnesota and South Dakota)

(Gen. Macomb's half-sister was the wife of Peter Flandraugh, defender against the Sioux Uprising (1861) and later Governor of Minnesota)

Will of Maj. Gen. Alexander Macomb

(dtd. Feb. 27, 1841, probated July 9, 1841; Book 5, pp. 218-219;

O.S. 2283; Box 15)

All real estate to wife for her lifetime, and after her death to children: Alexander A. Macomb; William H. Macomb; Catharine Mason; Alexandrine Staunton; Czarina Macomb; Sarah Macomb; and Jane Octavia Miller, and their heirs, to be equally divided between them.

My house on I St., City of Washington, in which I now reside, and the lots adjoining having been purchased from William Williamson with the separate funds of my wife, I consider as solely her property; to wife, all my personal estate except those legacies hereinafter mentioned.

To sons Alexander and William Macomb, my military equipment, trophies, medals and swords presented by the U.S., the first to have the gold medal presented to me by Congress in consideration of my service at Plattsburgh in the month of June 1814; the second, William to have the sword presented for the same occasion.

To children, equally divided, a claim when recovered, against the general government for brevet pay which amounts to about $13,000 and which ought long since to have been paid.

Exrx.: Harriet B. Macomb, wife

Wits.: J.B.H. Smith; Samuel A. Houston; William P. Rodgers

Macomb, Mrs. Harriet B. Wilson d. 30 Mar 1842 R55/148

The Evening Star, Dec. 31, 1870

Sale of the residence of the late Mrs. General Macomb – Green and Williams yesterday sold the residence of the late Mrs. General Macomb, together with the ground attached containing 9,360 sq. ft. and situated on the northwest corner of 17th and I streets to R.C. Clary, Esq. for $17,950.

Source: Congressional Cemetery

Township's role remembered during War of 1812 bicentennial

Belleville played an important role in the war. The Belleville Gunpowder Mill was located on Mill Street and manufactured gunpowder for the U.S. Navy. The mill exploded in 1814 killing all 12 workers, four of whom are buried in the Belleville Reformed Church Cemetery.

Certainly the best known battle of the War of 1812 is the Battle of New Orleans fought in January of 1815, and its hero Andrew Jackson. But tragically for those involved, the war had already ended, word had not reached the commanders in time. The most important battle of the war was actually fought in New York in a town called Plattsburgh on the banks of Lake Champlain.

It was the intention of Great Britain to extend their Canadian border as far south as possible. To accomplish this Britain sent its largest army ever across the Atlantic to invade the United States. Britain had just defeated Napoleon and this freed up thousands of the Duke of Wellington's finest troops for what the British War Department called "The Final Invasion."

The British War plan called for an attack on Washington and Baltimore to divert American attention from the true target which was to annex New England and New York. The bombardment of Fort McHenry and the attack on Plattsburgh occurred 48 hours apart. The rockets' red glare that Francis Scott Key would be witnessing in Baltimore harbor would be falling at the same time with much more ferocity over the American forces in Plattsburgh.

On Sept. 11, 1814, the largest invasion and attack in America history took place at Plattsburgh. There 15,000 British troops battled a tiny American force of 1,500 regular troops, supported by New York and Vermont militia volunteers, old and ill veterans and 20 schoolboys.

The heroic American resistance was led by General Alexander Macomb. While at the same time in Plattsburgh Bay, a large British fleet attacked a much smaller American fleet commanded by Commodore Thomas Macdonough.

Fortunately America as we know it was saved by a stunning victory at Plattsburgh. Brilliant naval strategy by Commodore Macdonough resulted in the surrender of the British fleet, and fierce resistance from General Macomb's vastly outnumbered troops resulted in a British retreat back to Canada. The British defeat was the turning point of the war and a peace treaty was signed in December.

Over a century later even Winston Churchill commented that the Battle of Plattsburgh "was the decisive battle of the war". And Franklin Roosevelt while assistant secretary of the Navy testified before Congress that the Battle of Plattsburgh should be celebrated on a national level.

Both Commodore Macdonough and General Macomb received national honors for their victory. Immediately after the battle President Madison promoted

Macomb to the rank of Major General. Congress awarded General Macomb a Gold Medal struck in his honor. Governor Tomkins of New York presented General Macomb with a ceremonial sword on behalf of the grateful people of the state of New York and in New York City, Mayor Dewitt Clinton presented Macomb with the Key to the City.

General Macomb, before returning to his post at Plattsburgh, was able to return to his home for a brief rest.

As reported in the New York Post, "Never, on the return of any hero to the peaceful bosom of his family was shown so universal a sense of sincere and heartfelt satisfaction." "The village was illuminated and he was received with the most gratifying tokens of respect, when he returned to his family at Belleville, New Jersey."

Courtesy Michael Perrone, Belleville Historical Society; first published Aug. 21, 2014.

200 Years After Macomb's Homecoming

It was 200 years ago this week that War of 1812 hero General Alexander Macomb, after a stunning victory over the British at the Battle of Plattsburgh, N.Y., made a triumphant return to his home in Belleville.

Macomb's family lived in a stately mansion then located at the corner of Main and Williams streets. Macomb had just been promoted to the rank of Major General by President Madison and awarded a Congressional Gold Medal. As he made his way home to Belleville he paid visits to Governor Tompkins of New York, who presented Macomb with a ceremonial sword, and then visited New York City to receive the Key to the City from Mayor Dewitt Clinton.

On the evening of Nov. 15 he arrived back in Belleville. The homecoming was described in a page 2 article in the New York Post. "The inhabitants of Belleville NJ on the return of Major General Macomb to his family received him a manner most gratifying and complimentary, as a testimony of their spirit and patriotism they fired a national salute (15 shots on a cannon, one for each state in the Union) and illuminated the village (with bonfires). The General came forward and courteously acknowledged the compliment....taking the villagers cordially by hand".

As a thank you to the villagers for the warm welcome which he received Macomb, who was accompanied home by his army band, ordered them to play for the enjoyment of the townspeople, playing "Hail Columbia and other patriotic tunes".

Author and historian Keith Herkalo, an authority on the Battle of Plattsburgh, noted that that the townspeople must have been very impressed with Macomb's band. The band's uniforms had been confiscated by the victorious Americans after the battle from the Brunswick Regiment of the British 104th Royal Infantry. The white uniforms with red cuffs and collars and gold braid were the most elaborate military uniforms at the time. Macomb replaced the British buttons with American artillery buttons and the band wore the standard U.S. Army hat.

After a brief stay at home in Belleville, Macomb returned to Plattsburgh to oversee operations there. The following year President Madison reassigned Macomb to the Detroit military district.

In 1828 President John Quincy Adams appointed Macomb Commanding General of the U.S. Army, the nation's highest military office. In modern times the title was changed to Army Chief of Staff.

Macomb held the office for 13 years, dying in office in 1841 at the age of 57. Macomb was the third longest serving Army chief in U.S. history. His funeral procession to the Congressional Cemetery was led by President John Tyler and former President John Quincy Adams.

The Belleville Historical Society is currently working on a project to establish an appropriate local memorial for General Macomb.

Courtesy Michael Perrone, Belleville Historical Society; first published Nov. 13, 2014.

Civil War

Henry Benson

Captain Henry Benson, of Belleville, died August 11 of wounds received on July 1, 1862, at the battle of Malvern Hill, Va., the sixth and last of the Seven Days Battles (Peninsula Campaign). On that day, Confederate Gen. Robert E. Lee launched a series of disjointed assaults on the nearly impregnable Union position on Malvern Hill.

Malvern Hill was one of the North's rare victories in the early years of the Civil War. The Battle of Malvern Hill, also known as the Battle of Poindexter's Farm, took place on July 1, 1862, in Henrico County, Va. Fought during the Peninsula Campaign, it proved the superiority of Union artillery, which together with Union troops under the able leadership of Gen. Philip Kearny, decisively repulsed Robert E. Lee's attempt to destroy the Army of the Potomac.

LOCAL INTELLIGENCE

CAPT. BENSON, U.S.A. – Among the sufferers placed on board the steamer Spaulding at Harrison's Landing, to be brought to Philadelphia, was Capt. Henry Benson, of the Second Regiment U.S. Artillery. He had a shell wound in the right thigh, received from one of his own guns at Malvern Hill on the 6th inst., from which, unfortunately, he died on board the boat. Captain Benson was from Belleville, in this State, and rose from the ranks. For his good qualities as a soldier he received a commission as a brevet second lieutenant of the Second Artillery, June 28th, 1848. In March, 1853, he was commissioned first lieutenant, and in May, 1861, captain. He was a fine artillery officer, and a favorite with Gen. McClellan and all with whom he was associated. The funeral will take place with military honors, to-morrow, at 3 P.M., from the Reformed Dutch Church in Belleville.

MILITARY FUNERAL AT BELLEVILE – A large concourse of people assembled yesterday at Belleville to pay their last respects to the memory of the late Capt. Benson, of the U.S. Army. The Pall Bearers were Maj. Gen. Runyon, Col. A.J. Johnson, Col. A.F. Munn, Col E.A. Carman, Lieut. Col. Swords, Lieut. Col. Corby of Bloomfield, Paymaster Ward, of Belleville, and Major Webster of Belleville. A detachment of 100 men from the 13th Regiment, a Company from Bloomfield, and one from Franklin formed the military escort. The remains were taken from the house to the Dutch Reformed Church, where the funeral ceremonies took place. After the services the body was carried to the grave yard in rear of the church, upon the shoulders of six men from the 13th Regiment, detailed for that purpose, and with measured step, and notes from the fife and drum, with the ceremonies of the Episcopal church, all that remains of the patriot was consigned to the grave – "dust to dust, ashes to ashes," there to remain until the resurrection. At the close of the services a volley of three rounds was fired over the grave by a platoon of men, and the vast assemblage retired, showing that the words of the text was verified "than thou destroyest the hope of man." *(Newark Daily Mercury, Aug.13.1862)*

The grave of Capt. Henry Benson, (November 20, 1824 to August 11, 1862), in the Dutch Reformed Church Cemetery, Belleville, N.J., is a few feet north of the marble obelisk marking the Benson family plot, located near the middle of the churchyard's western wall. His name appears on both the northern facade of the obelisk and on a separate marble headstone with Civil War imagery in its tympanum: a cannon, forager cap, and Old Glory.

The 38-year-old Civil War officer was a Belleville native, born in the Miller House, and was accorded his hometown's first military funeral. He was captain and commander of Battery M, 2nd United States Regular Light Artillery.

The battery between Forts Ripley and Mansfield, and west of Powder Mill Branch (Maryland) are to be called Battery Benson after Capt. Henry Benson, who died Aug. 11, 1982, of wounds received at the second engagement at Malvern Hill, Va., by order of Brig. Gen. George W. Cullum, Chief of Staff, March 16, 1863.

Another battery was named for Maj. Gen Philip Kearny, U.S. Volunteers, killed at the battle of Chantilly, Va.

Sources: American Civil War.com; Belleville: 150th-Anniversary Historical Highlights 1839-1989 by Robert B. Burnett and the Belleville 150th-Anniversary Committee Belleville, New Jersey. 1991. Newark Daily Mercury, Weds., August 13, 1862, Local Intelligence and Military Funeral at Belleville, courtesy of Glen Pierce. Wikipedia: http://en.wikipedia.org/wiki/Battle_of_Malvern_Hill; http://en.wikipedia.org/wiki/File:Benson%27s_Battery_M_at_Fair_Oaks_1862_-_LC-B815-433.JPG Find a Grave memorial; Created by: Nikita Barlow; Record added: Aug 01, 2002; Find A Grave Memorial# 6653672; http://www.findagrave.com/cgi-bin/fg.cgi?page=gr&GScid=1259891&GRid=6653672&

John J. Rogers (Rodgers)

John Rogers (Rodgers) was killed in action on April 8, 1865, at Fort Davis while defending Washington, D.C., shortly before the war ended.

Rogers, of Belleville, died of his wounds, according to the Civil War Diary of James C. Taylor of Belleville, Company F, 39th Regiment, New Jersey Volunteers, in the War to Save the Union of the United States of America.

In his diary, Taylor wrote on April 1: "At 11 last night 2 pieces of heavy artillery were brought into Fort Davis. This looks ominous. At 11:30 the regiment fell in and went out alongside the road where they waited there for hot coffee, and then we removed down to the front. We moved as far front as we could and then were ordered to lie flat on the ground. The enemy are firing lively with mortar shells and rifle shots. While lying flat, John Rodgers received a fatal wound."

Taylor enlisted in Captain John Hunkele's Company on Sept. 17, 1864, along with Rodgers, James M. Crisp, Linus Ackerman, Edmund Holmes, Charles Stanford, James McCluskey and Daniel McGinnis.

Before the war, the Union capital was a sleepy city of approximately 62,000 residents. The city sat almost completely unprotected, with Fort Washington, the lone fortification, being 12 miles south. Virginia, a Confederate state, lay on one side of the city, and Maryland, a slave-owning state, was on the other, leaving Washington dangerously vulnerable.

By 1865, the Defenses of Washington included 68 forts, supported by 93 detached batteries for field guns, 20 miles of rifle pits, and covered ways, wooden blockhouses at three key points, 32 miles of military roads, several stockaded bridgeheads, and four picket stations. Along the circumference of the 37-mile circle of fortifications were emplacements for a total of 1501 field and siege guns of which 807 guns and 98 mortars were in place. The defenseless city of 1860 had become one of the most heavily fortified cities of the world.

Private John J. Rogers enlisted Sept. 13, 1864, mustered in Sept. 25, 1864 for 1 year. He died at 3d Div. U. S. Army Gen. Hospital, Alexandria, Va., April 8, 1865, of wounds received in action before Petersburg, Va. He is buried at Alexandria National Cemetery, Alexandria, Alexandria City, Virginia, USA, and Plot: Company G, Thirty-ninth Regiment.

Sources: Civil War Diary of James C. Taylor of Belleville, Company F, 39th Regiment, New Jersey Volunteers, in the War to Save the Union of the United States of America, 1925. National Park Service http://www.nps.gov/cwdw/historyculture/fort-davis.htm Find A Grave Memorial# 10453303; Record added: Feb 10, 2005; http://www.findagrave.com/cgi-bin/fg.cgi?page=gr&GSln=Rogers&GSfn=John&GSmn=J.&GSbyrel=all&GSdy=18 65&GSdyrel=in&GScntry=4&GSob=c&GRid=10453303&df=all&

Thomas Stevens (Stephens)

Color Sergeant Thomas J. Stevens (Stephens), of Belleville, was killed June 27, 1862, in The Battle of Gaines's Mill, sometimes known as the First Battle of Cold Harbor or the Battle of Chickahominy River, took place on June 27, 1862, in Hanover County, Virginia, as the third of the Seven Days Battles (Peninsula Campaign).

A member of the First New Jersey Brigade, he served under 1st Lt. W. E. Blewett in the Second Regiment. A color sergeant is a sergeant who carries the regimental, battalion, or national colors as in a color guard.

"Friday, June 27th, 1862, the First New Jersey Brigade was ordered to Woodbury's Bridge over the Chickohominy, there to meet Gen. Porter's Division. ... Col. Tucker led out the remaining four companies, including Lt. Blewett's command with the rest of the Brigade. From Woodbury's Bridge this Brigade, with others, was sent to engage the enemy near Gaines's Mills and was soon in the thick of the fight. Porter's Division, in hand-to-hand conflict, held their position against overwhelming odds until reinforcements, long delayed, arrived, but owing to the fact that their position was unfavorable and to the superiority of the enemy in numbers, the Union troops were compelled to retire. ... The Second Regiment had the right of line, and though outnumbered and flanked by the enemy, they were the last to leave their station in the field. In this fight the regiment lost its colonel, Isaac M. Tucker, Capt. Charles Danforth, Color Sergeant Thomas Stevens of Belleville, and many others. ..."

Sources C.C. Hine And His Times, Woodside, Pages 244 and 245 (Belleville Public Library); FIRST NEW JERSEY BRIGADE, Page 443 (aka Stephens); Wikipedia http://en.wikipedia.org/wiki/Battle_of_Gaines%27s_Mill

DIARY OF JAMES C. TAYLOR
of Belleville, N. J.
In the War to Save the Union of the United States of America
Medal Grand Army of the Republic 1861 - Veteran – 1866

September 17th, 1864 - Enlisted in Captain John Hunkele's Co: F

39th Regiment, New Jersey Volunteers.

With me at the same time were enlisted John J. Rodgers, James M. Crisp, Linus Ackerman, Edmund Holmes, Charles Stanford, James McCluskey, Daniel McGinnis.

Sept. 19, 1864 All went to "Camp Frelinghuysen" on Roseville Ave., donned the Blue Uniform of the Union Army and all went home on a Pass.

Sept. 25 - Mustered into the United States Service.

Oct. 1st - In the evening we presented our Captain with a sword, sash, and belt; also our two Lieutenants.

Oct. 2nd - Got a pass and went home to see Mother and other friends. We were invited to the M. E. Church in the evening and each presented with a copy of the New Testament by the Pastor, Rev. D. R. Lowrie.

Oct. 3rd - Back in Camp by 9 A. M. and received a visit from several ladies, Mrs. Worthington, Mrs. Nuttall and others. At 5 P. M. a Dress Parade was held.

Oct. 4th - Marching Orders! Leave Camp at 9 A. M. Five Companies only, under the command of Lt. Col. James H.

Close marched down Broad St., and here I must digress. Leaving a widowed mother at home, and the main support being my brother, John, just recovering from Typhoid Fever, while sitting on the curb at Broad and Chestnut St., I thought of Mother, and was relieved that she did not appear to say good-bye, but it was better so. My mother was one of the best in the world in my estimation, and it would have saddened us both. Then some one touched me on the shoulder, I turned to look, and there was an elderly lady, - a cousin of my father's; she had trudged all down Broad St. to hand me a bag of cream puffs. I don't forget such acts as this, small as it may appear to others.

We finally resumed our March t0 the train at Chestnut St. Station, at 11 A. M. Locomotive got off the track at Elizabeth, got away at 4 P. M., arrived at Philadelphia at 10 P. M. where we were well fed by some of the best ladies at the aid Cooper Shop and off again at 1 A. M.

Oct. 5 - Arrived at Baltimore at 10 A. M. Stacked arms in street until 5 P. M., then marched into Fort Federal Hill and camped as well as we could, among the great guns which Gen. Butler had trained on the city long before. From here I mailed letters to my mother and my best girl.

Oct. 6 - 4 P. M. marched down to the docks and took the Transport, "Nellie Pentz" to City Point, Virginia.

Oct. 7 - Suspicions were aroused by the slow progress we were making down Chesapeake Bay and the engineer and the captain were put under arrest by an officer from the U. S. Gunboat "Dawn," who fired a shot, which caused our vessel to stop, and who declared us in distress. We were then taken in town by the "Steamer Lizzie" Baker at 2 P.M.

Oct. 8 - Anchored off Fortress Monroe last night. This morning put three (3) Companies on the Steamer George Weems, and off for City Point at last. At 11 A. M. passed the ruins of several houses at Harrison's Landing at 1 P. M. and at last arrived at City Point at 5 P. M., too late to land and go into Camp, so we were anchored out in the stream again.

Oct. 9 - Laid in the stream all last night. Landed at 9 A. M. New tents were issued to us and we went into camp on high ground in the afternoon.

Oct. 10 - Sent out to work on the breastworks with pick and shovel. I got sick ad was sent back to our camp. Ed. Holmes, and James Crisp are tenting with me; we call our tent the Hotel De Belleville.

Oct. 11 - Working on the trenches 8 hours a day and a gill of whiskey when we get through the day, for each man. Wrote to my best girl.

Oct. 12 - Still at work on the fortifications. About 11 A. M. the Engineer General rode by giving instructions; he looked more like a raw recruit, it was laughable to see him.

Oct. 13 - At the same work as before. Warm today, went to a farm house and got some butter milk, 2 canteens full.

Oct. 14 - Same work today but we take it easy. Some are complaining that they did not enlist to dig, and wish for a change. Most of us think the change will come soon enough.

Oct. 15th - This morning the program was changed, giving us a knapsack drill, worse a hundred times than the digging. We today also laid out our Co. Streets in the camp.

Oct. 16 - Today we had a Dress Parade and being Sunday, we had no work. Could hear heavy cannonading at Petersburg and Richmond. I begin to feel a sore throat, a case of "Quinsy."

Oct. 17 - Today it is worse and the Doctor excused me from all duty.

In the evening we could see the shells explode in the air up at the front.

Oct. 18 - Today our Colonel arrived and had his quarters put up, at 5 P. M. a Flag Raising and speeches by Col. & Lt. Col. My throat gets worse.

Oct. 19 - I am still off duty and can hardly eat or drink, am utterly miserable - my first attack of quinsy. Who wouldn't be a soldier?

Wrote a letter to Rev. Mr. Lowrie at Belleville.

Oct. 20 - Put on light camp duty today, about 1/2 hour work. Wrote to Rev. Mr. Smith, Bloomfield.

Oct. 21 - Again working in the trenches. In evening a large fire built in front of Col's tent and a prayer meeting held, very interesting indeed.

Oct. 22 - Went out to work as usual, but felt bad, throat worse and awful headache - our orderly sergeant told me to go into my tent, which I did.

Oct. 23 - This morning at 8 o'clock we broke camp and marched about five miles and took the box cars on Gen. Grant's Military railroad, got off at "Yellow Tavern," marched a few miles to Poplar Grove Church and encamped.

Oct. 24 - Spent the day putting up our tents, etc. so we now belong to the 1st Brigade and 2nd Division of the 9th Army Corps, Army of the Potomac, Major General John G. Parke, commanding.

Oct. 25 - Dress Parade 8:30 A. M., Company Drill, 10:30 to 11:30, then dinner. 2 P. M., Battalion Drill, then all at once marching orders, to where to we knew not.

Oct. 26 - Still in camp, expect to move soon.

Oct. 27 - At 2 A. M. as quiet as possible, we packed up everything and moved out toward the enemy. At daybreak General Meade and staff passed us, and the adjutant of our regiment joined us. Brisk firing down in the woods ahead of us, our regiment held in reserve. Here, I saw the wounded for the first time, some limping ... and blood" but able to walk, these were all the colored troops. Our regiment stood there, it seemed, for hours. I confess I felt rather shaky as I saw a fine looking officer brought near us, his left hip was horribly mangled and bloody. As the stretcher bearers were about to carry him further to the rear, he put his left hand own to feel the wound, then waved the right to us with a smile and a good-bye gentlemen.

Oct. 28 - Yesterday, I was with the regiment in another position in the evening turning one of the enemies abandoned breastworks and doing it in a heavy rain. That completed, I lay down for a little rest and sleep and slept from 2 to 4, then was called by the Corporal to go on duty as a Vidette and was placed down in the woods to watch and give alarm if I saw any thing, as the enemy was looked for in that direction. This whole movement was called a reconnaissance in force 3 or 4 Army Corps being engaged in it

Oct. 29 - We are back in our old camp and I am on the camp guard.

Nov. 10 - Brigade Drill lasting 3 hours - very tiresome.

Nov. 11 - News of Lincoln's re-election as President.

Nov. 13 - Letter from Brother John with some money and 24 post stamps.

Nov. 15 - Letter from Brother Henry enclosing money.

Nov. 17 - Brigade Drill.

Nov. 24 - Thanksgiving Day-Very little change in our dinner.

Nov. 27 - Went out to our picket line, curious to see how it looked and was told that Gen. Roger R. Pryon, Confederate, came into our line and gave himself up.

Nov. 28 - Battalion Drill by the Colonel.

Nov. 29 - Orders this A. M. for a General Review instead of which we packed up and marched down to front of Petersburg, laid in woods all night.

Nov. 30 - Laid out our Camp and pitched tents in the rear of "Fort Hell" and was known as "Camp Blackwater."

Dec. 3 - For the first time I am in the picket trenches: go on at 5 P. M. for 24 hours duty.

Dec. 4 - This is a bright and sunny morning, can hear the church bells in Petersburg; at 5 p. m. we are relieved by a new detail and return to our camp. A stray shot hits a man in camp.

Dec. 8 - A letter and photograph from my best girl.

Dec. 9 - On picket again and a cold hail and sleet storm, which froze to everything it touched. What a long, long night it was. I shall not forget it as long as life and mind last. My boots made to order before leaving home, costing $12.00, had to be cut off my feet. The Regiment during this time had gone on a mud march and suffered intensely.

Dec. 10 - The Regiment got back and were ordered out again and had to go and view the hanging of two young fellows of a N. Y. Regiment (Deserters).

Dec. 11 - Had a rest all day, it being Sunday, then had 24 more hours in the trenches - very cold and windy.

Dec. 15 - On Picket again.

Dec. 16 - The enemy throwing shells quite lively.

Dec. 18 - This morning our Forts are firing a salute for some recent victory.

Dec. 19 - On picket again, were shelled very lively, very difficult to get to our rifle pits.

Dec. 22 - Turned out in a hurry at 5 A. M. Nothing came of it.

Dec. 23 - Charley Stanford received a box of good things from his Belleville home.

Dec. 24 - Dan McGinnis went on Picket and had the end of one of his thumbs shot away. John Rodgers went on Picket with only 2 hardtack.

Dec. 25 - Christmas: Mailed Letters to Brother George, Henry Coeyman and John McCluskey. There is a scarcity of rations, even of hard tack.

Dec. 26 - A dispatch from Gen. Sherman read to the Regiment.

Dec. 27 - Battalion Drill today.

Dec. 28 - I am on Picket today with Rodgers and Holmes. Heavy shelling in afternoon, two shells came very near striking us as we went out by "Fort Hell."

Dec. 30 - I go on the Alarm Guard in afternoon.

Dec. 31 - Cold and stormy on Alarm Guard, which is a line of defense between our camp and the outer picket line. Came into camp at 4 P. M. mustered for pay and got some hot milk punch from our good Capt. John Hunkele.

1865

Jan. 3 - On Picket in same Rifle Pit with Private Klemme; who just at dusk was badly wounded in the shoulder, we believed by a sharp shooter. Holmes and Elder in same rifle pit.

Jan. 6 - Regiment ordered out to witness the execution of a deserter.

Jan. 9 - Wrote a letter to Polk Crisp's father to inform him that his son was on the sick list.

Jan. 13 - Went to Division Hospital to see Polk Crisp at the Division Hospital and found that he had been removed to the 9th Army Corps hospital at City Point. I received a letter for him from his father.

Jan. 17 - News of the capture of Fort Fisher and a salute fired at the enemy with shotted guns in honor of it.

Jan. 18 - At 5 P. M. go on picket in the trenches.

Jan. 22 - Received a welcome box of good things from mother with cigars and smoking tobacco from Mr. Gasherie DeWitt, of Belleville. Box had been broken in transit and the rain spoiled nearly all of it.

Jan. 29 - Today I am on the Alarm Guard. Mailed a letter of thanks to Mr. DeWitt, Belleville.

Jan. 31 - Regiment on monthly inspection. Mailed a letter to Bro. John, containing one to Cousin Mary, Bolton, England.

Feb. 1 - On Picket with Privates Deurr and McCluskey. In the afternoon there was great shouting and the pickets of both armies perched on top of their rifle pits. It turned out that a Flag of Truce was out, and (3) three Commissioners from the Confederate side were passing through our lines to confer with Lincoln and others to see what terms could be made to close the war - I shall never forget it.

Feb. 2 - I received a letter from Miss Annie Benson to James M. Crisp - 9th Corps. Hospital.

Feb. 3 - Sent the above and 3 other letters to him and one to his father at Belleville, N. J.

Feb. 5 - Capt. Hunkele returned from his furlough at his home in Newark, N. J. We received light marching orders and 4 days rations. Went to Church in evening and heard a Massachusetts chaplain.

Feb. 11 - We broke camp at Blackwater at 3 A. M. and occupied "Fort Davis" which was close by Had our quarters finished at 11 A. M.

Feb. 13 - Letter from G. DeWitt and Brother Henry.

Feb. 16 - A letter from Mr. Crisp to his son. Stanford and I procured passes on the Grand railroad to City Point and saw him there in our 9th Corps Hospital. While waiting for train, met our Lieut. Lange and he loaned be $2.00 without asking it, which was very welcome. I found that Crisp was well on the road to recovery but he said he did so much want the taste of an apple. I went out and after quite a search found a sutler with a few small ones and bought a half dozen. Now this was contrary to the surgeon's orders, but I sneaked them in to him. Many times since he told me that I saved his life.

Feb. 17 - A very heavy rain kept us all last night at the hospital and arrived back in camp at 12 noon and was called for the picket line at 4 P. M.

Feb. 20 - Cheer for the capture of Charleston, S. C., by Gen. Sherman's Army.

Feb. 22 - Washington's Birthday. Heavy shelling on the Appomattox River. Fort Mahone was opposite to us and for the first time they open fire on our relief of 100 on their way out to the trenches. No one was killed, but they had to scatter and finally got out all right.

Feb. 23 - At 11 P. M. saw quite a fire in Petersburg.

Feb. 24 - On Alarm Guard. A rainy night, 8 deserters came into our lines. Brisk shelling from both sides and our Regiment under arms most of the night.

Feb. 25 - Five months in the service today. It was reported that about 500 deserters came into our lines, 16 on our front. Signed pay roll and received $35.45.

Feb. 26 - Went down to Hancock Station and had a good square Dinner for $1.00. Saw about 70 deserters from the enemy.

March 4 - President takes the chair for 4 years more.

March 8 - Picked up a pocket book containing $9.25, advertised it as much as possible, so not finding an owner, used it.

March 15 - All sutlers are ordered to the rear which indicates a movement of some kind and go on Alarm Guard with Rodgers.

March 16 - All sutlers are moving back. Went to church in evening.

March 17 - Am on the picket lines again with Lance and Reiss. Singular occurrence during the evening - a half-grown toad hopped into our rifle pits and into our little fire which we always kept burning.

March 19 - A letter came to me to Crisp from his father and I mailed one to Dr. Arthur Ward, of Belleville. A new recruit came into my tent, from Newark, Louis Ayres, by name.

March 20 - Terrible shelling this P. M., our regiment just about formed for a Dress Parade, when the enemy spotted us and broke up the show. Our Major and Alonzo (Pop) Van Riper from Belleville, and our Left Guide of the regiment, had a close call from a shell which fell in the sand close to them, but failed to explode.

March 21 - A spy of the enemy caught in our lines last night. I am on camp guard today. Extra Pickets sent out tonight and John Duerr shot at 11 P. M. One Deserter in our guard house all night.

March 23 - Changed my residence to the next door with Obermann, Fruend and Veltpush. Heavy wind and trees blown down inside of our Fort Davis.

March 24 - A visit from Conrad Bein of the 40th N. J. Regiment Volunteers. Two deserters came into our lines and said we would be attacked before morning.

March 25 - At 4:30 A. M. the attack was made with 3 Brigades of the enemy, they got inside our lines, but were finally driven out with great loss and a great failure for General J. B. Gordon.

March 26 - Whole regiment turned out at 3 A. M. We then stacked arms and turned in again, but were told not to remove our equipment until the morning roll call.

March 27 - Sheridan's Cavalry came and encamped near us.

March 28 - Called out at 3:15 A. M. A visit from Jack McCluskey of the 3rd N. J. Cavalry, went on a Battalion Drill and were shelled by the enemy. On Alarm Guard in the afternoon, was placed to the left of Fort Davis and close by it. At

8 P. M. the long roll was beat and the regiment was under arms again; the climax seems to be near.

March 29 - The heavy picket firing last night which called the regiment out was caused by some deserters being fired on by their own side.

March 30 - Long roll beat last night at 10:30. Very rapid mortar shelling, under arms at 4 this A. M., go on picket in the trenches at 5 P. M.

March 31 - Our regiment posted in rear of Fort Rice until noon expecting an attack.

April 1 - At 11 last night 2 pieces of heavy artillery were brought into Fort Davis. This looks ominous. At 11:30 the regiment fell in and went out alongside the road where they waited there for hot coffee, and then we removed down to the front. We moved as far front as we could and then were ordered to lie flat on the ground. The enemy are firing lively with mortar shells and rifle shots. While lying flat, John Rogers received a fatal wound.

April 2 - At day-light the order to charge the enemy is given and we go and head for Fort Mahone, which we take and get inside but find they have a strong inner line and can get no further. Our Colonel orders us to retreat so we go back and use the front of the fort for a breastwork and hold the fort all day - at dusk - they retreated and never came back. The regiment retired at dusk to go back into our lines and into our home (Fort Davis) for the Night. Many of our regiment were killed and wounded. I had but one hour of sleep since coming off picket the previous day, so I slept like a stone on this night. I write home a few lines, all this was on Sunday - April 2nd.

April 3 - I am 22 today - yesterday I never expected to see it - go outside the Fort and see the pile of dead that had been brought in during the night, some of whom I recognized. One of the Belleville boys had been sent to the hospital but 5 days, then I saw Sergt. John Kehoe on a stretcher with one leg off. Michael McGuire, a Belleville man had gone out after dark and found him helpless, got him on his back and brought him in. It was a long distance to carry him. Now you can see what one comrade in the stress of war can do for another. Noble McGuire.

We are ordered to pack up after breakfast and leave Fort Davis, our late home, forever, and follow the retreating Confederates and just outside of Petersburg we are turned off the road, stacked our guns and rested for some time.

Our President Lincoln passed by on horseback with a small body guard. We all rushed to the roadside and greeted him. He has just crossed the very ground we had fought over the previous day. We had all gathered from rows of peach and pear trees near by, the pink and the white blossoms, which we made into small bouquets and put them in the muzzle of our guns, then we started off again and an the Brigade Music was massed in front. It was like a great moving bed of flowers.

As we approached the city we were greeted by 3 or 4 fine looking slaves I presume, but nearly white all of them. They waved their arms and called out, "Welcome Princes of Peace, we've been looking for yer dis long time but now wese looking right at yer." Then we passed on, all the drums playing "The Lass O' Gowrie," this I cannot ever forget - we soon passed through the city, it was at noon, and camped in a nice grove 10 miles away.

April 4 - 8 A. M. we go on the march again. During the day we met a rebel Brigade Gen. and Staff who are prisoners; go into camp at dark near a railroad, and here I discarded my overcoat.

April 5 - We resumed our march out following the Southside railroad. Now we meet a rebel Col. and 300 prisoners guarded by a company of our Cavalry. Sheridan is at our front and gives the enemy no rest.

April 6 - We are having a long march today and can hear the artillery firing which seems about 10 miles away. Pass Nottoway Court House and stop for the night about 11 P. M. This was the most lengthy and fatiguing march of my career, fully two thirds of the regiment fell out and took a rest on our own account, and most of these did not join the front until about 9 next morning. We finally get to Burksville Railroad Junction. Saw a lot of wounded "rebs" here. Saw, too, here a Union and Reb surgeon amputating limbs and they were very busy.

April 7 - We stop here all day. Holmes and I are drawn for picket duty.

April 8 - We draw rations. John Rodgers died today of his wounds.

April 9 - On the march again, and camp about 9 P. M.

April 10 - Off again at 7 A. M. and at noon we enter Farmville and cross a bridge into a paved street, the main street. As we got on to this pavement, a lone cavalry man passed and announced, "take your time boys! the War is over, Lee surrendered yesterday at 2 P. M. Many would not believe it. I was one that did. We turned off after a while and went into camp in a nice grove.

There was great joy at this news, and some of the boys went for a Fire Engine, got it out and paraded through the town cheering. Bells were rung wherever found. It was a hilarious time all the evening.

April 11 - Lee's men had to see the U. S. Provost Marshall, who occupied a place on the main street, there to sign a paper not to again take up arms. Then they had rations issued to all of them, which were very much needed.

April 12 - Saw the 6th, 2nd and part of the 25th Corps of our Army on their way back towards home. They made a grand sight for us.

April 13 - Men from Lee's army coming in here from all directions and I talked with several.

April 15 - Our Co. F were sent off on a special detail.

April 16 - Co. F got back at noon today. News that Gen. Johnston had surrendered to Sherman. Went to the M. E. Church at 2 P. M.

Heard that Pres. Lincoln had been shot.

April 18 - Part of the 24th Army Corps passed through on their way toward home. Dress Parade at 4:30 P. M., an Official Order was read of the death of President Lincoln by assassination.

April 19 - This is Wednesday, and is to be observed by all the U. S. Army, no work being done on account of funeral of Abraham Lincoln, the President.

April 20 - Eggs for breakfast. Struck out tents at 9 A. M. and marched back to Rice's Station, rested for dinner. Very hot and tiresome. Camp near Burkeville Junction for the night.

April 21 - Off again and reach Nottoway Court House at noon, I fell out and made coffee for dinner. My feet very sore, heard we were on the way to Washington, D.C., to be mustered out.

April 22 - Camped out last night 14 miles from Petersburg at the railroad water tank. There we slept on the ground.

April 23 - Sunday - Our 1st Brigade came along at 9 A. M. and we fell into our proper places and marched into Petersburg. A few of us went out to look over our battleground of April 2nd. This was where I expected to meet my death, but I really think an overruling power was watching over me at that time and also many times since.

April 24 - Off at 7 A. M. crossed the old lines of trenches near our Fort Steadman and camped at noon near City Point.

April 25 - Inspection of Arms and Knapsacks.

April 26 - Broke camp, went to the Point and took the steamer "Nereus."

April 27 - Sailed at Sunrise for Washington, D. C., passed Fortress Munroe at noon. Anchored in the mouth of the Potomac at night.

April 28 - At 4:30 A. M. off again; at Alexandria 3 P. M., go ashore and march to the High Ground at the back of the town and into camp.

April 29 - Received letters from home and one from Cousin Mary in Bolton, England.

April 30 - Inspection for muster at 11 A. M.

May 2 - James Crisp and I after our coffee started on foot for Mount Vernon, and saw "Washington's Tomb."

May 3 - Drilling all kinds now every day.

May 12 - Nothing of note until today - when in the evening all the camps lit up with candles.

May 13 - No drill today so cleaned and brightened up my rifle.

May 14 - News was received of the capture of Jefferson Davis and his staff at 9:30 A. M. and a brigade review at 3 P. M.

May 16 - Brigade Dress Parade. A quarrel broke out in Co. G. The fact is we are all getting tired of nothing but drill and want to be mustered out and start for home.

May 18 - We received news that a Grand Review of all the Army of the Potomac is ordered to be held in Washington on May 23rd, and the Western Army under Gen. Sherman on May 24th. Most all the regiment were sent down to guard paroled prisoners.

May 22 - Monday, Rose early to get ready for the march to the capital. Mailed a letter to my mother, and one other younger lady. Then we started on one more march to Washington, and arrived there at 12 noon. Stacked arms east of the Capitol and that was our camp for the night.

May 23 - This was the most wonderful parade that ever went down Pennsylvania Avenue, about 75,000 men and why? Because it was what was left of the Union Army. It drew to the reviewing stand in front of the White House many notable men from various parts of the world - President Lincoln was not there which caused a void in the hearts of the private soldiers now passing. It was now President Andrew Johnson. Our Regiment marched 16 files front, 32 to each Co. It received its first "Baptism of Fire" on the 2nd of April, 1865.

May 25 - 8 months in the service today.

May 28 - Helped Lawrence Burns to Hospital.

May 30 - Am on guard at Brigade Headquarters today.

May 31 - Visit from Joe Brooks and Jack McCluskey. Went down to the Potomac River for a swim. Marcus L. Ward, of Newark, known as the soldiers' friend, also visited our regiment and made a speech,

June 1 - Roberts, McCluskey and I walked down to Mt. Vernon and visited Washington's Tomb.

June 2 - Went fishing with Sam Hampson, got no fish; he tried to jab a water snake with his knife but was bitten on the thumb.

June 3 - A review of our 2nd Division today.

June 4 - Inspection at 7 A. M. Very hot.

June 5 - Brigade Review at 6 P. M. By our old Commander John G. Curtin, in tears as he rode along at his farewell.

June 6 - Our Company got its muster out roll. Looks like home. In the evening the 36th Mass. Regiment serenaded the 45th Pennsylvania and other Regiments of our Brigade as they were to leave for home.

June 7 - Our muster out rolls are being made today.

June 9 - 35th Mass. Regiment left for home this A. M. Our Regiment fell in and cheered them.

June 10 - The 7th Rhode Island and 36th Mass. left for home today. Our Col. Wildrick is acting Brigadier General.

June 11 - Got a pass to go to Alexandria - Saw Larry Burns in hospital there. Met his father also.

June 12 - A visit of 3 members of the 3rd N. J. Cavalry, John McCluskey, John McDonald and Lt. Ackerman.

June 13 - A good square meal of beef steak and onions was enjoyed by Polk Crisp and me tonight.

June 14 - Two members of our Company caught a live eagle and brought it into camp.

June 17 - The recruits which came to us were transferred to the 33rd N.J. Regiment. At about 1 P. M. the 39th was mustered out and we expect to leave for home tomorrow.

June 18 - Last night we had a grand illumination and paid our respects to the other regiments of the brigade. At midnight we turned in and so on to Washington, D.C. Took train to Baltimore arrived by the 4th and 7th R.I. Regiments, marched down to Alexandria our tents and at 6 A. M. left our last camp in Virginia, escorted there 2 P. M.

June 19 - Arrived in Philadelphia at 11:30 A. M. Had a good meal at the "Old Cooper Shop," attended by the ladies of the city. In the early evening we marched through the streets, where we were greatly cheered by the ladies especially, windows were all occupied and our eagle was carried on a perch and caused quite a sensation. We then took the train and arrived at Trenton. Marched out of station to a vacant spot near by. Stacked our guns and awaited a breakfast which the ladies of the vicinity served to us. We later on marched down State street, Trenton. Gov. Parker had invited m all to a luncheon at noon and made a speech of welcome.

June 20 - I arrived home in Belleville at 7:30 P. M. had a thorough bath and donned my citizen suit and made a call on one outside my own family.

In conclusion will say that I had a good (yes a very good) Captain in John Hunkele of Newark, N. J., and notwithstanding all the dangers and hardships that I successfully passed through, I did not get as much as a scratch. "Close Call," yes several that I was aware of at the time, and I am the only one left of the eight that enlisted from Belleville, N. J.

JAMES C. TAYLOR.

Aug. 24, 1925.

Presented to Belleville Historical Society, 1971, by Anna Underwood.

De Witt Press Print

115 Roseville Avenue

Newark, N.J.

William E. Blewett

Born in New York City, William E. Blewett came to Belleville at an early age.

In the spring of 1861, just after the Civil War broke out, he organized a company of volunteer troops for service in the Union Army.

The 101-man company, comprised mostly of Belleville men, arrived in Washington, D.C., in May.

Blewett's company, part of the First New Jersey Brigade, helped to cover the retreat of the Union Army after the first battle of Bull Run in Virginia two months later.

A second lieutenant in 1861, Blewett was made a first lieutenant by order of General Philip Kearny (for whom the town across the Passaic River is named) in 1862.

At the Battle of Gaines' Mill in June 1862, the Union troops sustained losses of nearly 6,000 killed and wounded at the hands of the Confederate Army; one of the dead was Color Sergeant Thomas Stevens of Belleville.

Blewett was shot in the chest but the bullet traveled down and lodged in his side. While returning to the rear for medical treatment, an exploding shell blew off his belt.

Blewett came home to Belleville on the Fourth of July. The fact that the bullet could not be located and removed prevented him from returning to active service.

Blewett served in the New Jersey National Guard and rose through the ranks to become a captain, major, and lieutenant colonel before resigning in 1874.

A jeweler by trade, William E. Blewett died in 1913.

Sources: American Civil War.com; Belleville: 150th-Anniversary Historical Highlights 1839-1989 by Robert B. Burnett and the Belleville 150th-Anniversary Committee Belleville, New Jersey. 1991

Maj. Gen. Daniel Henry Rucker

Major General, US Army (Arlington National Cemetery)

Born on April 28, 1812 at Belleville, New Jersey. As a young man, he moved to Grosse Ile, Michigan, a village near Detroit, and it was from Michigan that he was commissioned directly into the Army as a Second Lieutenant of Dragoons on October 13, 1837.

Source: http://www.arlingtoncemetery.net/dhrucker.htm

Died January 6, 1910, Washington DC

Pre-War Profession: Commissioned as 2nd Lt. in 1st Dragoons in 1837, Mexican war, quartermaster duty.

War Service August 1861 Major in Quartermasters Department, retained in a staff duties in Quartermaster's Department throughout the war, May 1863 appointed Brig. Gen. of Volunteers.

Brevet Promotions Maj. Gen. U.S.V. March 13, 1865, Maj. Gen. U.S.A. March 13, 1865.

Post War Career Army service in the Quartermaster's Dept., retired 1882 after forty-five years of duty.

Source: US Civil War Generals at http://sunsite.utk.edu/civil-war/ung_r.html

Capt. Aaron Young

Company F, Second Regiment. Aaron Young Captain May 28, '61 May 28, '61 3 Yrs Died of typhoid fever at Belleville, N. J., June 4, '62.

Sources: N.J. Civil War Record: Page 126, NEW JERSEY VOLUNTEERS. *http://www.njstatelib.org/plweb-dbs/civilwar/docoutputs/NJCWn126.html*

Stephen V.C. Van Renssalaer

Birth: unknown Death: May. 20, 1885 Burial: Christ Church Cemetery, Belleville, N.J.

Civil War Union Army Officer. Commissioned Captain and commander of Company A, 13th New Jersey Volunteer Infantry on August 22, 1861, and fought with his unit at the battles of Antietam, Fredericksburg, Chancellorsville and Gettysburg. On December 28, 1863 he was transferred to the 3rd New Jersey Volunteer cavalry, and was promoted to Major. Served with the cavalry until his resignation from the service on October 18, 1864.

Sources: Find a Grave – Christ Church at http://www.findagrave.com/cgi-bin/fg.cgi?page=cr&GRid=6405218&CRid=125991&pt=Stephen+Van+Renssalaer &

39th Regiment - Infantry - Volunteers

The 39th Regiment was organized under the provisions of an Act of Congress, approved July 22, 1861, and an Act of Congress, approved July 4, 1864, as set forth in General Orders No. 224, dated War Department, Adjutant General's Office, Washington, D. C., July 6, 1864, and under authority received from the War Department for the raising of two regiments of Infantry, and promulgated in General Orders No. 4, dated Office of Adjutant General, Trenton, N. J., August 24, 1864.

The Regiment was organized under the provisions of General Orders No. 110, War Department, Adjutant General's Office, Washington, D. C., April 29, 1863. Instructions were issued and recruiting for the Regiment immediately commenced. The Headquarters of the Regiment was established at Camp Frelinghuysen, Newark, N. J., and active measures were put forth to complete the organization at an early day.

The required number of men to complete the Regiment was soon raised and mustered into the service of the United States, by companies, for one year.

Company A was mustered in October 11; Company B, September 30; Company C, October 8; Company D, October 3; Company E, September 23; Company F, September 25; Company G, September 23; Company H, September 26; Company I, October 1; Company K, September 23, 1864, at Camp Frelinghuysen, Newark, N. J., by William O. Douglass, Second Lieutenant, Fourteenth Infantry, United States Army.

Soon after the commencement of this regiment, authority was issued for the raising of another regiment of Infantry, to be known as the 41st, recruiting being dull it failed of success - the men that had been enlisted for it were transferred to and joined this regiment.

The Regiment was fully completed and organized by the 11th day of October, 1864, having a full complement of men. Officers, 39; Non-Commissioned Officers and Privates, 973. Total, 1012.

It left the State by detachments. Companies E, F, G, H, and K, left October 4, 1864, under the command of Lieutenant-Colonel James H. Close; Company D, left October 9th, under the command of Captain Fowler Merrill; Companies B and I, left October 10th, under the command of Major William T. Cornish, and Companies A, C, and Field and Staff, left October 14, 1864, under the command of Colonel Abram C. Wildrick, and proceeded under orders direct to the front.

Arriving at City Point, Va., it was temporarily assigned to duty with General Benham's Brigade of Engineers, within the fortifications around Petersburg.

It remained in this connection but a short time; when it was assigned to the Ninth Army Corps. During the months of March and April, 1865, the strength of the Regiment was increased by the joining from Draft Rendezvous, Trenton, N. J., of a large number of recruits.

The Regiment continued its organization and remained in active service until the close of the war, and those not entitled to discharge under the provisions of General Orders No. 77, War Department, Adjutant General's Office, Washington, D. C., April 28, 1865, were transferred to the Thirty-third Regiment, in compliance with Special Orders No. 45, dated Headquarters, Ninth Army Corps, June 15, 1865, and were discharged with that regiment.

The remainder were mustered out of service near Alexandria, Va., June 17, 1865, under provisions of special orders from War Department, Adjutant General's Office, Washington, D. C., dated May 18, 1865, by Edward Rose, First Lieutenant Fifty-sixth Infantry, Massachusetts Volunteers, Assistant Commissary of Musters, Second Division, Ninth Army Corps.

The Regiment was first attached to General Benham's Brigade of Engineers, Army of the James - then to the First Brigade, Second Division, Ninth Army Corps.

The Regiment took part in the following engagements: Before Petersburg, Va., (Capture of Fort Mahone), April 2, 1865.

Source: NJ State Library, NJ Civil War Record, Page 1129

World War I

1917-1918

According to the American Battle Monuments Commission, of the 136,516 Americans that lost their lives during World War I, there were 4,452 Missing In Action. The population of Belleville in 1920 was 15,696. These 20 Belleville Sons are known to have died in the Great War. They are listed on the monument located in front of town hall.

Victory statue in front of Town Hall honors the Belleville sons "who served in the World War, and in perpetual memory of those of their number who gave their lives in the service and whose names are here inscribed."

> **William Charles Bain Jr., Harry Benjamin Blekicki (Smith), Carmine Caruccio, Edward J. Crowell, Gregory Mc Pherson Davey, George Eyre, Michael Flynn, Harry Melvin Garside, Henry Charles Hoag, George Kalvio, Edward Joseph Kane, Charles Mc Ginty, Charles Edgar Morgan, Michael John Murray, Charles Aloysius Schaffer, George S. Smith, William T. Smith, Fred W. Stockham, George A. Younginger**

Not listed: **Carmelo Sarno**

William Charles Bain Jr.

Private William C. Bain, Jr., 25, of 55 Dewitt Avenue, died of kidney failure on October 3, 1918. Born November 26, 1892 in Allegheny City, Pa., he was inducted at Newark on July 5, 1918, and assigned to combat engineers. He is survived by his mother Mrs. William Bain.

Sources: *State of New Jersey Dept. of State Div. of Archives & Records Management: World War I Casualties: Descriptive Cards and Photographs.*

Carman Caruccio

Born in Gaggiano, Salerno, Italy, Carman Caruccio (aka Carmine Corviccio, Caruscio) of Belleville was killed in action.

Sources: *State of New Jersey Dept. of State Div. of Archives & Records Management: World War I Casualties: Descriptive Cards and Photographs.*

George Eyre

Private George Eyre was killed in action on Oct. 19, 1918. He joined the Army from New Jersey. Pvt. Eyre served with the 312th Infantry Regiment, Eighth Infantry Division. He is buried at Plot E, Row 08, Grave 12, at Meuse-Argonne American Cemetery, Romagne, France.

Source: American Battle Monuments Commission

Henry Charles Hoag

Sgt. Henry C. Hoag, 25, died of lobar pneumonia at Fort Sam Houston, Texas, on October 14, 1919. He enlisted in the Army at Fort Slocum on Feb. 11, 1915. Hoag was promoted to corporal on June 1, 1917, and to sergeant on June 13, 1917. He listed his residence as West Orange, he was born in Newark. He is survived by his aunt Mrs. Margaret McGill of S. 14th Street, Newark.

Sources: *State of New Jersey Dept. of State Div. of Archives & Records Management: World War I Casualties: Descriptive Cards and Photographs.*

George Kalvio

(Jan. 11, 1919) – Private George John Kalvio, 22, died from pneumonia in France on Oct. 24. His sister, Miss Toinie Kalvio of Hillside Avenue, Nutley, said no details were given by the War Department. Kalvio graduated Nutley High School with the Class of 1914. His family has dispersed since he was inducted into the service last May.

New Jersey records indicate Pvt. Kalvio died of bronchopneumonia. He was born in New York City, and joined the Army at Newark on April 2, 1918. He served overseas from May 20, ,1918, to his death. He is survived by his father, Peter Kalvio of 10 Oak Street, Belleville.

Kalvio was in Headquarters Company, 312th Infantry Regiment, 78th Infantry Division. Pvt. Kalvio is buried at St. Mihiel American Cemetery, Thiaucourt, France, Plot A, Row 19, Grave 29.

Sources: *The Nutley Sun, American Battle Monuments Commission; State of New Jersey Dept. of State Div. of Archives & Records Management: World War I Casualties: Descriptive Cards and Photographs.*

Charles Mc Ginty

Private Charles Mc Ginty, 25, was killed in action on Sept. 29, 1918. He joined the Army from New Jersey. Pvt. Mc Ginty served with the 147th Infantry Regiment, 37th Infantry Division. He is survived by his sister Mrs. Lillie Schroeder of 126 Courtlandt Street, Belleville. He is listed as Missing in Action or Buried at Sea on the Tablets of the Missing at Meuse-Argonne American Cemetery, Romagne, France.

Source: American Battle Monuments Commission; State of New Jersey Dept. of State Div. of Archives & Records Management: World War I Casualties: Descriptive Cards and Photographs.

Thomas J. Mooney

Private First Class Thomas Joseph Mooney, 25, of 3 Cedar Hill Avenue, was killed in action on Sept. 27, 1918. He joined the Army on Sept. 22, 1917, from Brooklyn, New York. Pvt. Mooney served with the 106th Infantry Regiment, 27th Infantry Division. He is survived by a sister, Mrs. Catherine Huggins of No. 6th St., Newark. He is buried at Plot B, Row 02, Grave 02, at Somme American Cemetery, Bony, France.

Source: American Battle Monuments Commission; State of New Jersey Dept. of State Div. of Archives & Records Management: World War I Casualties: Descriptive Cards and Photographs.

Charles Edgar Morgan

Private Charles Edgar Morgan, 20, of 492 Joralemon Street, died of bronchopneumonia on May 19, 1917. He is survived by his father William B. Morgan of the same address. Born in Newark, Pvt. Morgan joined the Army at Ft. Slocum, N.Y., on April 29, 1917, where he served in the cavalry until his death.

Sources: State of New Jersey Dept. of State Div. of Archives & Records Management: World War I Casualties: Descriptive Cards and Photographs.

Michael John Murray

Pvt. Michael J. Murray, 27, died of lobar pneumonia on Oct. 5, 1918. Murray joined the Army at Ft. Slocum, N.Y., on May 25, 1917. He served in the 57th infantry. He is survived by his mother Mrs. Mary Murray of 52 Elliot St., Newark.

Sources: State of New Jersey Dept. of State Div. of Archives & Records Management: World War I Casualties: Descriptive Cards and Photographs.

Carmelo Sarno

Private Carmelo Sarno, 27, of 80 Heckel Street drowned on July 21, 1918. Born May in Volura, Italy, he entered service at Newark on May 26, 1918.

Sources: State of New Jersey Dept. of State Div. of Archives & Records Management: World War I Casualties: Descriptive Cards and Photographs.

Charles Aloysius Schaffer

Private Charles Schaffer, 27, of 10 Smith Street, Belleville, died of pneumonia on Oct. 4, 1918. Born in Ivanhoe, Va., Schaffer was inducted at Newark on July 5, 1918. He served in Company A, 5th Engineers at Camp Humphreys, Va. He is survived by his sister Elizabeth Schaffer of 55 Oriental Terrace, Newark.

Sources: State of New Jersey Dept. of State Div. of Archives & Records Management: World War I Casualties: Descriptive Cards and Photographs.

George S. Smith

Private George Stuart Smith, 24, of 34 Isaac St., Belleville, was killed in action on Nov. 1, 1918. He joined the Army from New Jersey and was inducted at Fort Slocum, N.Y. Pvt. Smith served with the Ninth Infantry Regiment, 2nd Infantry Division. He served in engagements at Verdun; Marne; Soissons; St. Mihiel; Mont Blanc Ridge and the Argonne Forest. He is survived by his mother Mrs. Marie Vreeland of the same address. Pvt. Smith is buried at Plot E, Row 39, Grave 34, at Meuse-Argonne American Cemetery, Romagne, France.

Source: American Battle Monuments Commission; State of New Jersey Dept. of State Div. of Archives & Records Management: World War I Casualties: Descriptive Cards and Photographs.

William T. Smith

Private First Class William Thomas Smith, 26, of 4 Harrison Street, Belleville, was killed in action on Oct. 23, 1918. He joined the Army from New Jersey. Pfc. Smith served with the 312th Infantry Regiment, 78th Infantry Division. Smith served overseas from May 20, 1918 to his death. He is survived by his father Christopher Smith of the same address. Pfc. Smith is buried at Plot B, Row 20, Grave 37, at Meuse-Argonne American Cemetery, Romagne, France.

Source: American Battle Monuments Commission; State of New Jersey Dept. of State Div. of Archives & Records Management: World War I Casualties: Descriptive Cards and Photographs.

George A. Younginger

Private George A. Younginger, 28, of 44 Wilson Place, Belleville, was killed in action on June 5, 1918. He served overseas from April 2, 1918, to his death. He joined the Army at Newark on Nov. 19, 1917.

Sources: State of New Jersey Dept. of State Div. of Archives & Records Management: World War I Casualties: Descriptive Cards and Photographs.

Edward Joseph Crowell – Michael Augustine Flynn

Belleville paid final tribute to two of its war heroes yesterday at the joint military funerals of Private Edward Joseph Crowell, Jr. son of Mr. and Mrs. Edward J.

Crowell, 19 Factory Street, and Private Michael A. Flynn, son of Police Chief Flynn, 11 Washington Street.

Throngs lined Washington Avenue as the cortege proceeded from St. Peter's Catholic Church to St. Peter's Cemetery. The bodies were borne on gun caissons. The photo shows the body of Private Flynn in the foreground, as the procession was passing the Town Hall.

Chums in boyhood, comrades in enlisting in the army, these two youths who made the supreme sacrifice in accidents far from the battle fronts after participating in some of the fiercest engagements of the war, went together to their graves, which lie side by side.

To honor these heroes, both of whom had been decorated for valorous conduct in fighting, the American Legion Post and the George Younginger and Abraham Lincoln Posts, Veterans of Foreign Wars, united yesterday to form the escort for the procession.

Source: Newark Star-Eagle

Belleville Buddies Die Overseas

Mr. and Mrs. Edward Crowell of 19 Factory Street, Belleville, last night received a telegram from the War Department that their son, Private Edward Crowell Jr., 23, had died of wounds in Brest, August 4, 1919. The soldier had been wounded in action, but was believed to have fully recovered.

He was a member of the Fifty-ninth Infantry and had been in France two years.

Private Crowell was wounded on Nov. 4, but took part in the victory parades in both London and Paris. He was twenty-six years old, was born in Belleville and was a member of the Belleville Democratic Club and St. Peter's Catholic Club.

Besides his parents he is survived by two brothers, Martin, who is in the Navy, and James of Belleville; and two sisters, Mrs. James Lockwood of Haskell and Mrs. George Machete of Forest Hill.

Source: Undated newspaper clipping.

Edward J. Crowell

Edward Joseph Crowell, Jr. was born on March 9, 1894, in Belleville, N.J. He was baptized on March 25, 1894 in St. Peter's Church in Belleville. He lived at 19 Factory Street.

As a boy growing up, Edward had a friend, Michael Flynn Jr., and as best friends go, these two boys were inseparable.

Then in 1916, every parent's nightmare was realized in the wake of World War I. Yet to young men like Edward and Michael, it was a time of honor and duty.

Edward enlisted in the Army on June 17, 1917 and was sent to Fort Slocum, N.Y. Eddie wanted his childhood friend to enlist with him, but Mikey was rejected because of his teeth. Flynn saved his money to have his teeth fixed and later reapplied and was accepted into the Army.

Later Edward was assigned to a training camp at Syracuse, N.Y. From here he was sent overseas.

While in Europe, the two friends were reunited and had a picture taken together with a John Grant of Boston who was Flynn's bunk mate. Pvt. Edward J. Crowell was a member of the 59th Infantry.

Crowell's grandnephew, Ed Morrows recalls his grandmother and Edward's sister, Catherine Machette, saying that her brother had the nickname of "Whitey". When I asked why was this his nickname, she said that the war had turned his hair white.

According to accounts, both tragically died after the war was over but before returning home. Eddie was in a bar the night before he was to sail home to America.

Another soldier was drunk and said some nasty remarks about Eddie's mother. A fight ensued and Eddie was stabbed in the temple. He died the next day, on August 4, 1919, as the ship he was to be on sailed from the harbor.

Michael Flynn

Michael Flynn, 20, was said to have been riding on a train in a boxcar with other soldiers. They were horsing around when Michael fell off and under the train and was killed instantly.

Throughout their lives they were inseparable and now both were honored in a joint funeral in Belleville. They were buried side by side in St. Peter's Cemetery.

Source: Written by Ed Morrows, grandnephew of Edward Crowell, Used with permission; State of New Jersey Dept. of State Div. of Archives & Records Management: World War I Casualties: Descriptive Cards and Photographs.

The following is from St. Peter's Church, Belleville, New Jersey - 150 Years

"On October 5, 1923, the Reverend Edwin Field was appointed to the post of pastor at St. Peter's Church in Belleville, New Jersey.

Father Field was a deeply patriotic man, and envisioned a monument to be constructed in memory of the men of the military and naval forces who had lost their lives in the "several wars."

With his objective in mind, he set off a section of the rectory grounds at the corner of William and Dow Streets as the place for this monument, and it was dedicated on May 30, 1929.

Five thousand people attended the ceremonies including John Barrett, the last of the Civil War veterans in Belleville; veterans of the Spanish American War and World War I; and members of the American Legion and its Ladies Auxiliary, as well as several other organizations.

The ceremony was described as beautiful and moving. The address of presentation to the church was made by John A. Matthews, and the speech of acceptance made by a former congressman, James Hammill.

Five thousand voices were raised to sing the "Star Spangled Banner," while Lt. Edward J. Lister of the Foreign Legion raised the flag to the top of the monument. Bishop Walsh led the congregation in the salute to the flag, and then the crowd sang "Holy God We Praise Thy Name."

Taps were sounded in memory of the war dead, and a salute fired under the direction of Lt. Commander Morrow of the U.S. Navy.

Names of those inscribed in the monument who lay down their lives for their country included Harry Benjamin Blekike, Carmen Carruccio, Edward Crowell, Michael Augustus Flynn, Henry Charles Hoag, Edward Joseph Kane, Charles McGinty, Thomas Joseph Mooney, Michael John Murray, Charles Aloysius Schaffer, William Thomas Smith, Edward W. Stockham, and George John Kalvio. This monument has since been relocated to a place of honor at the main entrance to the cemetery."

World War II

In 1940, the population of Belleville, N.J., was 28,167. Our township lost 117 sons in World War II.

According to Belleville: 150th Anniversary Highlights, nearly 3,500 Belleville citizens participated in WWII. According to the American Battle Monuments Commission, of the 405,399 Americans that lost their lives during World War II, there were 78,976 missing in action.

Gilmer E. Adams

(May 10, 1945) – Seaman 1/c Gilmer Eugene Adams was killed in action in the Pacific where he was serving with amphibious Navy forces. "Bucky" Adams, was the son of Mr. and Mrs. Willie Adams of May Street.

His parents received a telegram from the Navy on April 28, but the notice did not detail his reported date of death.

Born in North Carolina, Adams was 21 when he enlisted in 1942. He spent 2-1/2 years in the Atlantic. He transferred to the Pacific Theater of Operations six months ago.

Source: The Belleville Times

1st Lt. Ernest H. Alden

(Nov. 29, 1945) – 1st Lt. Ernest H. Alden, of Prospect Street, was reported killed in action in Austria in March. Alden was a navigator and radio operator on B-24 Bomber. He had been previously reported missing and is now officially presumed to be dead. The notification of his death was received by his wife Mrs. Nora Stevens Alden, of Phoenix, Ariz., on Armistice Day, his 25th birthday. Lt. Alden had been stationed with the 15th Army Air Force in Italy. He was awarded the Air Medal with cluster and the Purple Heart.

Source: The Belleville Times

Peter Andrusyn

Marine Private Peter Andrusyn was killed in action on Feb. 26, 1945. Andrusyn was awarded the Purple Heart. He is honored on the Tablets of the Missing at Honolulu Memorial, Honolulu, Hawaii.

Source: American Battle Monuments Commission

Joseph Antonik

U.S. Naval Reserve Aviation Ordnanceman 3/c Joseph Antonik was killed in action during World War II. He is the son of Mr. and Mrs. John Antonik, Ralph Street.

Sources: World War II Honor List of Dead and Missing, State of New Jersey, War Dept. June 1946.

Antonik brothers in service, 1944.

Walter J. Antonik

(Jan. 11, 1945) – Walter J. Antonik, 20, was killed Jan. 3, in a crash of a Liberator bomber on which he was a gunner and ordnanceman. He is the son of Mr. and Mrs. John Antonik of Ralph Street.

The patrol bomber, VPB-105, serial No. 38947, was returning from an operational mission and had been diverted to Exeter Airport due to bad weather, including patches of rain, sleet and snow flurries at its home base at Fleet Air Wing 7, Dunkeswell Airfield.

The pilot, Lt. George E. Pantano, had made contact with the field lights and asked for landing instructions.

Upon starting turn to base leg, the plane, during a downwind landing at night struck 50 feet from the top of a 600-foot Beacon Hill, Sidmouth, near Honiton.

The aircraft slid along for 175 yards before coming to a rest and burning.

Killed were Pilot Pantano, Ensign M. W. Garber, Walter Antonik, Ammf3c G. A. Matta, Sea1c A. R. Pelath, Amm 3c A. E. Simmons.

Crew members who escaped with minor injuries were Ensign Walter T. Wilson, Amm1c Joseph C. Juhasz, Arm3c Clarke R. Willey, Jr., and Arm3c Dean G. Ludlow.

The U.S. Navy and U.S. Army Air Force operated from Dunkeswell Airfield, England, during WWII, protecting the convoys and keeping open the vital sea lanes from America to Great Britain.

Antonik graduated from Belleville High School in 1942.

He entered the Navy in Jan. 29, 1943. He received his boot training at Sampson and his radar/gunner training at Memphis, Tenn., Jacksonville, Fla., Chincoteague, Va., and Boca Chica, Fla.

Antonik went overseas in October.

He is survived by brothers John and Bronislaw, both presently in service.

(March 23, 1944) -- Aviation ordnanceman 3/c Walter Antonik reported this week to Chincoteague, Va., for further training.

Antonik wears the American Theatre campaign bar, and submarine patrol ribbon, and member of combat air crew.

(Aug. 2, 1945) – A memorial dedicated by Fleet Air Wing Seven and contained the names of 182 U.S. Navy men – including Walter J. Antonik, who lost their lives while operating from the Air Station.

The memorial is located at the U.S. Naval Air Facility at Dunkeswell, England. The site is five miles inland from the English Channel, near Exeter, Devon. It is the only U.S. Naval Air Station in England.

A memorial organ in Kuneswell Parish Church has the names of the men on a bronze tablet.

Sources: The Belleville Times; Fleet Air Wing-Seven History by Gene McIntyre; National World War II Memorial; Newark Evening News, Feb. 6, 1945; MISHAPS: 03 JAN 45 A/C: PB4Y-1L; http://www.vpnavy.com/vp105_mishap.html, Terence Geary; http://www.usn-dunkeswell.info/; http://home.att.net/~jbaugher/thirdseries4.html; PB4Y-1 Liberator Bureau Numbers, http://www.air-navy.com/pb4y-1_buno.htm;

Patrick J. Barbone

(June 22, 1944) – Sgt. Patrick J. Barbone, of 61 Eugene Place, was killed in a pre-invasion bombing over France on June 2.

According to the Eighth Air Force history, the role of the heavy bombers from June 2-5 in preparation for the invasion of Normandy on June 6 included continuation of attacks against transportation and airfield targets in northern France and the institution of a series of blows against coastal defenses, mainly located in the Pas de Calais coastal area, to deceive the enemy as to the sector to be invaded.

The history contains the following about two missions on Friday, June 2.

Mission 384: In the morning, 521 of 633 B-17s and 284 of 293 B-24s hit V-weapon sites in the Pas de Calais area; 11 B-17s are damaged; 1 airman is killed in action, 1 wounded in action and 1 missing in action.

Mission 385: In the afternoon, 242 B-17s are dispatched to railroad targets in the Paris area; 163 hit the primaries, 49 hit Conches Airfield, 12 hit Beaumont-sur-Oise Airfield and 1 hits Caen/Carpiquet Airfield; 77 B-24s are dispatched to Bretigny Airfield in France; 13 hit the primary target, 47 hit Creil Airfield and 14 hit Villeneuve Airfield; 2 B-17s and 5 B-24s are lost, 2 B-24s are damaged beyond repair and 90 B-17s and 37 B-24s damaged; 1 airman is killed in action, 4 wounded in action and 68 missing in action.

According to the 489th bomb group, crewmen for the mission on June 2 to Bretigny and Creil, France, were: 2nd Lt. Peter H. Fiero, pilot;

2nd Lt. James W. Houtchens, co-pilot; 1st Lt. John D. Van Winkle, navigator; 1st Lt. Jack P. Blanton, bombardier; SSgt. Anthony J. Wisinski, engineer; Sgt. Patrick J. Barbone, radio operator; Sgt. George E. Zaprala, gunner; Sgt. Everett E. Hensley, gunner; Sgt. Thomas N. Dodds, gunner;

Sgt. Edward R. Kantner, gunner.

The aircraft was hit in the #3 engine which exploded and tore off the right wing. All aboard were lost.

Sgt. Barbone had been listed as missing in action since June. The telegram notifying his family that he had been killed in action came Jan. 12, 1945.

Sgt. Barbone was 1939 graduate of Belleville High School.

He was born Sept. 13, 1920, and enlisted in the Army in August 1942.

Sgt. Barbone was a radioman-gunner on a B-24 Liberator. He studied radio at Chicago and received his wings at Fort Myers, Fla.

He served with the 489th Bomb Group, Eighth Air Force, in the European Theater of Operations.

The Barbone-Mosco Post #7 Italian American War Veterans was incorporated and established in Belleville.

He is buried at Mount Olivet Cemetery, Bloomfield.

Sources: The Belleville Times; Remembrance - George Sbarra Belleville Times: June 22, 1944, March 15, 1945; National World War II Memorial; Newark Evening News, July, 12, 1944, Eighth Air Force History; Jim Woods 489th Bomb Group association.

Joseph Bengivengo

Corporal Joseph Bengivengo was killed in action about May 1945. His service number is 1210977

Sources: National World War II Monument, Leo Fracasso

Giavanni Bocchino

(Dec. 14, 1944) – Private Giavanni Bocchino, 20, was killed in action on Leyte on Oct. 25, 1944. He had been overseas with the Army 170th Engineer Combat Battalion engineers for three months. Bocchino entered active duty July 17, 1942. The son of Anthony and Michelina Bocchino of Lake Street, he had seven brothers and one sister.

Pvt. Bocchino is survived by his wife, Mary Gammaro, son Anthony, daughter Michelina. A son, John, was born Jan. 3, 1945, three months after his father died.

Bocchino is buried at Plot D, Row 12, Grave 137, in the American Cemetery, Manila, Philippines. He was awarded the Purple Heart.

Sources: American Battle Monuments Commission, The Belleville Times, Remembrance - George Sbarra

Charles R. Braun

Fireman 1st Class Charles R. Braun was killed in action on June 5, 1943.

Braun joined the U.S. Navy from New York. He is memorialized on the Tablets of the Missing at Honolulu Memorial, Honolulu, Hawaii.

Source: American Battle Monuments Commission

Alvin C. Brown

(Nov. 7, 1945) – The Veterans of Foreign Wars commemorated the Brown-Marshall VFW Post at 82 Broad Street, Bloomfield in honor of John Marshall and Alvin Brown.

Alvin Brown was killed in action while serving with the same outfit in April 6, 1945. He had previously served six years in the National Guard before entering the Army. According to the American Battle Monuments Commission, 7 Alvin C. Brown, served in the 370th Infantry Regiment, 92nd Infantry Division. He entered service from New Jersey.

Pvt. Brown was awarded the Purple Heart. He is buried at Plot B, Row 3, Grave 13, in the Florence American Cemetery, Florence, Italy.

Sources: The Belleville Times, American Battle Monuments Commission

John Brown

(June 21, 1945) – Corporal John Brown, 23, died May 28 in Manchusen Austria.

The son of Mr. and Mrs. Frank Brown of Hornblower Avenue, Cpl. Brown was a member of the medical detachment of the 21st Armored Infantry Battalion in General George Patton's Third Army. Cpl. Brown was recently awarded a Bronze Star for his efforts during the Third Army's march through France into Germany. Brown graduated Belleville High School in 1940. He entered the service in 1942, and went to Fort Dix., N.J., and then to Camp Polk, La., for additional training. He also trained in Texas and California. Brown went overseas in September 1944.

Source: The Belleville Times

2nd Lt. Victor R. Bruegman

(Aug. 9, 1945) -- 2nd Lt. Victor Bruegman, 26, was killed over Hungary on July 2, 1944.

Bruegman served in the 744th Bomber Squadron, 456th Bomber Group, Heavy which operated out of the Stornara Airfield located near Cerignola, Italy.

The target that day was the Shell Oil refinery at Budapest. Thirty planes from the 456th Bomber Group left for the mission, and eight did not return.

According to B-24 pilot Robert C. Alexander, his aircraft, #42-78072, was shot down over Budapest. Five of the men on board were killed, the rest - co-pilot, radio operator, navigator, nose gunner and engineer were - taken prisoner.

Alexander was the only member of the crew uninjured.

In a letter written to his dad on Oct. 9, 1944, Alexander "writing from Stalag Luft III ... I don't know if you knew but both "P.C." (Page Hendrickson, pilot) and "Brugie," (Victor Bruegman, bombardier) were killed. From all the information I have I seem to be the only one on my crew that got out with no injuries."

The crew comprised:

Pilot: Page C. Hendrickson - Wheeling, W. Va.

Co Pilot: Robert C. Alexander - Warrendale, Pa.

Navigator: Edward B. Wagner - Portland Ore., or Woodland, Calif.

Bombardier: Victor Bruegman - Belleville, N.J.

Top Gunner: Glenn W. Constable - Johnstown, Pa.

Engineer: Arthur A. Pope - Lombard Ill. (Pope did not fly that day. His replacement was a man named Plath)

Ball Gunner: John L. Weidrich - Buffalo, N.Y.

Nose Gunner: J. T. Phillips - Belmont, N.C.

Tail Gunner: Robert P. Mack - Milwaukee, Wis.

Radio Operator: Earl E. Richardson - Christiansburg, Va.

From a letter dated Nov 8, 1944, Alexander wrote from the POW camp:

"Dear Dad and Louise,

Just lately I've been getting my mail. On the 31st I received 8. (4 from you and one each from Rose Marie, Eula & Cliff, Frank Beveridge, and Mrs. Betty Bruegman.) Betty had a baby (a boy) on Sept. 22. Did she get my address from you. I don't think she knows yet that "Vic" is dead...."

According to Fred Riley, 746th Squadron:

Victor Bruegman was a bombardier in the 744th Squadron, I was a bombardier in the 746th Squadron and at Group Headquarters Victor graduated from the Big Spring Texas Bombardiers school in the class of 43-18 and I graduated from the Midland Texas Bombardiers school with the class of 43-11 on 4 August 1943. As I recall a class graduated every two weeks so he would have graduated about 14 weeks later, probably in November. I too was on that mission to Budapest, probably the worst of the war for the 456th Bomb Group. That day we lost six planes and crews. 2 July 1944, Group mission No. 77, the target Shell oil refinery at Budapest Hungary. Thirty six bombers carrying 67.38 tons of GP bombs attack the facility with good results reported. The flak at the target was heavy, intense and accurate. The air engagement was very intense with sixty enemy aircraft reported, of which twenty six were destroyed, eight probably destroyed and four damaged. The 456th group lost six planes and crews. Combat flight time was 6:25 hours. The Shell oil refinery and storage area at Budapest Hungary, was the target during the 744th Bombardment Squadron's most tragic mission of W.W.II. Eight of its B-24's flew out with the 456th Bomb Group and only two returned. As the bombers broke away after the bomb run a waiting formation of FW-190's and ME-109's attack with devastating accuracy. Six bombers from Baker box were seen shot down in the target area. Reporting crews, were unable to distinguish between these aircraft as to number, as a result a definite report could not be made on the individual planes. It was reported however, two ships were seen to disintegrate in mid-air, two were seen going down with engines afire, one with a wing broken off and another with the tail broken off. All reported seeing chutes open, varying from four to five, but were unable to tell from which aircraft. The bombing was successful however, and the 456th Bomb Group was awarded its second Distinguished Unit Citation as a result of this mission. Sixty one crewmen were reported as MIA, one KIA and four gunners wounded. These numbers were later determined to be much greater.

The sixth 744th plane lost was A/C #42-78072, piloted by Lt. Page Hendrickson and crew. The Crew: Pilot - 2nd Lt. Page C. Henderickson -KIA

Co-pilot - 2nd Lt. Robert C. Alexander - POW - Deceased 2/26/97

Bombardier - 2nd Lt. Victor R. Bruegman - KIA

Upper Turret - S/Sgt. Glenn W. Constable - KIA

Ball Turret - Sgt. Robert R. Mack - MIA - KIA

Radio Operator - S/Sgt. Carl E. Richardson - POW - Current Status Unknown.

Navigator - 2nd Lt. Edward B. Wagner - POW - Deceased 1985

Nose Turret - Sgt. John L. Weidrich - POW – Current Status Unknown.

Engineer - T/Sgt. Louis C. Plath - POW – Deceased 7/21/44

Victor Bruegman was interred in the American Military Cemetery, Lorraine France Plot K, Row 9, Grave 14.

Bruegman enlisted in the Army on April 2, 1941. He served 1-1/2 years in the infantry before transferring to the Air Corps in 1943. He received his wings at Big Spring Bombardier School in Texas on Dec. 25, 1943. He went overseas in May and landed in Italy on June 6, 1944.

Second Lt. Victor R. Bruegman, U.S. Army Air Forces, serial number O-703441, of the 744th Bomber Squadron, 456th Bomber Group, Heavy, entered the service from New Jersey.

Bruegman, a 1937 graduate of Belleville High School is the son of Mr. and Mrs. Alvin Bruegman of Malone Avenue. His brother Richard is serving in the South Pacific.

His family was notified that he was missing in action on July 27, 1944. He is survived by his wife Betty, and has a son, Victor Jr. whom he never saw.

2nd Lt. Victor Bruegman, who received the Air Medal and the Purple Heart, is buried at Plot K, Row 9, Grave 14, in the Lorraine American Cemetery, St. Avold, Moselle, France.

Sources: American Battle Monuments Commission; One Soldier's Story - A Collection of War Stories by Robert W. Reichard; The Belleville Times: July 27, 1944, Aug. 9, 1945; 456th Bomber Group; Richard Bruegman, brother, Oct. 23, 2003; Robert C. Alexander - Catherine Alexander; National World War II Memorial.

Arthur Burke

(Nov. 30, 1944) -- Staff/Sgt. Arthur Burke, 33, the son of John and Anna Burke of Washington Avenue, was killed June 9 in the English Channel. He is believed to have perished when his landing craft was attacked during the early days of the Normandy landing. Burke is survived by brothers Harry and John; and four sisters, Dorothy, Hazel (Rowe), Ethel (Connolly) and Kathleen (Neal); and uncle to 18 nieces and nephews.

Company. He entered the Service from New Jersey, and died on June 9, 1944.Burke is listed on the Missing in Action or Buried at Sea Tablets of the Missing at Normandy American Cemetery, Colleville-sur-Mer, France. He was awarded the Purple Heart.

According to American Battle Monuments Commission, Burke, U.S. Army serial No. 32148158, served in the 3422nd Ordnance Automotive Maintenance Three Belleville sons, Sgt. Edward Henris,

Burke and Sgt. Carmine Olivo were likely on the same ship as all three served in 3422nd Ordnance Automotive Maintenance Company. The families were notified in July, November and December 1944, respectively.

Sources: American Battle Monuments Commission; The Belleville Times, Nov. 30, 1944; National World War II Memorial; Mary Ann Rowe, Niece (June 11, 2004).

NAP1 42 GOVT=DUX WASHINGTON DC JUN 21 1048P
MRS A BURKE=
    577 WASHINGTON AVE

THE SECRETARY OF WAR DESIRES ME TO EXPRESS HIS DEEP REGRET THAT YOUR SON PRIVATE ARTHUR BURKE HAS BEEN REPORTED MISSING IN ACTION SINCE NINE JUNE IN EUROPEAN AREA IF FURTHER DETAILS OR OTHER INFORMATION ARE RECEIVED YOU WILL BE PROMPTLY NOTIFIED=
    ULIO THE ADJUTANT GENERAL.
        734A JUN22.

NAP45 46 GOVT=DUX WASHINGTON DC NOV 21 1206P
MRS A BURKE=
    577 WASHINGTON AVE

THE SECRETARY OF WAR ASKS THAT I ASSURE YOU OF HIS DEEP SYMPATHY IN THE LOSS OF YOUR SON PRIVATE ARTHUR BURKE WHO WAS PREVIOUSLY REPORTED MISSING IN ACTION REPORT NOW RECEIVED STATES HE WAS KILLED IN ACTION NINE JUNE IN THE EUROPEAN AREA LETTER FOLLOWS=
    DUNLOP ACTING THE ADJUTANT GENERAL.
        134P.

Joseph Burlazzi

Private Joseph L. Burlazzi, 25, of Mt. Pleasant Avenue, the "first local war casualty" who was killed in action on March 23, 1943, near Tunisia, was posthumously awarded the Distinguished Service Cross. Pvt. Burlazzi, 25, earned the service cross during his last encounter.

Brigadier General E. L. Ford said, " ... during assault on enemy forces ... Burlazzi and another man volunteered ... into the face of enemy fire to take up an abandoned machine gun position ... they were responsible for turning an enemy assault into a retreat and allowing our own troops to advance... (they) moved (the) machine gun position ... Burlazzi went up with his rifle to provide security for his companion and was struck and killed by artillery fire."

His brother Guido accepted the award.

Pvt. Burlazzi enlisted in the Army in 1940. He trained at Fort Devons, Mass. He went overseas more than a year ago and was stationed in England, until the invasion last fall of North Africa. A veteran of ten successive battles, he aided in the capture of German prisoners.

Burlazzi was born in Smith's Mills, Pa.

Source: The Belleville Times, April 15, Oct. 7, 1943

Morris C. Catalano

(June 29, 1944) – Private Morris C. Catalano of Belleville Avenue, was killed in action at Anzio, Italy, on May 14. The Anzio beachhead invasion began in May 1944. Allied troops were held on the beachhead for five months.

Catalano, 28, was born in Brooklyn, and lived most of his life in Belleville. He attended Silver Lake School. He entered the Army in September 1943. He attended basic training at Camp Croft, S.C. He is survived by his parents. His wife and a 22-month-old son, Robert, live in Newark. His service number is 42009073

Sources: Belleville Times, June 29, 1944; Remembrance - George Sbarra; Tiscali Reference Encyclopedia – Hutchinson

Lt. Kenneth A. Chewey

(Aug. 16, 1945) – Lt. Kenneth Andrew Chewey died in Manila, Philippines, after a few days of illness on July 23. Lt. Chewey received two battle stars for action in the Leyte and Luzon campaigns.

He is the son of Mr. and Mrs. Stephen Chewey of Malone Avenue. Lt. Chewey is a 1940 graduate of Belleville High School. Chewey attended Rutgers University for three years.

He entered the service Oct. 2, 1942, and was commissioned 2nd lieutenant on May 20,1944. He enlisted in the Signal Corps Reserve. Chewey transferred to the Army and then attended basic training at Camp Crowder, and Officer Candidate School at Fort Monmouth. He trained at Camp Crowder, Md., and was deployed overseas in January 1945. He served with the Signal Corps in New Guinea and the Dutch East Indies and the Philippines. He participated in the invasions of Leyte and Luzon. He was stationed at a Signal Service Battalion at Santa Mesa, Philippines when he became ill. He died shortly after in a Manila hospital.

While at Rutgers, Kenneth majored in Electrical Engineering. He was a master concert violinist and served as president of Tau Kappa Epsilon.

A member of the Black Fifty, Kenneth attended Officer Candidate School at Fort Monmouth in 1944.

Sources: The Belleville Times, Aug. 16, 1945, Rutgers University Oral History

Joseph J. Cifrodella

(Nov. 30, 1944) – Torpedoman's Mate 2/c Joseph J. Cifrodella, 22, of Magnolia Street was presumed killed in action Nov. 14, when his ship, the Escolar, one of 52 submarines lost during the war, failed to return from a patrol on the Yellow Sea.

The USS Escolar was a Balao class submarine carrying a crew of 6 officers and 60 enlisted men.

Cifrodella, of 282 No. Belmont Ave, first served on a heavy cruiser, then volunteered for submarine duty. Born Feb. 5, 1922, he left school to enlist in the Navy in 1940. His service number is 2238292. In his honor, the people of Silver Lake founded the Joseph Cifrodella Amvets Post #26. His parents are Mr. and Mrs. John Cifrodella.

He was awarded the Purple Heart. He is listed with the Missing in Action or Buried at Sea on the Tablets of the Missing at Manila American Cemetery, Manila, Philippines

THE SECRETARY OF THE NAVY
WASHINGTON
223 B2 92
5 December 1945

Mr. and Mrs. John Cifrodella
Magnolia Street
Belleville, New Jersey

My dear Mr. and Mrs. Cifrodella:

Your son, Joseph John Cifrodella, Torpedoman's Mate second class, U. S. Navy was officially determined to be missing in action as of 13 November 1944. He was serving aboard the USS ESCOLAR when that submarine was reported overdue and presumed to be lost. The exact date the vessel was lost is not known.

On 13 September 1944, the ESCOLAR departed from Pearl Harbor on a war patrol in the Yellow Sea and failed to return. The last communication received from the submarine was on 17 October 1944. To date no further information has been received by the Navy Department regarding the ESCOLAR or any member of her crew.

In view of the strong probability that the submarine sank as a result of enemy action in waters known to be controlled by the enemy, and that your son was lost with his ship, because no official nor unconfirmed reports have been received that he survived, because his name has not appeared on any lists or reports of personnel liberated from Japanese prisoner of war camps, and in view of the length of time that has elapsed since he was determined to be missing in action, I am reluctantly forced to the conclusion that he is deceased. In compliance with Section 5 of Public law 490, 77th Congress, as amended, the death of your son is, for the purposes of termination of pay and allowances, settlement of accounts, and payment of death gratuities, presumed to have occurred on 14 November 1945, which is the day following the expiration of twelve months in the missing status.

I know what little solace the formal and written word can be to help meet the burden of your loss, but in spite of that knowledge, I cannot refrain from saying very simply, that I am sorry. It is hoped that you may find comfort in the thought that your son gave his life for his country, upholding the highest traditions of the Navy.

Sincerely yours,

James Forrestal (signed)

Sources: American Battle Monuments Commission; Belleville Times; Remembrance - George Sbarra; World War II Honor List of Dead and Missing, State of New Jersey, War Dept. June 1946

Clatie R. Cunningham Jr.

Staff Sgt. Clatie Ray Cunningham, Jr. was killed on a mission over the Mekong River in French Indo-China (Vietnam), on July 23, 1945, when the B-24 in which he was the flight engineer crashed after a bombing run scored a direct hit on an enemy barge.

The explosion of the barge was so bad that the B-24 was damaged. The pilot then headed to a point assigned to a lifeguard submarine.

Cunningham and nine other crewmen bailed out, however, only three crewmen survived. One was picked up on July 26 by a Catalina seaplane. Separate submarines picked up two crewmen.

According to the 868th Bombardment Squadron Unit History, supplied by Clatie Cunningham III, the B-24 was based at Morotai in the South Pacific.

That day's mission sent three B-24s on a "snooper mission" staged through Palawan in the Philippines. Their primary target was to search out the Bassac and Mekong rivers in French Indo-China (now Vietnam).

Lt. Walter Low piloted aircraft No. 808, Cunningham's bomber. Three bombs were dropped on a 200-foot coastal steamer from an altitude of 100 feet, scoring direct hits immediately sinking the vessel.

Three bombs were dropped on Sugar Charlie Sugar, 130 feet in length, scoring near misses with no visible damage resulting. The vessel was sunk later by Aircraft No. 780.

Two oil barges, 120 feet in length, being towed by a tug, were attacked with three bombs being dropped from 100 to 200 feet. Direct hits were scored, exploding both barges, with orange flames and smoke to 1500 feet.

Although four to five second delay fuses were used, the force of the explosions blew out the waist windows of the attacking B-24, and the pilot was thrown from his seat.

Soon thereafter, the No. 2 engine was afire and had to be feathered, or shut down, necessitating a bail-out of the entire crew at sea.

Low radioed to Aircraft No. 780 nearby that they had insufficient gas supply to get back to Palawan.

Aircraft No. 780 made sub contact and received instructions to have the crew of the distressed aircraft bail out at a certain location.

THE CREW -- Back row, from left, S/SSgt Clatie R. Cunningham, Tenn.; S/Sgt. Nicholas Meriage, Pa.; A.S. Pitt, Conn.; S/Sgt. John W. Knigga, Ky.; Sgt. Charles E. Carroll, Mass.; Sgt. Lyle D. Kowalske, Mich.; S/Sgt. Roy E. Hayes, Ill.; Front row, from left, Lt. Ed Gingerich, Mich.; Lt. Walter N. Low, Maine; Lt. Don McDermott, Ga.; Lt. Stanley L Reed, Sea Girt, N.J. Photo taken January 1, 1945. Crew members not shown: Sgt. Clifton E. Leach (replaced A.S. Pitt) <Photos courtesy Clatie R. Cunningham III.>

Three men bailed out on the first pass over the given position. Five men bailed out on the second pass over the same position. Two men bailed out on the third and last pass over the same position.

Bail-out was made and all ten chutes were seen to open. Witnesses said that all ten chutes landed with 3 miles.

Edward Ginerich was picked up by a Catalina on July 26.

Low was rescued by submarine Hammerhead on July 27.

Lt. Stanley Reed was picked up by submarine Sidonet on July 28.

No trace of the rest of the crew was ever found.

Lost were: 2nd Lt. Donald C. McDermott, S. Sgt. Clatie R. Cunningham, Sgt. Charles E. Carroll, S. Sgt. Roy E. Hayes, S. Sgt. John W. Knigga, S. Sgt. Nicholas Meriage and Sgt. E. Clifton Leach.

Sgt. Cunningham, who was all of 138 pounds at 5'10", with blue eyes and red hair, attended Casey Jones School of Aeronautics in Newark, N.J., from Sept. 26, 1941 to March 21, 1942.

While there, he met Alice, the daughter of John William and Helen Rose Papartis of Stephens Street, Belleville.

They were married in Union, N.J., on Feb. 9, 1944.

Sgt. Cunningham, 23, was survived by his wife Alice Sylvia, of Stephens Street, Belleville; twin sons Clatie III and John W., born June 5, 1945, in Glen Ridge, N.J.; his mother, Laura Cunningham and a brother Billy Joe, both of Chattanooga, Tenn.

Sgt. Cunningham was awarded the Air Medal with oak leaf cluster, and the Purple Heart.

He is listed as Missing in Action or Buried at Sea on the Tablets of the Missing at Manila American Cemetery, Manila, Philippines.

Sources: American Battle Monuments Commission; 868th Bombardment Squadron Unit History; Clatie R. Cunningham III; National Archives and Records Administration; Naval Museum and Naval Historical Center; Newark Evening News, March 20, 1946; U.S. Army Forces Western Pacific casualty information, July 1946; US Air Force Historical Research Agency; War Department - Report of Death; Lost in the Victory – Reflections of American War Orphans of World War II – by Calvin L. Christman

Joseph J. Curran

Technical Sergeant Joseph J. Curran was declared killed in action on March 1, 1946. He served with the 18th Infantry Regiment, First Infantry Division. He entered the service from New Jersey. Sgt. Curran is listed as Missing in Action or Buried at Sea on the Tablets of the Missing at Netherlands American Cemetery, Margraten, Netherlands. He was awarded the Silver Star, Bronze Star, and the Purple Heart.

Sources: American Battle Monuments Commission; Newark Evening News, July 9, 1943, March 6, 1946

Lt. John J. Daly, Jr.

(Aug. 10, 1944) – Lt. John J. Daly, Jr., was killed in action in Normandy on July 4. Lt. Daly commanded a paratroop company. In April 1942, he attended Officer's Candidate School at Ft. Benning, Ga. He has been overseas since last Christmas.

After Officers Candidate School, John volunteered for Jump School. He was well prepared for his leadership role in the newly formed 508th Parachute Infantry Regiment, of the 82nd Airborne Division. John and the entire 508th were sent overseas to Nottingham, England, in December of 1943. According to the unit history, they jumped from 300 feet over Normandy at 2:40 A.M. on June 6, 1944. John was killed in action while leading his men in the invasion of Normandy.

At the time of his death, Lt. Daly and his wife Doris, were expecting a child.

Daly was graduated from Belleville High School in 1932. He played football there and at Manhattan College in Riverdale, N.Y. While at Manhattan he was a star catcher and team described "spark plug" of the spirited Jasper baseball team. Under John's leadership Manhattan enjoyed a 6 win, 3 loss, 1 tie 1938 season. The Jaspers bested such great teams as Michigan State, Georgetown, Detroit, North Carolina State, Niagara and St. Bonaventure. For his talent, determination and sheer tenacity, John was voted best athlete of 1938.

Daly was vice president of "The New Jersey Club," an off-campus organization of Manhattan College students from across the Hudson River in New Jersey. Among the firsts for John and The 1938 New Jersey Club was an annual dinner dance held at a hunting lodge on The Palisades in New Jersey, which was the first Manhattan College dance to be broadcast live over the radio, direct from the floor of the event.

After graduating from Manhattan College in 1938, Daly played for the Jersey City Giants. The Jersey City Giants were a popular local attraction and a minor league farm team of The New York Giants. Daly also was an assistant coach at Belleville High School.

Daly's U.S. Army enlistment information shows that he enlisted on April 2, 1941. His Serial Number was 32064820. His branch alpha and branch code was "Branch Immaterial - Warrant Officers, USA." It also indicates that his civilian occupation was as a teacher.

He is interred at Beverly National Cemetery, Burlington County, N.J. Plot: I, 0, 197

Sources: The Belleville Times, Aug. 10, 1944; Newark Evening News, Aug. 5, Oct. 21, 1944; William Lynch of Millstone Township, N.J.; Dick O'Donnell and the members of The 508th Parachute Infantry Regiment http://www.508pir.org; http://www.findagrave.com/cgi-bin/fg.cgi?page=gr&GRid=551684

William H. Deighan

Sergeant William Deighan, U.S. Army Air Forces, 568th Bomber Squadron, 390th Bomber Group, was the engineer/top turret gunner aboard the B-17 heavy bomber #232026, nicknamed "Tis a Mystery" piloted by 1st Lt. Duane

G. H. Sweeny of Iowa. All members of the Sweeny crew were killed in action on December 30, 1944.

The Missing Air Crew Report, #11247, consists of four pages – none of which give any detail as to the crash of the aircraft into the sea except as quoted below:

"A/C 026, flying #3 position of lead squadron took off as brief at 08:34 hours climbing in pattern and disappeared into the clouds over the base which were from 3,000 to 9,500 ft., with moderate to severe icing conditions reported at about 7,000 ft. A/C 026 was not seen nor heard from after entering clouds."

(Jan. 25, 1946) – A high mass of requiem for Sgt. William H. Deighan, son of Mr. and Mrs. John Deighan of Centre Street, Nutley, listed as missing over Kassel, Germany, since December 30, 1944, and now officially declared dead, will be held in St. Peter's Church, Belleville on Feb. 2.

Sgt. Deighan had been in service two years and had trained in Texas before going overseas where he served as gun crew chief on a B-17 with the Eighth Air Force.

Born in Belleville, Sgt. Deighan attended Belleville High School and Bloomfield Vocational school and had been employed at the Viking Tool Company, Belleville, before entering service.

He was awarded an Air Medal and a Purple Heart. Deighan is memorialized at the Cambridge American Cemetery, Cambridge, England.

Sources: American Battle Monuments Commission; National World War II Memorial; Newark Evening News, Jan. 19, 1946; The Nutley Sun, Jan. 25, 1946; 390th Bomber Group Memorial Museum, Research Dept.

Edward DiCarlo

(Nov. 15, 1945) – A new pipe organ will be dedicated on Sunday in honor of 53 members of the Silver Lake Baptist Church who are serving in the Armed Forces and in memory of Sgt. Edward DiCarlo who was killed in action in Guam. DiCarlo, who entered the service in 1942, saw action in the South Pacific and died June 26.

His mother died in 1937. His father died this past January, when the Sergeant was home on emergency furlough. He is survived by his brothers Guy, Joseph and William.

Sgt. DiCarlo in a letter from Guam asked Rev. Benedetto Pascale about a stained glass in memory of his parents.

The First Italian Baptist Church of Silver Lake was originally dedicated Nov. 21, 1914 with Rev. Pascale who was its pastor for 75 years.

Sources: The Belleville Times; Belleville: 150th-Anniversary Historical Highlights 1839-1989 by Robert B. Burnett and the Belleville 150th-Anniversary Committee Belleville, New Jersey. 1991

John Del Grosso

Marine Master Tech. Sgt. John Del Grosso of Cleveland Street, died in San Diego, Calif. on Nov. 8, 1943.

He had been under treatment for pernicious anemia - a blood disease, and in spite of several blood transfusions, succumbed suddenly after a short illness. A Marine for four years before the war, and honorably discharged, Del Grosso re-enlisted shortly after Pearl Harbor. He had learned to fly in Nutley, and hoped for overseas service. He was stationed, however, at the Naval Air Base at Santiago, Calif., as a technical instructor where he his family joined him about a year ago. There was plenty of action even in California, for Sgt. Del Grosso was on flight duty, making repairs and testing planes. With him in California, were his wife, the former Blanche Orlando of Race Street, and his sons Jack, 11, and Bob, 9. He is also survived by his mother, Mrs. Minnie Del Grosso of Newark.

According to his son, John R. Del Grosso, the Marine was stationed at the North Island U.S. Naval Air Station in San Diego, at the time of his death, not Santiago. He passed away in the Balboa Naval Hospital in San Diego.

"My dad died when I was age 10 and my brother Robert (Bob) was age 8. Our mother Blanche (his only wife) was age 36. Dad grew up on Cleveland Street in Belleville. His father was Genaro Del Grosso and his mother was Minnie. He had 13 siblings.

"Dad ran away from home and joined the Marines at age 16 and served in a Haitian Campaign during the 1920's. After his hitch he became a master auto mechanic and also a watch maker.

"He met my mother and they married at his age 26, they had us two sons and we lived in Harrison, NJ for a short time and then moved on to Nutley. He also became a civilian pilot, soloing in 1939 at the Lincoln Airport in Caldwell, NJ.

"When the Japs bombed Pearl Harbor, he immediately reenlisted in the Marines and was given the rank of staff sergeant. His first assignment was at Quantico, Va., and after a few months there he moved us to Fredericksburg, Va., where he came home to be with us each night.

"He was then assigned to the North Island Naval Base at San Diego, Calif., where now at the rank of Master Sergeant he was in charge of instrument repair for the damaged Grumman Wildcat's, TBF's and Catalina Aircraft for the Navy and Marines.

"One day I remember seeing the USS Hornet Carrier there with shot up Wildcats on its deck as my mother would sometimes take us to North Island to visit him there. We lived at 201 Ash St. in San Diego until his death. He repaired watches there nights for extra money. I know one of his hobbies was to play the piano by ear and he also built a midget racing car while in Nutley before entering the Marines again in 1939.

"Over the years people have told me he was a very happy and good family man. I am 75 now and have never heard a bad word spoken against him and am proud he was my father."

Sources: *The Nutley Sun*, Nov. 12, 1942, *The Belleville Times*, Aug. 31, 1944; (Jack) John R. Del Grosso, May 26, 2008, November 26, 2008

Nicholas Del Grosso

(April 6, 1944) – Pfc. Nicholas Del Grosso, 19, son of Mr. and Mrs. Ignazio Del Grosso of Mt. Prospect, was reported killed in action around Feb. 20. Del Grosso entered the Army in April 1943. He was stationed in North Africa before going to Italy. He was graduated from Belleville High School in 1941, where he played on the school basketball team.

Del Grosso served in the 52nd Quartermaster Battalion. According to the American Battle Monuments Commission, he died April 30, 1945. He is listed as Missing in Action or Buried at Sea on the Tablets of the Missing at Florence American Cemetery, Florence, Italy. Del Grosso was awarded the Purple Heart.

Nicholas J. Del Grosso was the youngest of six children born to Ignazio and Adeline Del Grosso, who emigrated in 1905 from Benevento, Italy, to Belleville.

He attended Belleville School Eight and was graduated from Belleville High School, Class of 1941.

He was described as good kid and an excellent baseball player. After high school he was employed by American Precision Company on Cortlandt Street in Belleville until he was inducted into the Army on April 8, 1943.

He received his Basic and Advanced Infantry training at Camp Croft, Spartanburg, S. C., until August when he had a ten-day furlough, his last visit home before going overseas.

He embarked on a troop ship at Fort Patrick Henry, Newport News, Va., in September 1943 and was in a replacement unit in Oran, North Africa, in October. He then was transported by ship to Naples, Italy, where he was assigned to the 3rd Infantry Division, 30th Regiment, Company E.

He was in the vicinity of Mount Rotundo near Mignano, Italy, during the Cassino campaign when he was "slightly injured in action on November 14."

He was then recuperating from his injuries for approximately six weeks in a field convalescent hospital near Naples.

He rejoined Company E in late December, and then participated in the Anzio invasion on Jan. 22, 1944.

He was in the Anzio beachhead for nearly a month when on Feb. 19, his 30th Regiment was called on to push back the intensive German attack that was threatening to push the Allied beachhead into the sea. All the officers, the sergeant and half of Company E were killed on this day. Del Grosso was listed as killed in action on Feb. 20, near Carano, Italy.

This counterattack was fought so courageously that it was credited with saving the beachhead and resulted in the enemy assuming a defensive posture for the remainder of the Anzio Beachhead campaign.

Del Grosso was buried in the Nettuno cemetery on Feb. 23. His body was repatriated to St. Peter's Roman Catholic Church Cemetery in August 1948, where he lays with his parents today. His tragic death also contributed to his mother's untimely death of a cerebral hemorrhage in December 1944.

Inspired by his great sacrifice of service to our country, several nephews went on to become officers and men in the Marine Corps, Navy, Air Force and Army. His Del Grosso nephews are continuing to conduct extensive research into the Anzio Beachhead campaign in an effort to gain additional understanding as to the circumstances surrounding his death.

The "Nephews of Pvt. Nicholas J. Del Grosso Association" can be contacted by calling the principle researcher, Frank Marano, LCDR, US Navy, Ret., (BHS '71, USNA '75) at 973-715-9336.

Sources: American Battle Monuments Commission, Belleville Times; Nephews of Pvt. Nicholas J. Del Grosso Association.

2nd Lt. Hermann M. Doell

2nd Lt. Herman M. Doell, U.S. Army Air Forces, 26, Seventh Bomber Squadron, 34th Bomber Group, Heavy, was killed in action over England on D-Day, June 6, 1944. Doell, of 169 Linden Avenue, was a B-24 pilot.

He entered the Army in 1941 from New Jersey, and rose to sergeant in the infantry. He transferred to the Army Air Corps a year and a half later. He was commissioned at Ellington Field, Houston, Texas. He took specialized training at Blythe, Calif. His service number is O-687561.

Doell was a member of the Glee club and was a graduate of the Belleville High School class of 1933. He worked as a teller at First National bank immediately after completing his studies.

He was awarded the Purple Heart. Lt. Doell is buried at Plot B, Row 1, Grave 30, Cambridge American Cemetery, Cambridge, England.

Sources: American Battle Monuments Commission, The Belleville Times, June 22, June 29, Aug. 31, 1944

George R. Fredericks

Private George R. Fredericks of Montgomery St. was killed in service during WWII while serving in the U.S. Army. His service number is 12126603.

Sources: Remembrance - George Sbarra; World War II Honor List of Dead and Missing, State of New Jersey, War Dept. June 1946

Harry C. Fredericks Jr.

(June 4, 1942) – Coxswain Harry Carl Fredericks Jr., 26, of Montgomery Place was killed in action in the Gulf of Mexico on May 19. The son of Mr. and Mrs. Harry Fredericks, he served in the Navy's Armed Guard service.

The Armed Guard was created by the Navy during World War I, and it was reactivated during World War II. Its members served on more than 6,000 merchant ships, and nearly 2,000 members were killed.

Fredericks was in charge of a gun crew aboard a U.S. merchant, the freighter Ogontz, ship when it was sunk by Nazi sub U-103. On board were two armed guards and a crew of 17. Records indicate he was one of a crew of 20 lost when the ship went down. The ship sank bow first. The stern smokestack struck the captain's lifeboat and pushed it under. Only one of the 20 in the lifeboat survived. Coxswain Fredericks joined the Navy four years ago and was discharged from service in December. He then re-enlisted after war was declared.

He has two brothers, Sgt. William Fredericks of the Army Air Corps, and Sgt. Clifford of the Engineering Corps. Coxswain

Fredericks is listed among the Missing in Action or Buried at Sea, on the Tablets of the Missing at East Coast Memorial, NY. He was awarded the Purple Heart.

His service number is 02385643. The American Battle Monuments Commission lists him as declared dead on May 20, 1943.

Sources: American Battle Monuments Commission; Belleville Times, June 4, 1942; May 18, 1944; The Philadelphia Enquirer July 8, 1998: Armed Guard Veterans Finally Get Their Thanks, by Lacy McCrary; Remembrance - George Sbarra; U.S. Merchant Marines –

Armed Guards; U.S. Merchant Marines Ships Sunk 1942; World War II Honor List of Dead and Missing, State of New Jersey, War Dept. June 1946

Lt. William Fredericks

(June 14, 1945) – Lt. William Fredericks, 27, of the Army Air Forces, a B-29 co-pilot was listed as missing in action after a raid on Guam in the South Pacific. He is the son of Mrs. Ruth Fredericks of Montgomery Place. Lt. Fredericks entered the service in 1940 as a member of the National Guard. He was assigned to the 44th Division Field Artillery, and transferred to the Air Corps in 1941.

His brother Coxswain Harry C. Fredericks was killed in action in the Gulf of Mexico on May 19, 1942. It was the first reported Belleville Gold Star casualty of the war.

(May 23, 1946) – Lt. William Fredericks, who was declared missing in action a year ago May 5, has been declared killed in action. Lt. Fredericks was the co-pilot of a B-29 shot down over Kyushu, Japan. The pilot of the plane was found alive as a prisoner of war held by Japan. Fredericks leaves a wife and 8-month-old son, William Jr.

Sources: The Belleville Times; Remembrance - George Sbarra

Michael G. Froehlich

S/Sgt. Michael Froehlich, Jr., 30, of DeWitt Avenue has been reported missing in action since June 11, 1943, according to a telegram received by his family. In April 1943, he went to England. In May, on a mission over Wilhelmshafen, his plane was shot up, and was last seen 10 miles off the northwest coast of Germany. Sgt. Froehlich entered the Air Forces on August 1942. His service number is 32458436. He received his wings as a Flying Fortress tail gunner at Tindall Field, Fla.

Sgt. Froehlich has been overseas since May 1. He had been stationed in England with the 524th Bomber Squadron, 379th Bomber Group, Heavy. Sgt. Froehlich was awarded a Purple Heart. He is buried at Plot A, Row 28, Grave 21, Ardennes American Cemetery, Nupre, Belgium.

Sources: American Battle Monuments Commission, The Belleville Times, July 8, 1943, June 22, Aug. 31, 1944

Gerald J. Fuselle

(Oct. 7, 1943) – Corporal Gerald J. Fuselle was reported missing in action since Sept. 2 in the North African Theater of Operations. The 24-year-old soldier had recently written "we're in sight of the city (probably Bizerte) but not allowed to go there ..." He had been overseas since the end of June. Fuselle served with the 157th Infantry Regiment, 45th Infantry Division.

(Aug. 31, 1944) – Cpl. Gerald J. Fuselle, 24, of Belmont Avenue, died on July 10, 1943, in Tunisia, North Africa. He was overseas less than one month before he died. The infantryman lost his life in action during the last furious fighting before Rommel's Nazi hordes were swept out of Tunisia in the Mediterranean. He graduated Belleville High School in 1936, and served in the National Guard for three years. Fuselle enlisted in the Army in February 1942. His service number is 32237101. He was awarded the Purple Heart. Fuselle is buried at Plot F, Row 3, Grave 54, Sicily-Rome American Cemetery, Nettuno, Italy.

Sources: American Battle Monuments Commission, Belleville Times, Oct. 7, 1943, Aug. 31, 1944, Remembrance - George Sbarra

William Gaydos

Merchant Marine William Gaydos, a messman, of Cortlandt Street, was killed when his freighter the Yorkmar was hit by a torpedo and sank in the North Atlantic on Oct. 9, 1943, killing all 22 aboard. Gaydos joined the Merchant Marine on July 15. He went on active duty in September. He trained at Sheepshead Bay, Brooklyn. Gaydos, who grew up in East Rutherford, has been married since January 1935 to Anna, nee Kinsley. Among other survivors is his brother Joseph.

Sources: The Belleville Times, Oct. 14, 28, 1943; U.S. Merchant Marine Casualties – Listing; U.S. Merchant Marine Casualties During WWII

Angelo Guarino

(Aug. 10, 1944) – Pfc. Angelo Guarino, 25, of Carmer Avenue, was killed in action in France on July 18.

His parents received an undelivered letter stamped "deceased" followed by a war department telegram confirmation. A 1937 graduate of Belleville High School, Guarino enlisted in the infantry April 1941. He was a machine gun instructor at Camp Forrest, Tenn., and went overseas to Ireland last December.

According to the American Battle Monuments

Commission, Private First Class Angelo Guarino, U.S. Army Serial No. 32064795m served in the 13th Infantry Regiment, 8th Infantry Division. He entered the service from New Jersey, and was killed in action on July 18, 1944. Private Guarino is buried at: Plot G, Row 9, Grave 36, at Normandy American Cemetery, St. Laurent-sur-Mer, France. He was awarded the Purple Heart.

Sources: American Battle Monuments Commission, Belleville Times, August 10, 1944; Remembrance - George Sbarra; Photo courtesy of Verona Heroes - Robert Caruso, used with permission.

Stanley Guzik

(May 31, 1945) – Corporal Stanley Guzik was killed in action in the Philippines. He had been overseas 14 months, and had received a Purple Heart at Guam. Guzik had lived with his sister Mrs. Albert Miskiewicz of Cortlandt Street. His other family members live in Wilkes Barre, Pa.

Source: The Belleville Times

William Hamilton

(May 3, 1945) – Sgt. William Hamilton was killed in action in Germany on April 2. He served with the Seventh Army and has been buried in West Germany. Sgt. Hamilton grew up in Newark but lived on Arthur Street for five years before he entered the service in 1942. He went overseas in February. He is survived by his wife Pearl, and 22-month-old daughter Joyce Pearl; and his parents Mr. and Mrs. David Hamilton.

(source & date unknown, newspaper clipping, probably Belleville Times:)

Memorial services were held Sunday in St. James Church, Newark for Sgt. William Hamilton, formerly of 15 Arthur Street, who was reported killed in action in Germany April 2.

A war department notification was received by his wife, Mrs. Pearl A. Hamilton of Kearny.

Sgt. Hamilton is also survived by a twenty-two month old daughter Joyce Pearl, and his parents, Mr. and Mrs. David Hamilton of Newark who lived at the Arthur Street address until last November.

His brother, Cpl. Edward Hamilton is with the 5th Army in Italy. Two sisters are Mrs. Thomas Burns of Orange and Mrs. Frank Wunsch of Irvington.

Mrs. Hamilton was notified that her husband, who was a squad leader attached to the 7th Army was killed in Germany and buried with United States forces in West Germany.

He had gone overseas in February, just three years after entering service. He was born in Newark but had lived here more than five years before entering service. A graduate of Boys' Vocational school, Sgt. Hamilton was employed by Tung-Sol Lamp works in Newark in civilian life.

Rev. Perry Olton, pastor of St. James church, conducted the memorial.

Hamilton did not waste his sympathies on the Nazi soldiers. "The Jerries are getting a dose of their own medicine now, and they certainly deserve all they're getting," he wrote in his last letter home.

Besides his parents, he leaves his wife Pearl and a 22-month-old daughter Joyce, of Kearny; a brother Cpl. Edward, 20, with the Fifth Army in Italy, and two sisters, Mrs. Thomas Burns, Orange, and Mrs. Frank Wunsch of Irvington.

June 19, 1945 - Chaplain's Letter

Dear Mrs. Wunsch,

I am in possession of your letter requesting more information concerning your brother who was killed in action. I am happy to share with you all the facts that I have been able to gather, even though they are meagre (sic).

The battalion was engaged in offensive action against the town of Stein, Germany, north of Heilbronn. Capture of the town was essential to the advance of our troops. It was heavily defended because it was a key position to a huge underground concentration of Germany supplies. William's company pushed off at dawn. While passing through woods on the approach to the town the company encountered heavy enemy artillery and machinegun fire. They halted and called for artillery support and tanks. It was in this woods amid bursting shells and crackling machinegun bullets that your brother was struck down. There were Medical Corpsmen on the spot but there was nothing they could do to save William's life. He died instantly, as I am sure we would all have preferred him to, since it had to be. I might add that the ensuing action captured the town and opened the way for a break-through for our forces. It was his efforts and the work of others like William that gained the victory. He made the greatest sacrifice possible, but, praise God, he did not die in vain. He is buried in the U. S. Military Cemetery in Bensheim, Germany.

May our Lord comfort your heart and heal this shock to your love.

Sincerely yours,

Gordon C. Curty, Chaplain (Capt.)

253rd Infantry

Joyce Pearl Hamilton traveled to Germany and met Mr. Albert Rosser in Stein and explained that she was trying to get factual information about her father's death. Rosser researched all in Heidelburg. When Ms. Hamilton returned four months, Rosser told her the skirmish was in Tiefenback, not Stein, according to U.S. records. Rosser also spoke with a 90-year-old man who was THERE in 1945 and he said it happened at a Catholic Church. The U.S. soldiers spent the night in the church, emerged and started up the small grassy embankment where they encountered German soldiers. All the Germans died. This information coincides with information from Joyce's mother's cousin who was close by & had once told Joyce he saw her father's body. On Dec. 9, 1948, William Hamilton was re-interred with a military funeral at Beverly National Cemetery, Beverly, N.J.

Sources: The Belleville Times, May 3, 1945; Hamilton family letters, courtesy Muriel & Edward Hamilton; Joyce Pearl Hamilton

Donald B. Hartley

Seaman 1/c Donald Buddell Hartley, 20, of Mertz Avenue, was killed while on his first voyage, when his ship collided with another in the North Atlantic on Aug. 18, 1943. He is the son of Mr. & Mrs. Alonzo Albert Hartley of Mertz Avenue. Seaman Hartley, USNR, was an armed guard aboard the Panama-class tanker J. H. Senior. The Navy created the Armed Guard during World War I, and reactivated it during World War II. Its members served on more than 6,000 merchant ships, and nearly 2,000 members were killed. The Navy reported few survivors from either ship. Ships involved in the North Atlantic incident were: J. H. Senior Tanker (Panama) Collision/fire Damaged, Crew 41; AG 28; J. Pinckney Henderson, Liberty, Collision/fire Total loss, Crew 38; AG 25 Theodore Dwight Weld, Liberty, Collision

Hartley, who was graduated from Belleville High School in 1941, enlisted in the Navy in November 1942. He received his boot training at Sampson, N.Y., his radio and signaling training at Bedford, Pa., and his Special Signals Corps training at Noroton, Conn. Seaman Hartley was reported missing in action to his family in September 1943. He is listed as missing in action or buried at sea on the Tablets of the Missing at East Coast Memorial, New York.

Sources: American Battle Monuments Commission; Belleville Times, Sept. 9, 1943; Oct. 12, 1944; The Philadelphia Enquirer July 8, 1998: Armed Guard Veterans Finally Get Their Thanks, by Lacy McCrary; U.S. Merchant Marines Navy Armed Guard Casualties; U.S. Merchant Marines Casualties during WWII; World War II Honor List of Dead and Missing, State of New Jersey, War Dept. June 1946

Lt. Richard T. Hayes

Lieutenant Junior Grade Richard Thomas Hayes, was killed in action April 27, 1945. He is survived by his wife Margaret Flewellyn Hayes of Washington Avenue. He was awarded the Air Medal with Gold Star. Lt. Hayes joined the

United States Naval Reserve from Ohio. His service number is 0-176597. He is listed as missing in action or buried at sea on the Tablets of the Missing at Honolulu Memorial, Honolulu, Hawaii.

Sources: American Battle Monuments Commission; World War II Honor List of Dead and Missing, State of New Jersey, War Dept. June 1946

Edward R. Henris

(July 27, 1944) -- Sgt. Edward Henris, son of Minnie Henris, of Washington Avenue, has been missing in action in Europe since June 9. The family moved to Belleville 15 years ago when he was 22. Henris joined the Army in 1940 and was released as "overage." He was recalled after Pearl Harbor. Sgt. Henris went overseas September 1942.

(Aug. 17, 1944) -- Sgt. Edward Henris was killed in action in France three days after the Allied invasion. The 37-year-old sergeant was a native of Kansas. According to the American Battle Monuments Commission, Technician 4th Class Edward R. Henris, U.S. Army serial No. 32148220, served in the 3422nd Ordnance Automotive Maintenance Company. Henris entered the service from New Jersey, and died on June 9, 1944. He is listed on the Missing in Action or Buried at Sea Tablets of the Missing at Cambridge American Cemetery, Cambridge, England. He was awarded the Purple Heart.

Three Belleville sons, Henris, Staff Sgt. Arthur Burke and Sgt. Carmine Olivo were likely on the same ship as all three served in 3422nd Ordnance Automotive Maintenance Company. The families were notified in July, November and December 1944, respectively.

Sources: American Battle Monuments Commission, The Belleville Times, July 27, Aug. 17, 31, 1944: Miller Killed On Saipan, Vic Bruegman Missing; Three Soldiers Perish On Fields Of France.

Patrick J. Hoey

(August 2, 1945) – Technical Sgt. Patrick J. Hoey, 25, was killed in action on Dec. 14, while serving with the First Army in Germany.

Born in Long Island, Hoey lived with his aunt and uncle for 10 years in Belleville.

Hoey was wounded in Tunisia in 1943, and awarded the Legion of Merit. Hoey was also wounded during the Normandy campaign. He was awarded the Purple Heart.

Acting Adjutant General Maj. Gen. Edward F. Witsell presented the Silver Star and Bronze Star to the young soldier's aunt, Mrs. Daniel Hoey of Prospect

Street. The Silver Star was presented "for distinguishing himself and disregard for personal safety on Dec. 12, 1944, during the campaign ... which reflects highest credit upon himself and the Armed Forces of the United States."

The Bronze Star: "...during the period July 5 1944, to Sept. 30, 1944, in the European Theatre of Operations ... took over as platoon sergeant when his platoon sergeant had a casualty." Hoey was inducted into the service January 1941.

Sgt. Hoey served with the 60th Infantry Regiment, Ninth Infantry Division. He is buried at Plot G, Row 12, Grave 49, Henri-Chapelle American Cemetery, Henri-Chapelle, Belgium.

Sources: American Battle Monuments Commission, The Belleville Times.

William A. Hourigan

(Dec. 7, 1944) – Seaman 2/c William A. Hourigan, 18, formerly of Tiona Avenue, was killed in action in the invasion of the Philippines about Nov. 5. He enlisted in the service in February 1943. Hourigan last resided in Newport Beach, Calif., after living in Belleville until 1936. He entered the service from California. Hourigan was awarded the Purple Heart. He is listed as missing in action or buried at sea on the Tablets of the Missing at Manila American Cemetery, Manila, Philippines.

Sources: American Battle Monuments Commission, The Belleville Times

Capt. Louis J. Jannarone

(Nov. 2, 1944) – Captain Louis H. Jannarone of Passaic Avenue, died at Walter Reed General Hospital in Washington on Oct. 31. Army doctors said the cause of death was "battle fatigue brought on by his refusal to leave wounded on battlefield." Capt. Jannarone was with the Army Medical Corps and landed in France on D-Day. He worked day and night through the push across that country. Capt. Jannarone was stricken during the siege of Aachen, which is on the western border of Germany, near the eastern border of Belgium. It is about 50 miles west of Cologne & Bonn, Germany.

He was a 1931 graduate of Belleville High School. He graduated medical school at the University of Maryland in 1939. Capt. Jannarone joined the medical corps in October 1941. He served at Fort Benning, Ga., Camp Gordon, S.C., and went overseas on Jan. 6. Capt. Jannarone is survived by his wife, a nurse in Baltimore.

Source: The Belleville Times

John Johnson

(Aug. 16, 1945) – Seaman 2/c John Johnson, 18, died from a fractured skull sustained in an accident aboard an aircraft carrier in the Pacific on August 4. The son of Mr. and Mrs. John Johnson of Greylock Parkway, he left Belleville High School last March to enlist in the Navy. He was awarded his diploma in June.

Johnson trained in Sampson, N.Y. He was on the carrier about a month when he slipped and fractured his skull. He was rushed to the Navy hospital in Oakland, Calif. He died five days later, three days after his mother arrived. The Red Cross was praised for its efforts and assistance in the mother and child reunion.

Source: The Belleville Times

1st Lt. William B. Jones

(June 16, 1945) – 1st Lt. William Brewster Jones, 26, died over Europe on May 27, 1944.

Here is the account, according to Web Birds:

Taking off at 1903 hours, the lead ship, piloted by Capt. Dunbar, was hit by the last ship in a formation of P-51's passing over the field, and both ships crashed and burst into flames.

Accounts by the first arrivals on the scene of the crash vary, and the sole survivor of the accident, S/Sgt. Mattei, Capt. Dunbar's turret gunner, is not unnaturally confused about what happened after the crash. He was badly burned while attempting to get Captain Dunbar out of the cockpit of the flaming plane.

It is believed that Capt. Dunbar, his bombagator, Lt. Merrill, and Lt. William B. Jones, the Group Photographic Officer, who was flying as tunnel gunner, were killed by the crash.

Mrs. Elizabeth Ann Everitt, housewife from nearby Paddle Wharf Farm, and a passing cyclist, Sgt. John P. Hartman of the 78th Fighter Group, were killed in the explosion of bombs in the wreckage as they sought to extricate members of the crew.

1st Lt. William B. Jones, U.S. Army Air Forces, serial No. O-581917, served in the Headquarters, 409th Bomber Group, Light. He entered the service from New Jersey. Jones enlisted 15 months before Pearl Harbor was attacked by Japan. He attended AAF Intelligence School in Harrisburg, Pa., specializing in photo interpretation. The Army Intelligence Officer went overseas in February. Jones was a graduate of the Belleville High School Class of 1936. He competed regionally with the rowing club. He is buried at Plot E, Row 6, Grave 112,

Cambridge American Cemetery, Cambridge, England His grandfather, Charles Granville Jones, an architect, drew plans for The Belleville Town Hall, public library and high school (now the middle school.)

Sources: American Battle Monuments Commission, The Belleville Times, June 15, Aug. 31, 1944; Belleville: 150th-Anniversary Historical Highlights 1839-1989 by Robert B. Burnett and the Belleville 150th-Anniversary Committee. 1991; Web-birds 9th 409 May

Warren C. Jordan

Marine Corporal Warren C. Jordan, son of Arthur J. Jordon (sic) of Belleville Avenue, was killed in action on March 7, 1945. His service number is 00424998. He was awarded the Purple Heart with Gold Star. He is memorialized at the Honolulu Memorial, Honolulu, Hawaii.

Sources: American Battle Monuments Commission; World War II Honor List of Dead and Missing, State of New Jersey, War Dept. June 1946

John J. Kant

(July 30, 1942) – Seaman 2/c John J. Kant, 20, of DeWitt Avenue, was reported missing in action, the Navy notified his family this week. Kant, the son of a World War I vet who served in the Ninth Infantry of the Second Division, enlisted in the Navy six months ago. He trained at Newport, R.I. Kant was born in Belleville. He attended Good Counsel and then Bloomfield High School.

Source: The Belleville Times

John F. Kirwin

(Sept. 28, 1944) – Ordnanceman 3/c John Francis Kirwin of Forest Street was killed in the South Pacific when his patrol plane crashed at sea on Sept. 5. "Jack" Kirwin was 19 when he enlisted in the Navy in February 1943. He didn't finish high school. He went as a senior to boot training at Sampson. Kirwin received his specialized training in Tennessee, Florida and California before going overseas in July 1944. His twin brother, James E., is believed to be serving overseas.

Seaman 1/c Kirwin is the son of John F. Kirwin of Forest Street. He is listed as missing in action or buried at sea on the Tablets of the Missing at Honolulu Memorial, Honolulu, Hawaii.

Sources: American Battle Monuments Commission; Belleville Times, Sept. 28, 1944; World War II Honor List of Dead and Missing, State of New Jersey, War Dept. June 1946; James Kirwin, August 2003.

Joseph Klimchock

(June 8, 1944) – Pfc. Joseph Klimchock of Clinton Street, who had been reported missing since Dec. 2, has been declared dead following the fierce fighting through the mountains of the Italian peninsula. Born in Newark, he moved to Belleville before the war. Klimchock entered the Army in 1942, and took his Basic Training at Fort Hancock. He went overseas as an ambulance driver. He served with the 61st Station Hospital. Klimchock has two brothers serving in the South Pacific. He was awarded the Purple Heart. He is listed as missing in action or buried at sea on the Tablets of the Missing at Tablets of the Missing at Sicily-Rome American Cemetery, Nettuno, Italy.

Sources: American Battle Monuments Commission, The Belleville Times, June 8, Aug. 31, 1944

Thomas E. Lamb

(March 29, 1945) – Seaman 2/c Thomas Edward Lamb died of his wounds in the Pacific. He is survived by his wife Danetta Lamb of Union Avenue. Lamb grew up in Montclair where his parents still live. Seaman Lamb entered the U.S. Naval Reserve in May 1944, and trained at Sampson, N.Y., and Newport, R.I. He had been assigned to a cargo attack ship last November. Seaman Lamb returned from his first tour a month later, then sailed out again after temporarily being assigned in California.

Sources: Belleville Times; World War II Honor List of Dead and Missing, State of New Jersey, War Dept. June 1946

Joseph M. LaPenta

Private Joseph M. LaPenta of Eugene Place was killed in combat in Italy on January 21, 1944. Born in 1925, LaPenta served in the 36th Infantry Division, 143rd Infantry Regiment. His service number is 32925501. He was awarded the Purple Heart. He is buried at Mount Olivet Cemetery, Bloomfield.

Sources: The Belleville Times, March 9, 16, Aug. 31, 1944; Remembrance - George Sbarra

Albert H. Lariviere

(Oct. 5, 1944) – Private Albert H. Lariviere, 30, was killed in action on June 6, D-Day. He was in the first wave to hit the Normandy beaches. Lariviere's unit, the 112th Engineer Combat Battalion, objective on D-Day was to create gaps for U.S. ships by destroying obstacles, included those rigged with explosives, on the approach to the beaches.

Lariviere was inducted into the service in May 1943, and went overseas last September. His parents live on Tappan Avenue. His wife and daughter live in Garfield.

According to the American Battle Monument Commission, Private Albert H. Lariviere, U.S. Army Serial No. 32925495, served in the 112th Engineer Combat Battalion. He entered the service from New Jersey, and was killed in action on June 6, 1944. Lariviere is buried at Plot H, Row 18, Grave 4, Normandy American Cemetery, St. Laurent-sur-Mer, France. He was awarded the Purple Heart.

Note: Spelling variations include Larivere and Lariviero

Sources: American Battle Monuments Commission; The Belleville Times, Oct. 5, 1944; National Archives & Records Administration; Richard Grout - 60 years later – Record Eagle; Photo courtesy of Verona Heroes - Robert Caruso; ANNEX NO. 1, Omaha Beachhead Unit Citations (Published in War Department General Orders up to 15 September 1945) 112th Engineer Combat Battalion; U. S. Army Center of Military History; American D-Day (Stone!)

Ralph E. Ledogar

Staff Sgt. Ralph E. Ledogar, 20, formerly of Floyd Street, was killed in action May 30, when the Flying Fortress in which he was a radio operator was shot down over Germany. Ledogar served with the 359th Bomber Squadron, 303rd Bomber Group, Heavy, Eighth Air Force as a radio operator and gunner on a B-17 of Hell's Angels Squadron. Ledogar and his Van Weelden crew were assigned to the 359th BS/ 303rd BG(H) at Molesworth, England on May 4, 1944. The B-17 bomber #42-31213, nicknamed "Pistol Packin Mama" was piloted by 2nd Lt. Douglas C. Van Weelden on a mission to Halberstadt, Germany when it crashed on May 30, 1944. Co-pilot 2nd Lt. William A. Sysel, Sgt. Ledogar, Waist Gunner S/Sgt. William K. Forsythe and tail gunner Sgt. John K. Barry are believed to have been shot by Germans. The report that the four KIA crewmen had been shot (murdered) by Germans was the opinion of the crew's pilot Van Weelden and it has not been verified from any official sources. Crewmen taken prisoner were S/Sgt. Philip Olander, Sgt. Urban L.

Raterman, 1st Lt. Robert Saumsiegle, 2nd Lt. Van Weelden, Flight Officer Ronald Vincent, and Sgt. John R. Welch.

Sgt. Ledogar flew on the following nine 303rd BG(H) combat missions:

154 - 15 May 44 to Mimoyecques, France

157 - 22 May 44 to Kiel, Germany

158 - 23 May 44 to Saarbrucken, Germany

159 - 24 May 44 to Berlin, Germany

160 - 25 May 44 to Blainville, France

161 - 27 May 44 to Mannheim, Germany

162 - 28 May 44 to Cologne, Germany

164 - 29 May 44 to Posen, Poland

165 - 30 May 44 to Halberstadt, Germany

Ledogar enlisted in U.S. Army Air Forces in February 1943. He went overseas one month before he was killed. Ledogar graduated Belleville High School in 1941. He was awarded the Air Medal and the Purple Heart. He is buried at Plot C, Row 2, Grave 39, at the Ardennes American Cemetery, Neupre, Belgium.

Sources: American Battle Monuments Commission, The Belleville Times – Dec. 21, 1944, Hell's Angels - 303rd Bomb Group Assn., Harry D. Gobrecht,
http://www.303rdbga.com/359vanweelden.html
http://www.303rdbga.com/.359vanweelden.html http://www.303rdbga.com/p-rost-uvzz.html
http://www.303rdbga.com/murder.html
Additional information of the above combat missions and about the 303rd BG(H)
http://www.303rdbga.com/cd-records.html

Arthur Leithauser

(Dec. 29, 1944) – Private Arthur Leithauser, 34, of Ridge Road, Nutley, has been listed among those killed in action in France, according to official War Department telegrams. Mrs. Leithauser, the former Madeline Witck of Belleville, received word two weeks ago today that her husband had been killed Nov. 2. Several weeks previous she had received a telegram that he was missing. Leithauser, an assistant auditor with Globe Indemnity Insurance company of New York City, was drafted Jan. 28, and was home on his only furlough in June. He then went to Camp Meade, Md., and Camp Patrick Henry, Va., where his wife journeyed in an unsuccessful attempt to see him before he went overseas with an infantry unit. He arrived in France ten days before the date he is said to have been killed. Besides his wife, he leaves a two-year-old son Arthur, Jr. and his mother Mrs. Ella Leithauser, of Belleville. The family moved to town 14 years ago from East Orange.

Sources: The Belleville Times: Nov. 30, Dec. 28, 1944, The Nutley Sun

Emil M. Liloia

(April 13, 1945) – Pfc. Emil M. Liloia, 21, son of Mr. and Mrs. Vito Frank Liloia of Passaic Avenue, Nutley, was killed in action March 1 on Iwo Jima while serving with the Third Marines.

Liloia entered service Feb. 6, 1942, taking his basic training at Parris Island. He later was stationed at Philadelphia, guarding prisoners. When sent overseas a year ago, he first went to Hawaii and then to Iwo Jima. Born in Belleville, Pfc. Liloia came to Nutley when he was three. He went through Nutley schools and while in high school starred on the football team. As a result of his activities on this team and as a basketball player he was voted the best athlete. Upon high school graduation, he received a scholarship to Temple University in Philadelphia and had played there only one year when he went into service. Pfc. Liloia has four sisters, Ann, Ruth, Marie and Dorothy. A brother, SK 3/c Pat Liloia, has been in the Navy two and one half years and is at present on an oil tanker in the South Pacific.

Source: The Nutley Sun

Benjamin Lucas

(October 25, 1945) – Corporal Benjamin Lucas, 23, was killed in a plane crash in China on Sept. 28. Lucas, son of Mrs. Louise Lucas of Newark Place, was on his way home when the plane was destroyed in a crash.

Cpl. Lucas had completed two years in the Far East, most recently stationed at the headquarters of Chinese Combat Command. He enlisted in the Army in March 1942. Cpl. Lucas was first stationed in India. He went through the reopening of the Burma Road and was with the Mars Task Force.

The young man had three battle stars, and had been shot by Jap snipers in the past. Among his survivors are his brother Pfc. Andrew Lucas who was in Europe. The two brothers exchanged 500 letters while separated.

Source: The Belleville Times

Arthur H. Lundgren

Sgt. Arthur H. Lundgren, of Smith Street, died at Fort Dix, in September 1942.

Source: The Belleville Times, May 18, Aug. 31, 1944

George Malizia, Jr.

(May 3, 1945) – Sgt. George Malizia, Jr., was killed in Germany on April 7, 1945. He was the son of Anna and George Malizia of Conover Avenue. Sgt. Malizia entered the service May 5, 1944, and had served in England and France.

Source: The Belleville Times

John Marshall

(Aug. 9, 1945) – John Marshall, 33, was killed in Italy when stored mines exploded on July 8. Marshall was attached to the Headquarters station of the 92nd Infantry Division when the mines stored in an adjacent building exploded.

He is the son of Mr. and Mrs. Gus Marshall of Ralph Street. Marshall was in the Army two years, and went overseas in October. In February he was awarded the Combat Infantryman's Badge for outstanding performance of duty in action against the enemy. He is survived by his wife Mary, also of Ralph Street. In November, the Veterans of Foreign Wars commemorated the Brown-Marshall VFW Post at 82 Broad Street, Bloomfield, in honor of John Marshall and Alvin Brown.

Source: The Belleville Times, Aug. 9, Nov. 7, 1945

Joseph A. Masi

(Dec. 14, 1944) – Private Joseph A. Masi, of Lake Street, was killed in action in France on October 25. Born on January 1, 1920, he enlisted in the Army in 1942. He served with the 45th Infantry Division. Masi served two months in Italy before heading to France. He was awarded the Purple Heart and the Gold Star Citation. His service number is 32597268. A 1939 graduate of Belleville High School, he is buried at Mount Olivet Cemetery, Bloomfield.

Sources: The Belleville Times, Remembrance - George Sbarra

Ronald F. McCormack

(July 20, 1945) – Official word of the death of Seaman Second Class Ronald F. McCormack has been received by his parents, Mr. and Mrs. R. F. McCormack of Church Street, Nutley, it was revealed this week. The McCormacks are former residents of Belleville. Seaman McCormack was reported missing on June 9, 1944, after he participated in the D-Day invasion of Normandy. He was aboard LST 314. According to the report made by the Secretary of the Navy, "there were 5 LST ships in the group. They had made one successful trip across, but on the second, were hit by a torpedo from a German "E" boat, causing great fires and explosions. Three of the five ships were sunk." The attack occurred at night and according to some of the survivors, McCormack was believed to have been asleep at the time of the attack and went down with the ship. McCormack was a graduate of Belleville High School. Besides his parents, he is survived by a sister, Muriel.

Sources: The Belleville Times, July 19, 1945, The Nutley Sun

Joseph McDermott

Sgt. Joseph L. McDermott was killed in action during World War II. His serial number is 32599662.

According to his descendants, McDermott enlisted in the Army in 1942 taking basic training at Fort Dix, and further training in Colorado before heading to England.

He participated in the Normandy landing on D-Day, June 6, 1944.

Sgt. McDermott, 23, suffered a fatal concussion from a bomb explosion. He is buried at St. Peter's Cemetery on William Street in Belleville.

McDermott was born in Belleville to Grace and Thomas McDermott. He is survived by brothers Bart and Edward.

Sources: World War II Honor List of Dead and Missing, State of New Jersey, War Dept. June 1946; Belleville Times, Aug. 10, 1944

Francis C. Mc Enery

Staff Sergeant Francis C. Mc Enery, of 34 Fairway Avenue, was killed in action on Jan. 4, 1944. He served with the U.S. Army Air Forces in the 325th Bomber Squadron, 92nd Bomber Group, Heavy. Sgt. Mc Enery was awarded the Purple Heart. He is buried at Plot B, Row 14, Grave 1, Ardennes American Cemetery, Neupre, Belgium.

Sources: American Battle Monuments Commission, The Belleville Times, Jan. 1944, Aug. 31, 1944

Edgar H. Mc Ginty

Water Tender, 2/c Edgar H. Mc Ginty, of 50 New Street, was killed in action on Dec. 15, 1945. His U.S. Navy service number is 02283303. Mc Ginty was awarded the Purple Heart. He is listed as missing in action or buried at sea on the Tablets of the Missing at Manila American Cemetery, Manila, Philippines.

Sources: *American Battle Monuments Commission, The Belleville Times, Aug. 6, 1942*

Hector McNeill

(July 13, 1944) – Corporal Hector McNeill was killed in action in the Anzio Beachhead on June 1. The battle of Anzio, Italy, a beachhead invasion began in May 1944. Allied troops were held on the beachhead for five months. The young man was a member of an anti-aircraft battalion. He had been in the Army for two years, and went overseas a year ago. McNeill, of Cedar Hill Avenue, came to America from Scotland 12 years ago.

Sources: *The Belleville Times, Tiscalo Encyclopedia – Hutchinson*

William J. Mears

(Nov. 30, 1944) – Marine Sgt. William J. Mears of Jefferson Street was killed in action in Peleliu on Palau Islands in the South Pacific on Sept. 15. Mears enlisted in the Marines the day after Pearl Harbor was attacked. During his tour he was cited as a demolitions expert. He was a veteran of Guadalcanal, Cape Gloucester, New Britain and Bougainville during his 28 months overseas. He was scheduled to return to the States to begin study at officer candidate school. The Palue Islands are in the westernmost cluster of the Caroline Islands, north of Australia and west of Micronesia. He was awarded a Purple Heart. He is listed as missing in action or buried at sea on the Tablets of the Missing at Manila American Cemetery, Manila, Philippines.

Sources: *American Battle Monuments Commission, The Belleville Times*

2nd Lt. Roger J. Mellion

(Jan. 18, 1945) – 2nd Lt. Roger J. Mellion, 21, was killed near Goose Bay, Labrador, when the B-24 on which he was a crewmember crashed. He is the son of Mr. and Mrs. Harry Mellion of Overlook Avenue. Lt. Mellion was on the first lap of a flight to Europe to begin active duty as a pilot of a heavy bomber.

He was graduated from Belleville High School in 1941. He enlisted in December 1942 as a sophomore from Ohio State University. Lt. Mellion was commissioned as an Army pilot in May 1944 at Turner Field, Albany, Ga. He took his B-24 transitional training in Westover Field, Mass., and Charleston, S.C.

Source: The Belleville Times

Frank H. Metzler

(Oct. 4, 1945) – Sgt. Frank H. Metzler, 21, was presumed dead on Sept. 10, the War Dept. notified his parents, Mr. and Mrs. John of Reservoir Place. Sgt. Metzler, a tail gunner on a Flying Fortress, had been overseas five weeks before being reported missing in Germany since March 8, 1944. He is survived by his brother Pfc. Charles Metzler of the First Army who returned after 13 months in the infantry in Europe.

Source: The Belleville Times, April 27, 1944

John Miller Jr.

(July 27, 1944) – Sgt. John J. Miller, Jr., was killed in action in bloody fighting on Saipan, the Navy told his father, John Sr. of Elmwood Avenue. The young man moved to Florida after high school, and joined the Marines in 1939. He was stationed in the Virgin Islands and then the South Pacific two years ago.

Sources: *Belleville Times; World War II Honor List of Dead and Missing, State of New Jersey, War Dept. June 1946*

Emanual J. Montalbano

Private Emanual J. Montalbano, of Belleville, was killed in action during World War II. His service number is 32563652. The National Archives and Records Administration lists his first name as Emanuel.

Sources: *National Archives & Records Administration; Remembrance - George Sbarra; World War II Honor List of Dead and Missing, State of New Jersey, War Dept. June 1946; Glendale headstone photo by Anthony Buccino.*

Mario Morano

(May 13, 1943) – Mrs. Josephine Maiorano, of Dow Street, was informed that her son Sgt. Mario Marano, was killed in action in North Africa. Morano had been drafted in January 1941, and stationed in North Africa since last October. He was engaged to Ann Petrosino of Mt. Pleasant Avenue. Various spelling: Maiorano, Marano, Morano

Sources: *The Belleville Times, May 13, 1943; May 18, Aug 31, 1944 Honor Rolls*

Steveno J. Mosco

The 28th Belleville son killed in action in this war was Pfc. Steveno Julio Mosco, 20, of Honiss Street who died in Normandy July 27, 1944. Mosco had been in France only two weeks when he was killed, according to his wife, Mrs. Rosemarie Cappetta Mosco, and his parents, Mr. and Mrs. Giro Mosco of Honiss street. Born in Belleville, he lived all his life here. While attending the high school he became well-known as "Ju Ju" Mosco, captain of the Panthers, intermediate basketball team. He was employed with the Atlantic Paper Tube Company of Belleville at the time of his induction into the Army March 8, 1943.

He went overseas with an infantry unit last May. In his last letter home on July 17, he wrote, "I'm in a new division, the 79th Infantry Division, the ones who took Cherbourg." Several weeks ago, he met a Belleville friend, Benjamin Petrillo, in France. "It was an awful place to meet a friend," he wrote, "but it was a meeting we'll always remember." He was placed in a machine-gun squad when he was sent to France. At the time Mosco was killed, he had been in Normandy about one month.

He was awarded the Purple Heart. He is buried at the Mount Olivet Cemetery, Bloomfield, N.J. His service number is 32771245. Besides his wife and parents, he leaves four brothers, Pvt. Charles P. Mosco in France, Harry, Salvatore Victor; and two sisters, Mrs. Nancy Teal, and Gloria. The Barbone-Mosco Post #7 Italian American War Veterans was incorporated and established in Belleville, N.J.

Sources: The Belleville Times, March 23, 1944, Aug. 17, 1944; Remembrance - George Sbarra; Unidentified newspaper clippings

Glenn C. Nelson

(Nov. 30, 1944) – Ship's cook 3/c Glenn Charles Nelson, 21, missing since his ship-destroyer Warrington went down off the Virginia coast Sept. 12 in what was to be known as the Great Atlantic Hurricane of Sept. 14, 1944.

Nelson enlisted in the Navy in August 1941. His wife Anna lives on Washington Avenue.

Nelson was also listed as Ship's Clerk 3/c, according to the American Battle Monuments Commission. He is listed as missing in action or buried at sea on the Tablets of the Missing at East Coast Memorial, New York.

Sources: American Battle Monuments Commission; Belleville Times; World War II Honor List of Dead and Missing, State of New Jersey, War Dept. June 1946

Vincent F. Nucci

(Dec. 16, 1943) – Seaman Vincent Nucci was reported missing in action by the Navy which said his ship, a destroyer, was involved in a crash with a tanker in the Atlantic almost two months ago.

Nucci was believed to have been on the crew of the U.S.S. Murphy DD 603, when the collision occurred on the night of Oct. 21. Both ships were operating without lights. The front half of the ship sank in 10 minutes with a crew of 35. The stern remained afloat and was towed to New York Harbor in 24 hours.

Nucci, 23, was graduated from Belleville High School in 1940. He entered the Navy one year later. He participated in the invasion of Sicily.

Nucci is listed as missing in action or buried at sea on the Tablets of the Missing at East Coast Memorial, New York. He is the son of Mr. & Mrs. Joseph Nucci of Cedar Hill Avenue.

Sources: American Battle Monuments Commission; The Belleville Times, Deep Explorers; Destroyers Histories; Navsource; World War II Honor List of Dead and Missing, State of New Jersey, War Dept. June 1946

2nd Lt. Anthony Noto

(May 31, 1945) – 2nd Lt. Anthony Noto, of Frederick Street, was killed in a plane crash en route to Rome for furlough after completing his 35th Combat Mission as a B-24 navigator on April 28. Lt. Noto was a passenger on the flight that crashed in dense fog killing all aboard in Nettuno, Italy. He is buried in the American Military Cemetery in Southern Italy. He enlisted in the Air Force in July 1943, and went overseas last October.

He served with the 459th Bombardment Group, 756th Bomber Squadron. Lt. Noto had an Air Medal and oak leaf clusters for his exploits. Noto is survived by his wife, Phippene Noto of Irvington. He is buried at Plot C, Row 13, Grave 27, Sicily-Rome American Cemetery, Nettuno, Italy.

Sources: American Battle Monuments Commission, The Belleville Times; Remembrance - George Sbarra.

Walter A. Nusbaum

(May 17, 1945) – Corporal Walter Nusbaum, 24, was killed in action in Germany on April 25. His sister, Mrs. Ellison Pardun of Union Avenue, received a telegram saying that he had been wounded on that day. A second telegram said he had died that day. Cpl. Nusbaum entered the Army in November 1943, and had been overseas since last October. Born in New Brunswick, he lived in Newark until age 13 when his parents died and he moved in with his sister. Tech. 5/c Nusbaum served with the 491st Field Artillery Battalion, 11th Armored Division He was awarded the Bronze Star and the Purple Heart. He is buried at Plot F, Row 8, Grave 25, Lorraine American Cemetery, St. Avold, France.

Sources: American Battle Monuments Commission, Belleville Times

Harry W. Nyegaard

(Sept. 14, 1944) – Marine Pfc. Harry Nyegaard, 19, of Main Street, was reported killed June 19 on the Tinian Islands, his parents, Mr. and Mrs. Harry J. Nyegaard, were told in September. Nyegaard enlisted in December 1942, and went overseas with a field communications unit. He was a veteran of Saipan, Kwajalein, Namur and Roi, all in the South Pacific.

(Oct. 18, 1945) – Pfc. Harry Nyegaard was killed in Saipan on June 19, 1944, while laying a communications wire between a battalion command post and a company in the field. Navy Secretary James Forrestal personally signed the citation for Nyegaard's Silver Star. Nyegaard had already received a Purple Heart and a copy of the Presidential Unit Citation in which the commanding general of the Fourth Marine Division gave recognition to the young Marine. Nyegaard graduated Belleville High School in 1942, and enlisted at age 17. His brother, Vincent, a Motor Machinist's Mate 3/c, serving aboard an LSM from Luzon to Japan, visited his brother's grave in Manila a month ago.

Sources: Belleville Times, Sept. 14, 1944, Oct. 18, 1945; World War II Honor List of Dead and Missing, State of New Jersey, War Dept. June 1946

Carmine E. Olivo

(Dec. 14, 1944) -- Sgt. Carmen Olivo, 29, of Magnolia Street, was killed when his ship was sunk in the English Channel during the invasion of Normandy, France. He had been overseas since the summer of 1942.

He joined the service 3 1/2 years ago. According to the American Battle Monuments Commission, Technician 3rd Class Carmine Olivo, U.S. Army serial No. 32148160, served in the 3422nd Ordnance Automotive Maintenance Company. He entered the service from New Jersey, and died on June 9, 1944. Olivo is listed on the Missing in Action or Buried at Sea Tablets of the Missing at Cambridge American Cemetery, Cambridge, England. He was awarded the Purple Heart.

Three Belleville Sons, Sgt. Edward Henris, Staff Sgt. Arthur Burke and Sgt. Olivo were likely on the same ship as all three served in 3422nd Ordnance Automotive Maintenance Company. The families were notified in July, November and December 1944, respectively.

Family name also spelled Olivio.

Sources: American Battle Monuments Commission; The Belleville Times, Remembrance - George Sbarra

2nd Lt. Emil Ostrowski

(June 22, 1944) – 2nd Lt. Emil Ostrowski, 23, of 540 Union Avenue, a B-26 Marauder copilot fighting with the Ninth Air Force in England was killed in action on D-Day, June 6.

Ostrowski enlisted in the Army in July 1942. The young airman trained at Maxwell Field, Ala., Bennettsville and Shaw Fields, S.C. He was commissioned last November at Turner Field, Albany, Ga., Lt. Ostrowski went overseas three months ago.

Born in South River, he was graduated from Plainfield High School, and moved to Belleville five years ago. He worked at his father's butcher shop at the Union Avenue address.

Sources: The Belleville Times, June 22, Aug. 31, 1944

Stephen R. Otozky

Merchant seaman Stephen Rogalo Otozky, an oiler, was killed when the Liberty ship Jeremiah Van Rensselaer was hit by a torpedo and sunk on Feb. 2, 1943, killing all 35 aboard.

Sources: Belleville Times, May 18, Aug. 31, 1944, U.S. Merchant Marines

John Paterno

(May 13, 1943) – Private John Paterno of King Street was reported killed in action in February according to a telegram from the War Department. His family later received a letter from him dated last November. In May, the War Department listed him among the missing in action. Paterno had been stationed at Fort Knox, Tenn., Ireland, and then Africa.

Source: The Belleville Times, May 13, 1943, Aug. 31, 1944

Thomas A. Peacock

(Oct. 14/Nov.18, 1943) – Seaman 2/c Thomas A. Peacock, 20, was killed in action and buried at sea in the area of Malta, in the invasion of Sicily on Sept. 11. Peacock was believed to be aboard the USS Savannah in the Mediterranean when it was attacked by Nazi dive bombers. He is the son of Mr. & Mrs. William E. Peacock of Harrison Street. A small memorial ceremony was held on Armistice Day (November 1943) in the Soho section of Belleville incorporating the Town's Honor Roll. He is listed as missing in action or buried at sea on the Tablets of the Missing at Sicily-Rome American Cemetery at Nettuno, Italy. His letters home do not reveal much. He left for North Africa in April. Another letter said he's part of the invasion of Sicily. He received a service bar for action in the South Pacific last winter. Peacock left Belleville High School in his junior year to enlist in the Navy in October 1942. He trained at Newport, R.I. His service number is 02251767.

Sources: American Battle Monuments Commission; The Belleville Times; Destroyers Histories, Navsource; World War II Honor List of Dead and Missing, State of New Jersey, War Dept. June 1946; Remembrance - George Sbarra

Angelo Patrizio

Pfc. Angelo Patrizio of Watchung Avenue was killed in action in the European Theater on May 16, 1945.

The son of Francesca and Gerardo Patrizio, he is survived by brothers Gerardo Jr., and Benedetto, and sisters Rose and Lena.

His family noted that the soldier was killed in the Normandy invasion while trying to reconnect communication lines.

His service number is 42014084. He was buried Jan. 17, 1949 at Glendale Cemetery, Bloomfield, following services at Spatola Funeral Home, Newark.

Sources: American Battle Monuments Commission, The Belleville Times; Remembrance - George Sbarra

Frank Pepitone

Pfc. Frank J. Pepitone died, non-battle, during World War II. His service number is 32055522.

Sources: World War II Honor List of Dead and Missing, State of New Jersey, War Dept. June 1946

Albert E. Pole

(Sept. 7, 1944) – Marine Pfc. Albert E. Pole, 22, of Washington Avenue, was killed in Guam on Aug. 7. He enlisted in the Marines in 1942. Pole was sent to the Pacific Theatre in January 1943. The Belleville son received a Purple Heart for wounds received Nov. 19, 1943, in the South Pacific. Pole enlisted in 1942, and trained at Parris Island N.C. He went overseas in January. He is listed on the Honolulu Memorial, Honolulu, Hawaii. Pole was awarded the Purple Heart with Gold Star.

Sources: American Battle Monuments Commission; The Belleville Times, Dec. 16, 1943; Sept. 7, 1944; Newark Evening News, Feb. 26, Sept. 23, 1944.

Frank Rankin

Sgt. Frank Rankin, 24, of 18 Hornblower Avenue, was declared missing in action over France on March 26 and later declared killed in action on April 11. Gail Catherine, his baby's due date was March 6.

Sgt. Rankin was killed returning from his 17th combat mission when his plane was separated from its squadron in haze and crashed in France on March 6. He served as an engineer gunner of aboard an A-20 Light Bomber, Ninth Air Force and was stationed in France.

Sgt. Rankin received an oak leaf cluster to the Air Medal for meritorious service in the battle of the Belgium bulge.

He was the second member of the 'sandlot' team – the Emanons – to be killed in action. The first was Thomas Peacock who was killed in action in September 1943. A graduate of Belleville High School class of 1939, he went overseas last September.

Sgt. Rankin was buried with honors in Henri Chapell cemetery in Herze, Belgium. He was awarded the Air Medal, and a 2-oak leaf cluster, and a Purple Heart. His family noted that Rankin died exactly two years after enlisting.

Sources: The Belleville Times, April 19, May 31, 1945

1st Lt. Wilfred D. Potis

(May 17, 1945) – 1st Lt. Wilfred Potis, 28, son of Mrs. Charlotte H. Potis of Hornblower Avenue, was killed in England in an aircraft accident on April 26. His wife, Dorothy, received the telegram the day after V-E Day, when victory was declared in Europe. Lt. Potis was the pilot of a B-24 Liberator, stationed

with the Eighth Air Force in England. He served with the 706th Bomber Squadron, 446th Bomber Group, Heavy. His last letter was written April 25 after he completed his 34th mission, the finale for the Eighth Air Force. Reports said the Skoda works and Pilsen and rail targets at Birchtesgaden were targets. Potis said in his letter that on April 12 he saved his plane and crew from a collision with another plane in formation ... it had stripped a wing in "peeling off" and was falling towards him.

Potis enlisted March 5, 1941, and was assigned to the infantry division. He was in San Francisco on his way to the Philippines when Pearl Harbor was attacked. He was then sent to Hawaii for 8 months. Potis was sent Officer Candidate School at Ft. Benning, Ga. After six months as an infantry officer at Camp Claybourne, La., he switched to the Air Corps. He received his wings at Pampa, Texas. Lt. Potis is buried at: Plot F, Row 7, Grave 127, Cambridge American Cemetery, Cambridge, England He was awarded the Air Medal with 4 oak leaf clusters

Sources: American Battle Monuments Commission; The Belleville Times, May 17, 1945; Kenneth J. Potis, Esq.

Joseph A. Razes

(June 29, 1944) – Motor/Machinist's Mate 2/c Joseph Anthony Razes, 27, of Brighton Avenue, died of a ruptured aorta on June 2. He was buried in the South Pacific. Razes enlisted in the U. S. Navy on April 2, 1942. His service number is 02247949.

MoMM Razes, who entered the service from Pennsylvania, is honored on the Honolulu Memorial, Honolulu, Hawaii. Razes had lived with his aunt and uncle, Mr. and Mrs. Edward Petrauskas, of Brighton Avenue, after his parents died in McAdoo, Pa., when he was a baby. He attended Montgomery and Silver Lake Schools.

Sources: American Battle Monuments Commission; The Belleville Times; Newark Evening News, July 20, 1944; Remembrance - George Sbarra

Wallace E. Reed

(Sept. 14, Nov. 30, 1944) – Former resident Tech. Sgt. Wallace E. Reed, 27, was killed Aug. 6 in France. Reed lived on Van Houten Place before moving to Beech Street in Nutley. He was graduated from Barringer high school in Newark. Reed entered the Army 2 years ago. He served with the 47th Infantry

Regiment, Ninth Infantry Division. He participated in the invasion of North Africa, Sicily, Italy and France. He was awarded the Silver Star for leading his platoon against the Nazis. His service number is 32057432. Sgt. Reed is buried at Plot J, Row 11, Grave 2, Brittany American Cemetery, St. James, France. He was awarded the Silver Star, and Purple Heart with oak leaf cluster.

Sources: American Battle Monuments Commission; The Belleville Times, Sept. 14, Nov. 30, 1944; Newark Evening News, Sept. 15, 16, 18, Nov. 25, 1944

Stanley E. Reynolds

(May 7, 1942) – Private Stanley E. Reynolds, 27, of Malone Avenue was killed in an automobile accident in Nutley on May 3. A teacher was also killed in the accident and another person badly hurt. Pvt. Reynolds had been in the Army for two months. He had been stationed at Fort Belvoir, Va. He was home on furlough at the time of the accident.

Source: The Belleville Times

Joseph Rizzo

Staff/Sgt. Joseph Rizzo of Frederick Street was killed in action. His service number is 32300247.

Sources: Newark Evening News, Dec. 2, 1944 - (Returned to Action), Remembrance - George Sbarra

Lt. John F. Rogers

(Feb. 10, 1944) – Lt. John F. Rogers, 25, of 150 Birchwood Drive, was reported missing in the Gilbert and Ellice Island area of the South Pacific. He is believed to be a victim of a tropical hurricane that scattered the squadron of which he was the leader. Born in Newark, Capt. Rogers attended St. Benedict's preparatory school and was graduated with a B.S. degree from Notre Dame in 1940. H enlisted in the Marines in December 1940. The Marine captain is the son of Mrs. Frances V. Rogers.

Sources: The Belleville Times, Feb. 10, 1944; Newark Evening News, Feb. 5, 17, 1944; World War II Honor List of Dead and Missing, State of New Jersey, War Dept. June 1946

Frank J. Rosania

Private Frank J. Rosania was killed in action while serving with the U.S. Army in WWII. His service number is 32925440.

Source: National World War II Memorial

Lt. Edmund M. Sadlock

(March 22, 1945) – 2nd Lt. Edmund M. Sadlock, 28, of Adelaide Street, was killed in action on Luzon in the South Pacific on Feb. 19. Lt. Sadlock went overseas September 1943, three months before his son Edmond was born.

Sadlock, who lived in Belleville since 1931, enlisted in January 1941. He was commissioned a 2nd lieutenant at Fort Benning, Ga., in January 1942. He served in Hawaii and New Guinea before going to the Philippines.

At the time of his death, Lt. Sadlock was serving with the 149th Infantry Regiment, 38th Infantry Division. He had earned the Combat Infantryman's Badge. He was promoted to the rank of 1st Lieutenant posthumously.

He is buried at Plot N, Row 3, Grave 26, Manila American Cemetery, Manila, Philippines. He was awarded the Purple Heart.

Sources: American Battle Monuments Commission, The Belleville Times

William J. Salmon

(Oct. 26, 1944) – Marine Corporal William Joseph Salmon, 21, of Dewitt Avenue, was killed in action Sept. 23, on Peleliu on Palau Islands in the South Pacific. Salmon was a sniper-scout on the Guadalcanal, Cape Gloucester and New Guinea campaigns.

He is the son of Mr. and Mrs. Joseph Salmon of DeWitt Avenue. He left Belleville High School in his junior year to join the Civilian Conservation Corps.

While overseas, he met his brother on Guadalcanal in December 1941. The brothers both enlisted one week after Pearl Harbor was attacked.

The Palue Islands in what is now the Republic of Palau are in the westernmost cluster of the Caroline Islands, north of Australia and west of Micronesia.

Salmon is buried at Plot C, Row 12, Grave 57, Manila American Cemetery, Manila, Philippines. He was awarded the Purple Heart.

Sources: American Battle Monuments Commission; Belleville Times; World War II Honor List of Dead and Missing, State of New Jersey, War Dept. June 1946

1st Lt. Harry Salz

1st Lt. Harry Salz died at Fort Dix, N.J., on July 25, 1943.

Source: The Belleville Times, Aug. 31, 1944

Theodore P. Sanok

(March 15, 1945) – Pfc. Theodore P. Sanok, 29, was killed in an accident at Camp Blanding, Fla. No details of his death were released. He is the son of Mr. and Mrs. Joseph Sanok of Montgomery Street. His wife is the former Alice Syloski, in Bloomfield. He leaves behind a 3-month old daughter. He had been home for her birth.

He served at Fort Monmouth; Halloran Hospital, Staten Island; England General Hospital in Atlantic City; and Fort Lewis, Wash., before going to Camp Blanding.

Sources: The Belleville Times; Remembrance - George Sbarra

George J. Schemm

Quartermaster 3/c George J. Schemm was declared killed in action April 1, 1946. He is the son of Mr. and Mrs. William Joseph Schemm of 45 Division Avenue, Belleville.

His service number is 02244538. He entered the U.S. Navy. He is memorialized at Honolulu Memorial, Honolulu, Hawaii. He was awarded the Purple Heart.

Sources: American Battle Monuments Commission, National World War II Memorial; World War II Honor List of Dead and Missing, State of New Jersey, War Dept. June 1946

Salvatore N. Sena

Salvatore N. Sena, of Heckel Street, was killed in action at the beachhead assault, Anzio, Italy, on April 8, 1944. His is the township's 17th Gold Star.

Born on July 9, 1919, he enlisted in the Army and served with the 45th Infantry Division.

He was awarded the Purple Heart. His service number is 32910099. He is buried at Holy Cross Cemetery, North Arlington.

Sources: Newark Evening News, Feb. 17, 1945; Remembrance - George Sbarra

2nd Lt. George Skeen

(Nov. 21, 1944) – 2nd Lt. George Skeen, 22, died of wounds on Oct. 19, two days after his B-17 Flying Fortress was shot down. Lt. Skeen was reported missing Oct. 17 following a raid over Germany.

Skeen was commissioned on April 22 at Selman Field, Monroe, La.

At age 22, Skeen received the Air Medal for his work as a B-17 Flying Fortress navigator.

He entered the Army from 75 Van Houten Place, Belleville, on Jan. 29, 1943.

The son of Louis W. and Lillian C. Skeen, George Skeen was born Oct. 1, 1922, in Irvington, and was graduated from Irvington High School on Jan. 26, 1939. He had one sister Lois W. Skeen (Doyle).

2nd Lt. Skeen married Betty Ann Speight on July 16, 1944, at the chapel on the Air Base in Herington, Kansas. He was shipped overseas shortly afterward.

Betsy Sowers tells the story of her mother's courtship and first marriage:

While stationed in Kansas, George Skeen befriended Peter Sommer who was also in Army Air Corps' training. Peter invited George to be his Best Man at his wedding in Peoria, Ill. There George met Peter's first cousin Betty Speight. They had a whirlwind courtship, and a month later, as Peter and George heard rumors that they were about to be sent overseas, George sent word to Betty that he wanted to marry her before he left. Her own mother was ill, so her Aunt Bertha Wilson, and Mary Lou Sommer, Peter's new bride, accompanied her to the Air Base.

The women had to travel by troop train, and the train was full, so Aunt Bertha pretended to be disabled, and rode in a wheelchair, in order to get them on the train. They arrived in Kansas in the middle of the night, where an Army car and driver, along with George and Peter, picked them up and took them straight to the base chapel, which Mary Lou described as looking like a portable lean-to.

A soldier in the balcony played the wedding march on a phonograph, and the rings didn't fit. On their way to the hotel at 2 a.m., the only person on the street was a black man with a watermelon, which they bought, and ate on the curb as the "wedding reception." Both couples had two days in the local hotel, which was the honeymoon for all of them, because the men had their orders to depart. They took their brides back to the train for tearful farewells.

Two weeks later, they called from New Jersey to say they were on their way to England. That was the last they heard from them. Both George and Peter were killed, although they were not serving together at the time.

George's plane caught fire over Cologne, Germany, and he was shot attempting to parachute to safety. Peter bailed out of a crippled plane over the English Channel, and was never found.

2nd Lt. Skeen served with the 366th Bomber Squadron, 305th Bomber Group, Heavy. He is buried at Plot C, Row 28, Grave 13, Ardennes American Cemetery, Neupre, Belgium. He was awarded the Air Medal with oak leaf cluster and the Purple Heart.

Sources: American Battle Monuments Commission; Eileen Bellisario; Betsy Sowers; The Belleville Times, Nov. 21, Dec. 14, 1944.

2nd Lt. John J. Smith

(Jan. 18, 1945) – Army Air Force pilot 2nd Lt. John J. Smith, 28 of New Street, was killed over England when the B-17 he was flying collided with another Flying Fortress on Jan. 5. It was one of the first times piloting a B-17 for Smith, who had trained on B-24s. He served with the 848th Bomber Squadron, 490th Bomber Group, Large. Smith entered service on April 1943.

He trained at Kessler Field, Miss., Helena, Ark., Maxwell Field, Ala., Greenville, Miss, and Lawrenceville, Ill. He received six months additional training in Texas, Nebraska, and Idaho.

He last saw his wife and son on Nov. 28 before he left for overseas on Dec. 11. Lt. Smith was also known for his 4-piece orchestra "The Crestmen" at Belleville High School. He is buried at Plot F, Row 1, Grave 116, Cambridge American, Cemetery, Cambridge, England

Sources: American Battle Monuments Commission; The Belleville Times, Feb. 8, 1945; Newark Evening News, Feb. 1, 1945

Robert A. Stecker

(Sept. 21, 1944) – Robert A. Stecker, an Army engineer, was killed in action in France on Aug. 15. The young soldier leaves behind a 16-month-old daughter Carolyn who he never saw. Stecker joined the Army in 1942. He served in the Allied campaigns in North Africa, Sicily and Italy. He moved his family to Beech Street two years ago from Newark.

Source: The Belleville Times

Gerald Strigari

Seaman 2/c Gerald Strigari died in Brooklyn on Aug. 10, 1944.

Source: The Belleville Times, Aug. 31, 1944

Joseph C. Taibi

Private Joseph C. Taibi, of Frederick Street, was killed in action in Tunisia, North Africa, on April 8, 1943. Born on April 16, 1920, he served with the 47th Infantry, Ninth Division. His service number is 32057408. He is buried at Plot I, Row 17, Grave 8, North Africa American Cemetery, Carthage, Tunisia. He was awarded the Purple Heart. Taibi VFW Post #6265 was established in his honor in Belleville, N.J.

Sources: American Battle Monuments Commission; The Belleville Times, Aug. 31, 1944; Remembrance - George Sbarra; World War II Honor List of Dead and Missing, State of New Jersey, War Dept. June 1946

Robert C. Taylor

(Sept. 7, 1944) – Aviation radioman 2/c Robert C. Taylor, 24, of Bremond Street, was killed on a patrol mission off Hamilton, Bermuda, on Aug. 20. Seaman Taylor is the son of Mrs. Elizabeth Taylor, Bremond Street. Taylor entered the Navy in May 1942. Most of his Navy service was spent in Panama. On Aug. 20, 1944: Lieutenant (j.g.) Stanley C. Smith and seven crewmen were killed in a crash approximately 25 miles north of Bermuda while on an anti-submarine warfare practice bombing hop. Cause of the crash was unknown.

Crew members were: Pilot: Lt. (j.g.) Stanley Charles Smith, Joe Billy Longhorne, Marion Daniel Colvard, Fleming Whitney, Will Mitchel Haire, Robert Chester Taylor, Joseph Ellsworth Cook, James Lloyd Noel. Taylor was slated to return to States the next day to begin radio training. VPB-207 was Established as Patrol Squadron 207 (VP-207) on Dec. 1, 1942. It was redesignated Patrol Bombing Squadron 207 (VPB-207) on 1 Oct. 1, 1944. It was disestablished on June 26, 1945. The squadron's insignia featured an alligator holding a flaming bomb. No examples of the design exist in the records.

Taylor is listed as missing in action or buried at sea on the Tablets of the Missing at East Coast Memorial, N.Y.

Sources: American Battle Monuments Commission; The Belleville Times, Feb. 3, Sept. 7, Nov. 30, 1944; Nevins A. Frankel - VP Navy Web Site; Terence Geary - VP Navy Archives; Navy History, VP Navy Organization; World War II Honor List of Dead and Missing, State of New Jersey, War Dept. June 1946

Robert S. Taylor

(Feb. 3, 1944) – Radioman 2/c Robert S. Taylor of Joralemon Street was killed overseas before February 1944. He was a veteran of six major engagements in the South Pacific. His crew received a Presidential Citation for rescuing the crew of the Helena. He is a 1939 Belleville High School graduate.

Source: The Belleville Times

William E. Thetford Jr.

(May 17, 1945) – Pfc. William E. Thetford Jr., 27, of Linden Avenue, was killed in action in Germany on April 20. A member of the 63rd Infantry Division of the Seventh Army, Thetford recently wrote home that he liberated Allied soldiers from German prison camps. Thetford had been overseas since September 1943. He participated in campaigns in North Africa, Italy, France and Germany. Thetford trained at Camp Croft, S.C.

Source: The Belleville Times

Gus Frank Vaccaro

Coxswain Gus F. Vaccaro, was killed in action Feb. 26, 1945. He is the son of Mr. & Mrs. Natale Vaccaro, Holmes Street. His service number is 07102630. Vaccaro is listed as missing in action or buried at sea on the Tablets of the Missing at East Coast Memorial, New York.

Sources: American Battle Monuments Commission; World War II Honor List of Dead and Missing, State of New Jersey, War Dept. June 1946

John F. Verian

(Oct. 12, 1944) – Sgt. John F. Verian, 22, of 158 Washington Avenue, was killed in action in the midst of the Siegfried Line in Germany. Sgt. Verian landed in Oran, North Africa on Christmas Day 1942, six months after he entered the Army. He was wounded a month later in Tunisia serving in the 1st Division.

Sgt. Verian was also wounded in the invasion of Sicily on July 10, 1943. He was hospitalized for five months with severe wounds of the lower spine. In January, he went to England for five months of training in invasion tactics. He landed in Normandy on D-Day. Sgt. Verian joined the Army 25 years to the day after his father joined for World War I.

(June 24, 1943) – Corporal John F. Verian was awarded a Purple Heart while serving in North Africa. Verian has been in the Army since June 5, 1942. He has been stationed in Africa since December. He was recently hit in the leg by flying shrapnel. Classified as a minor injury, Verian just a few days later was doing Military Police duties. He then had taken part in a "final affair" in Africa in which the "Germans were cleaned up."

Source: The Belleville Times, June 24, 1943, Oct. 12, 1944

John Volinski

(April 2, 1942) – Private John Volinski, 21, died at Gorgas Hospital, Panama Canal Zone on March 28. Volinski, nicknamed "Windy" had been adopted by Mr. and Mrs. George Martin of Ralph Street. He was inducted into the Army in August 1941.

Source: The Belleville Times, April 2, 1942, Aug. 31, 1944

Louis Wagner

(Oct. 8, 1942) – Sgt. Louis Wagner, 24, of Stephens Street, was killed Oct. 2 following an auto crash in Macon, Ga. Wagner served with the 901st School Squadron at Cochran near Macon. Wagner had been in the service for 15 months. He was buried with military honors in Newark.

Source: The Belleville Times, Oct. 8, 1942, Aug. 31, 1944

Harry Ward, Jr.

(Nov. 29, 1945) – Sgt. Harry Ward Jr., of DeWitt Avenue, was reported killed in action in the Mindoro Islands in the Philippines on Dec. 21. He served with the 240th Engineer Construction Battalion. Ward entered the Army in January 1943, at age 18. Sgt. Ward took part in invasions of New Guinea, the Solomons, and Leyte. He was awarded the Purple Heart posthumously. He is listed as missing in action or buried at sea on the Tablets of the Missing at Manila American Cemetery, Manila, Philippines.

Sources: American Battle Monuments Commission, The Belleville Times

John N. Waters

(Feb. 21, 1946) – John N. Waters died Feb. 13, from injuries sustained while serving with the Marines, Second Division for 3 years in the South Pacific. Waters, who left Belleville High School to join the Marines, never took a furlough. He shipped out to the Pacific at the end of his basic training.

The young Marine served in battle campaigns including Tarawa, Peleliu, Tinian, Ie Shima – where newspaper writer Ernie Pyle was killed by a sniper – Okinawa and Saipan. Waters was sick with dengue fever, a tropical disease and had been hospitalized overseas. Waters received a Purple Heart, and was discharged last December. He died at home.

Source: The Belleville Times

James T. White

(Sept. 7, 1944) – James T. White, 24, of Holmes Street, was killed in action in Italy on Aug. 16. He had been overseas since January 1943.

White participated in campaigns in Tunisia, Sicily, Cassino and the Anzio beachhead. Born in Jersey City, he lived in Belleville for 14 years and graduated from Belleville High School in 1939.

White enlisted in July 1941, and served in the 67th Anti-Aircraft Gun Battalion. He is buried at Plot F, Row 7, Grave 31, Florence American Cemetery, Florence, Italy. He was awarded the Purple Heart.

Source: American Battle Monuments Commission, The Belleville Times

Lee O. White

(Aug. 10, 1944) – Water-tenderer 3/c Lee White of Ralph Street, Belleville, was killed during the invasion of France on June 8, 1944. The 26-year-old sailor was aboard the destroyer USS Meredith (DD-726) during invasion operations.

Early on June 6, Meredith screened the transports and landing craft to Utah Beach and provided pre-invasion shore bombardment. The Meredith was on patrol duty off the Bay of the Seine during June 7, when it struck an enemy mine.

Severely damaged, with a loss of seven killed and more than 50 wounded and missing, the Meredith was towed to anchorage at the Bay of the Seine. However, as the result of enemy bombing, the ship was blown apart, and broke in two without warning and sank June 9.

White had lived with his aunt, Mrs. Paul Ott of Ralph Street, after his parents died many years ago. His wife, Gloria Nero White, and his 3-month-old son, James Lee, whom he saw once before departure, live in Nutley.

White is listed as missing in action or buried at sea on the Tablets of the Missing, Normandy American Cemetery, St. Lauren-sur-Mer, France. He was awarded the Purple Heart.

Sources: American Battle Monuments Commission; The Belleville Times, The Nutley Sun; World War II Honor List of Dead and Missing, State of New Jersey, War Dept. June 1946; Alice and Lee White

William R. White

(Oct. 5, 1944) – Quartermaster 3/c William Russell White, 30, the son of Mrs. Caroline E. White of 63 Holmes Street, was presumed to be dead by the Navy.

White had not been heard from since his destroyer the USS Rowan was blown up off the beaches of Salerno, Italy, on Sept. 11, 1943.

He perished amidst terrific enemy barrages off the beaches of Salerno when, according to some reports, his destroyer exploded and went down in 36 seconds. It was his first trip abroad. White was born in Belleville and lived all his life here.

White enlisted in the U.S. Naval Reserve on Nov. 2, 1942. His service number is 07087795. He was called to active duty the following May. He was awarded the Purple Heart. White is listed among the missing in action or buried at sea on the Tablets of the Missing, Sicily-Rome American Cemetery, Nettuno, Italy.

Sources: American Battle Monuments Commission; The Belleville Times; Destroyers Organizations Histories; Navsource; USS Rowan; World War II Honor List of Dead and Missing, State of New Jersey, War Dept. June 1946

2nd Lt. Leonard R. Willette

(Jan. 18, 1945) – 2nd Lt. Leonard R. Willette, 22, was declared killed in action this week. Willette had been listed as missing in action since Sept. 22. He is the son of Newark Police Lt. and Mrs. Lawrence Willette, of Stephens Street.

The young man enlisted in the Army Air Corps while a student at New York University. He refused an appointment by the late Senator Barbour to West Point in order to get into active combat more quickly.

Willette received his wings at Tuskegee Army Air Field, Fla., in February 1944. He was a P-51 Mustang pilot based in Italy with the famed 99th Fighter Squadron, 332nd Fighter Group, under command of Col. Benjamin O. Davis.

He is buried at Plot J, Row 18, Grave 17, Lorraine American Cemetery, St. Avold, France. He was awarded the Air Medal with oak leaf cluster, and the Purple Heart. He is also survived by a brother, Lawrence.

According to W. F. Holton of the Tuskegee Airmen Inc., Leonard Willette graduated from Class 44-B-SE, on 2/8/44. Holton says records show that Flight Officer Willette was assigned to the 99th Fighter Squadron, 332nd Fighter Group, and was reported missing in action 9/22/44, while participating in a combat mission to Munich, Germany. His last known position was 10 to 15 miles North of Lake Chiem, Germany. He was flying is P-51, Mustang which he named "Wrong Woman."

One of the pilots of the 99th received a radio message from Willette, stating that he was having engine trouble and thought he would have to bail out. He was at 30,000 feet and losing altitude and his oil pressure was decreasing rapidly. When the pilot, Lt. Saunders, last saw Willette, he was disappearing through a hole in the clouds at about 20,000 feet.

A second pilot who was leading the mission, Herman Lawson, was flying at 30,000 feet when he received Willette's radio call that he would have to bail out. The time was 12:33 p.m. on Sept. 22, 1944.

Sources: W. F Holton, Tuskegee Airmen Inc.: American Battle Monuments Commission, The Belleville Times; Air Force Military Museum – Tuskegee Airmen, American Visionaries – Tuskegee Airmen; The Divided Skies by Jakeman; National Archives and Records Administration; The National Home of Tuskegee Airmen Inc.

Lt. Edward P. Wood

U.S. Naval Reserve Lt. Edward Parsons Wood, of 55 Berkeley Avenue, was killed in action in a bombing mission over occupied Europe on Jan. 10, 1944. His service number is O-100043. Lt. Wood is listed as missing in action or buried at sea on the Tablets of the Missing at North Africa American Cemetery Carthage, Tunisia. He is survived by his sister Amelia Elizabeth.

Sources: American Battle Monuments Commission; Belleville Times, Aug. 31, 1944; World War II Honor List of Dead and Missing, State of New Jersey, War Dept. June 1946

Fred R. Wyckoff, Jr.

(Sept. 9, 1943) – Staff Sergeant Fred Raymond Wyckoff, Jr. 28, of 481 Union Avenue, was killed in action in Tunisia in the North African Theater of Operations in August. Wyckoff was graduated from Belleville High School in 1933. He left town for the Army in January 1941. He received training at Fort Bragg, N.C. He was in the battle of Tunisia having landed with the first invasion force in North Africa last November. Among his survivors is a brother Sgt. Theodore Wyckoff, 24, in Colorado.

Source: The Belleville Times, Aug. 31, 1944

Joseph Zecca

Private Joseph Zecca, 19, of Fairway Avenue, was reported missing in action in Italy on Oct. 29, 1944. The killed in action notice came Jan. 23, 1945. Zecca left in his senior year at Belleville High School and entered the Army in 1943. He trained in Alabama. Zecca went overseas in March and was stationed in North Africa. He arrived in Italy in June. He served with the 133rd Infantry.

Source: The Belleville Times, Nov. 21, 1944, March 15, 1945

The Honor Roll board was erected on the southeast corner of Heckel and Honiss Streets by the patriotic citizens to show the servicemen that they were supported by the people of Silver Lake sections of Belleville. Source: Remembrance - George Sbarra.

BATAAN DEATH MARCH SURVIVOR TALE

Survivor of Bataan Death March Comes Home

Sgt. Michael Tortoriello, prisoner of Japs

Three-and-a-half-years, reveals horror tale;

Served seven years in Army

The phone rang in the home of Mr. and Mrs. Carmine Tortoriello of 88 Baldwin Place, Oct. 29, 1945, and Mrs. Tortoriello, answering the ring, heard a voice say: "Hello, Mom. This is Michael."

It was a voice Mrs. Tortoriello had not heard in seven long, anxious years, for Sgt. Mike Tortoriello was one of the survivors of the infamous Bataan Death March, and a Jap prisoner from April 9, 1942, to Sept. 17, 1945.

After going through years of torture, hardship and marked with death in its most horrid form, Mike is remarkably quiet and cool. Instead of a highly nervous, neurotic individual, which would be expected, he is restrained, but talks without hesitancy, showing an unusual capacity for remembering names, dates and places.

But the ordeal will never be forgotten, said Mike. Two little scars appear on each side of his cheeks, put there by Jap cigarette butts, one of their favorite forms of torture.

Captured one day after the fall of Bataan, Mike had been trying to reach the guerilla troops when Jap tanks caught up with him and several of his buddies. Then began a chain of horrendous nights and days.

FOUR DAYS MARCH IN SUN

For four days and nights the American soldiers and their Philippine cohorts were forced to march during the day under a blistering, tropical sun and at night with a ten minute rest period the only break along the torturous path. Men, driven crazy by thirst, ran off the road to attempt to reach one of the many artesian wells along the route, but were shot, clubbed or bayoneted to death by the brutal Jap guards.

"I kept a small pebble in my mouth, and kept rolling it around," said Tortoriello. "One instance I remember very well, in trying to get some water. We had reached Camp O'Donnell, a former American camp, and two Americans approached a Jap guard, and by using sign language asked if they could fill several canteens with water. The guard said to go ahead, and they disappeared into the undergrowth. That was the last we ever heard of them. Several Japs went into the bushes after them, while they were filling canteens, and killed both soldiers."

It was at O'Donnell that more than 32,000 Philippines died and several thousand Americans. A Jap commander, who sported a handlebar moustache, lined the survivors up, and through an interpreter, informed them there was no medicine available for them, and the sick would have to die. The Japs buried the dead in holes about two feet deep, and piled as many as twenty men in these holes, and then threw dirt on the pile. Along would come a rainstorm, wash away the dirt from the bodies and the wild dogs could be heard having a feast at night on the remains.

Then came Camp Cabanatuan in the Philippines. Upon reaching this side, in what was to become one of the famous Jap prisoner-of-war-camps, that more atrocities were committed.

MAKE CAMP LIVABLE

"We had to clean the place up," said Mike, "there was high grass all around and some dilapidated shacks that were falling apart. We built makeshift roads and constructed more livable quarters. When we first arrived, the Japs put up a fence with only a single strand of barbed wire. So many of the boys escaped, that the little men created the 'shooting squads.' The prisoners were divided into groups of ten, and if any one of them escaped, the others would be killed. We thought they were kidding, but one of the boys escaped, and the nine men left were all shot to death."

Tortoriello, when questioned about the food, related they were given 700 grams of rice a day. The Japs had a trick of filling bags of sand, piling them up with a few sacks of rice on top, and when the officer-in-charge of war prisoners made an inspection trip, he was shown the bags piled up, and what he thought was rice, was principally sand.

"We had gardens," said Mike, "but when there are 6,000 hungry men, and after the Japs got through confiscating a lot of the stuff we rised (sic), there wasn't much to go around."

In July 1944, the prisoners were shipped to Japan. Upon hearing of the move, the men were struck with the idea they would be better off, for they had heard that the prisoners in Japan at least had the benefit of the Red Cross packages. But conditions were very bad in Japan and they found they had been moved from the frying pan into the fire.

MEN CROWDED IN FREIGHTER

"There were 1,500 men crowded into the hold of this small Jap freighter going over," said Tortoriello, "and there was no sanitary facilities. We were in a convoy, right in the center, guarded by two carriers and a number of destroyers. But several days before we made port, I had occasion to go on the deck to use the only facility they made available for us. It was about two o'clock in the morning, and suddenly I saw through the cracks in the shack, four distinct flashes over the horizon. Our ship was going like mad, and we later learned that American subs had nailed two tankers and two freighters."

On August 4, 1944, the prisoners were marched into Camp Yawata, near the city of Moji, on the island of Kyushu. Shortly after arriving there, Tortoriello and some of his buddies were put to work in a steel mill, and then began the real battle of survival.

Sixteen hours a day, for three weeks straight, was the working schedule, and then came one day of rest. Mike operated an electric hammer and between dodging bombs from Yank B-29s and dipping into the Jap black market, became quite proficient in the language.

BLACK MARKET IN EVERYTHING

"The government controlled all the food, and you could not buy any in a store," he said, "consequently, there was black market in everything. Some of the extra clothing we had went into the market in exchange for soy beans, salt and money. We smuggled clothes out and food back in, but we were caught many times. Then came a little beating. One of the favorite tricks was the Water Cure. They put a hose in your mouth and loaded you up with water. Then when your stomach began to distend, they would jump on it or punch you."

The men were supposed to be paid for their work, but received practically nothing, as their money was just about worthless. The men learned that a plan had been drawn up in Tokyo to kill all the prisoners-of-war in the event of an invasion, and were kept on edge with this thought staring them in the face.

Then, one day a B-29 appeared and dropped a parachute with a package of food, and Mike said he never thought C and K rations could taste so good.

FLOWN HOME AFTER LIBERATION

The men were brought to Okinawa, after being released by American liberation troops, and from there (he) was flown home. Down to 125 pounds, Tortoriello was treated for malnutrition and most recently had been at the Rhoadea General Hospital in Utica, N.Y., before being released.

Sgt. Tortoriello was attached to the Air Force, and is now enjoying a 104-day furlough, upon completion of which he will go to California to be discharged.

A graduate of Bloomfield, Tortoriello was a star football player, playing in '36 and '37. He was employed at General Motors in Bloomfield, prior to enlisting in the Army for a two-year stretch in 1939.

Source: The Belleville Times

WWII POW - MIA

This listing is likely incomplete but it is a reminder of the additional sacrifices our Belleville sons paid for our freedom.

John J. Kant Jr. - MIA, recovered OK (7.30.42)

Pvt. Lawrence Ruzzo - POW, Italy, escaped (BT 3.18.43)

1st Lt. Edward T. Berlinski - POW, Italy (5.13.43)

Cpl. Raymond Squitieri, POW, Sicily (9.16.43)

Sgt. George Prezioso, MIA, Survived, (10.7.43)

Cpl. Anthony Bocchino - POW - Germany (11.11.43, 2.22.45)

Pvt. Joseph Ferraro Jr. - POW Germany (11.11.43)

Capt. John Rogers - MIA before February 1944.

Pvt. Joseph Bocchino - MIA/POW Sicily (4.6.44)

Sgt. Robert P. Leonard - MIA/POW, Germany (4.27, 6.29.44)

Lt. H. Clifford Schmutz - MIA Italy (5.11.44)

F/O John W. Barrett - MIA - Jugoslavia (5.11.44)

S/Sgt. Michael R. Ciano - MIA - Germany (5.11.44)

Pvt. Felix P. Mozeika - MIA - Italy (5.11.44)

Ronald McCormack - MIA - Normandy, June 9, 1944.

Lt. Wilbur M. Brean - MIA - France (6.8.44)

Al Culkin - POW - Germany 6.22, 7.13.44

Frederick Mason - MIA/POW - Germany (8.31, 10.12.44)

Glenn C. Nelson - missing in a hurricane 9.12.44.

Pvt. John C. Keller - MIA - Italy (11.2.44)

Joseph J. Cifrodella lost at sea on 11.4.44

Pvt. Joseph Zecca - MIA/KIA (11.21.44)

Arthur Leithauser - MIA/KIA (11.30.44)

Sgt. Harry Ward Jr. - MIA on 12.12.1944.

Sgt. Henry R. Candura - MIA (1.18.45)

Pfc. Edmond D. Kelly - MIA (1.18, 4.18.45)

Pvt. William J. Davis - MIA (1.18.45)

Michael Sbarra - MIA - (2.15.45)

Lt. Edward Stumpe - MIA, 4.25.45 (BT 5.17.45)

Pfc. Vincent Cassidy - POW - Home – 5.24.45

Cpl. Michael Tortoriello - POW - Japan, 10.4.45 (4.15.43)

Joseph Bocchino - POW (2.22.45)

Pfc. Arthur Schultz - POW - Released (4.18.45)

Pfc. Edmond Kelly - POW - Released (4.18.45)

Pvt. Joseph Gamarro - POW Released (4.18.45)

Pfc. Domenick Alberti - POW Released (4.18.45)

Pfc. James Wilkinson - POW Released (4.18.45)

Leonard R. Willette - MIA over Germany 9.22.45

LETTERS HOME TO BELLEVILLE

From Angelo Buccino

to Mitch Mosior

Next-door Neighbors

on Gless Avenue

April 25, 1942

Hello Met,

Its been a long time since I wrote hasn't it. Well how are you feeling these days. Begin training pigeons yet? Here's hoping you walk off with a few races in Young Birds. Sorry I couldn't see your loft last time I was home but I had a lot of things to do & only had one day to do it. You know the way it is when you looking the birds over. Time sure flies. I wish I had a few pair here. I saw some of the pigeons they have in Australia. I only saw them from the sidewalk, so I can't tell you much about them. If I'm lucky to return & stop back there I'll try bringing some home.

We left N.Y. a few days after you saw me and our voyage was on. We left N.Y. with a helluva cold spell & 4 days later we were stripped and taking Sun Baths. Going through Panama Canal was very interesting as I was always in the dark as to how the locks worked. This was the first chance we've had to mail letters, they were all censored, just as all our mail is.

Feb. 7th my one year was up and my girlfriend wrote & told me it was the same cold rainy weather as when I left. It was raining as we left the armory & we passed Charley's Washing Machine shop. I hollered across the street to him & he waved back. Next time you see him ask him if he still remembers. Then at Dix we got soaked walking from the train to our tents – that leaked like Eugene's pigeon coop (your kid brother). Ha ha. I almost landed in the same place again as we moved from Virginia to Dix. About 2 blocks away this time and again rain rain rain.

We kept sailing along, no one knows where we are going. So now I know how Columbus felt, sailing on & on, no one knowing where to. Then one day we got word we were Australia bound & we hit rough weather. I was sicker than a dog, the ships were going up & down and water was coming on deck. It felt good to set food on dry land – "just once more." (As I kept wishing all thru the trip.) In Australia we had a good time and we treated to the best Hospitality I've ever seen. But all this was too good to last and orders came through to sail again.

A few weeks later we land on an island called New Caledonia (betcha can't find it) in the Pacific. Up until now we haven't been able to mention where we are but the ban has been lifted. We are far from town, Met and its every once in a while your able to go. I personally don't care to go as there isn't anything there anyway. The way I feel the next time I want to see the town is homeward bound.

Letter-writer PFC Angelo Buccino served in Guadalcanal and the South Pacific.

We haven't the things here we had back in America. But we are getting used to conditions and learning ways to getting around them. I have some candy made by Charms Inc. in Bloomfield, as soon as I got the can, I wished I could be at the shop where it was made. We have a combination radio phonograph and along with it is about 150 records. I eat my heart out as I listen to them as they bring back memories of Better Days. But it's a good way to be reminded of back home.

Since we came here we worked in rain & heat. We got our positions up & everything's coming along fine. The rainy season is on here and never a day goes by without us getting rain One day last week we got a taste of what to expect when a real Tropical storm comes along. It rained 5 days straight without stopping. It's a good thing we have 8 sets of clothes.

There are few white people here, mostly natives and French Javanese. There are a lot of coconuts, oranges and bananas about the Island. What I hate about this place is the mosquitoes & ants. I wish I had taken up French in school, as I would be able to talk to the people here. That's another reason I stick around the camp. This is jungle country and it reminds me of the Tarzan pictures I used to see.

In spite of the heat, I'm feeling all right. And when I listen to an American broadcast, I feel even better, man my heart skips a few beats. From what I've seen, if I ever get back to America, I'll be like that guy hopping the Chattanooga Choo Choo. I'll never roam any more. There's nothing like the States. Met, take it from me. I can't understand why people spent money to go to Europe when there was so much to see in the States. Yeah man it's beyond me.

Your probably wondering when I'll be home. Well I can't say but with a prayer, and a little luck, I hope to be home Christmas. This is my opinion and I may be well be here for over a year. (Pardon me I just knocked on wood.) So Chet tied the knot eh! It sure was a surprise to hear about it from Sub (??) and my brother. Bruno was even a bigger surprise!

Marie tells me she mistook the draft list for the Radio Column. Its two full rows and they've just about cleaned out the 1st Ward in Newark. She also said you'd practically have to be a corpse to be rejected. I like Bernie Barnett know a thing like being rejected for teeth would never keep us out of the Army if War was declared. So I'm glad I came in when I did as I stand a 50 – 50 chance this way.

Does Bruno still get to Vuono's for a few with Charlie. How's the boys getting along. I heard a few joined the Navy. Pretty soon more will get drafted and good bye the ole gang!

Well Met, the sooner we get this mess over & done with the sooner we'll all get together. I met some fellows from Nutley about 3 weeks ago. Imagine meeting somebody you know from back home, way out here. There's about 21 hours difference in time, we're that much ahead of you.

Well Met, I think I'll close asking you to give my regards to the gang (what's left of them), And tell (ink stain) her. A lot of times the boys (ink stain) my mind & I wonder where they are and how they doing. But I hope we all meet again, someday and will celebrate.

So long Met, name a bird after me. He'll come thru. "Keep em Flying Kid."

Regards to the Gang and Family

Angelo

PS Did Charlie McIntyre leave for the Army yet? Ask his brother George next time you see him & also give him my regards!

How's Boom Boom (your sister) She's getting Fat I think!

Sept. 26, 1942

Hi There Metaslski,

I just received your letter of August 24th and I was glad too. We must have made a good connection that time as letters generally take 1 to 2 months to reach here.

Yes the Marines sure had a field day knocking them Japs out of the sky. This time the Japs were caught with their pants down. There's fighting going on there now but I haven't listened to a radio for over a week, so I don't know how things are up there.

I heard about the send off Val got & I also heard that he's in Washington now. They sure shipped him fast & far. That's the second time he's been to the West Coast. Well Met maybe when this reaches you you'll be in the Service also. It seems like every guy & his brother are in uniform these days.

So you're the Uncle to Judith Ann Mosior Eh? How does it feel. I've been an Uncle since I was two years old. My niece was married in April and her husband is in the Service too. So your engaged Met, well whatever you do don't get married before or while your in the Service. They say its much easier to leave a girlfriend behind than a wife. I guess they're right too. Wish you luck in getting into the Air Corps. Let me know how Chet makes out.

So Butchie came through and got 7th in the Club. Well he'll get his stride & bring home the bacon yet. Well you got 1st place in the other club so it ain't so bad is it?

Well Met all you said about Love & your girlfriend there isn't much that I can add except – Check! – Wish you luck in your affair. The jokes you wrote were good. I didn't hear them.

That's a date Met and we'll drink a toast when the introduction takes place. Don't build me up too much as she may be a little disappointed in what she sees. I said Maybe!

No Met I don't use the sign language on French girls instead I've bought a few books for beginners & now my vocabulary is about 40 words. Slow but sure. Honest Met you say hello to some of them & and they'll smile and answer you but some will stick up their nose as if they were the last woman God created. I never saw such a crazy bunch of gals in my life.

Your dam right, them Japs better stay the hell away from here if they ever want to see Tokyo or Yokohama again. We've been on this island a long time & all we've done is build & build and practice and what the hell not. We're ready anytime.

Thanks kid for saying a prayer for me. Up until a few weeks ago I used to attend church practically every Sunday but now – well something happened and I don' go. They say there are no Atheists in Fox holes. They're right there ain't.

Well kid I like your letters because they're nice and long and the dope it contains, so keep writing don't wait for an answer as then it will be a lot of time wasted for waiting. I'll do likewise Met. I'm sure you'll find it better this way. I'll write at least twice a month.

We are busy working, which isn't unusual to us anymore. But that's alright as it occupies your mind. Our soft ball has been cut out for awhile to as we often work the whole seven days.

I was on a detail in town for two weeks and I worked in a ship. It reminded of better times back home punching the time clock again. I saw a lot of the town in those two weeks. Yeah Man!

I guess I'll close now and glad to hear your using sense in waiting for this mess to be over before getting married. I heard from my cousin Val who is Ireland. He's a corporal now. But like us, we wish we were back in the good ole U.S. A. Yes we've learned to appreciate all the luxury & things of home. You don't miss em much until you have to do without it. So long now Met. Wish you luck in the Races, Air Corps, & with your girlfriend. Remember me to your friend (Butch!)

Angelo

P.S. Write my address plainer Met as the Battery F was underlined in red for not being plain enough. (maybe he needs glasses as I can read it plain enough.)

October 4, 1942

Hello Met, alias "Mitchell 2000"

Just a few lines to let you know I'm alright and hope your feeling the same. How are you and the girlfriend getting along? Fine I hope. It was a surprise to meal learning you were going steady. You never did care for women much anyway. But when she came along well your resistance was low, eh? They're all bound to fall some day no matter how much they dislike women.

How's Mike Siluk, I wrote to him several times but only got one answer and that was four months ago. Say Met have you ever seen Toot Bloomenshine around? How's Joe Metz, Charlie Chas, Metty, Silver Top (Chet's brother Johnny), Skippy & John Nuriki (Narucki)? I guess a lot of those guys are not around town anymore.

I'm sending you a snapshot of myself that I had taken several weeks ago. I thought you would like to have one being I have one of you & the girlfriend.

There's nothing much I can say about things here Met, but were busy as hell. We've had the past two Sundays off & a few guys got up a ball game. The weather is cool & windy, it keeps the mosquitoes inland. When we first landed here, they practically ate us alive. I've never seen them as thick as they are here. We have several boys in our outfit who come from Florida & they say the mosquitoes down at the "Keys" are much worse than these. The Natives don't seem to be bothered much by them.

Maybe they prefer white meat.

My girlfriend mentioned a clipping she saw in the paper a few months ago. It was about a girl writing to her boyfriend in Australia asking, "What have they got that we haven't." He answered, "Oh nothing, except they're over here." I don't think she could thing of an answer to that. But let me tell you Met I spent a week in Australia, yes they have their pretty women and all that but the American girls got it all over them as far as knowledge & being hip to the jive.

There are a lot of marriages taking place wherever Yanks are stationed. But that's the way it goes and I can't say as I blame them. But here's one guy that's coming home single, you can bet your last dollar on that. That is, if I come back at all, you know nothing is certain nowadays.

Today is Sunday & I go on guard duty tonight. We get a lot of that as we're {content cut from paper}. They'll never catch us napping Met. I don't know how the war is going except for what I read on the Bulletin board. But I hope to be home in the Spring or early Summer. But who knows?

There's about eight guys here in my outfit that come from Jersey, but most of them come from N.Y. and Tennessee. I haven't heard from Val as yet but I did get a letter about four days ago, but it was written Aug. 16th that was before he left for the Army.

Well Met I guess I'll be moving along now as I have a few more letters to write. I'll write again soon. Hoping this letter finds you all well and in the best of health. Give the Gang my regards and tell them to write.

So long

Your friend Angelo

October 16, 1942

Hello Met,

How are you Mitchell 2000? How's the girlfriend too? I wrote to you about two weeks ago & sent along a snapshot that I thought you'd like to have. Have you received it?

Well, how did "Pigeon Dealer Tiny" train the birds? In fact how did the Young Birds Series turn out? Racing in two clubs sure must increase the excitement on Sundays, eh? Did Butchie do any better later in the races? I stopped in to see some birds that they Army has here and it was just like ole times back home. Seeing them birds was sight for sore eyes.

Boy its getting hot here & it isn't even summer time yet. It's just the opposite of back home. We're still busy working on that project and in two months we should finish up.

Say Met I didn't know Muzz was in the Navy? How did Chet make out in trying for the Air Corps.? You have the same ideas eh? You know Tiny would stand a good chance being he's a licensed mechanic already. But I guess he's satisfied working at the Airport. Tell that guy Suhe (Mike) to leave the women alone for half hour and drop me a line. This guy Andy that stays with Charlie, is he in the Army yet? He was one of the first to go from the street but I guess I beat them all getting in. How the heck do you spell Charlie's last name? Micheski? Dolly tells me she's going out with Shum. The lucky stiff.

No kidding Met but its good to hear what's going on back home ... news about the old gang etc. Boy we're going to have some celebration when we get back. Met get me the addresses of Alex & Billy Duduck, Muzz any of the ole gang that you can. I'd like to drop them a line. Do you know any of the ships they're on?

How's that bit fellow Eugene, does he drive your car? Boom Boom is still having his legs run off eh? She was a regular fatstuff when I last seen her. Just wait till she gets a gander at this Fat Guy, 176 pounds Met. She'll have the laugh on me.

Well Met I haven't got anything else to say right now but I'll be back in a few weeks with another letter. I hope this reaches you before Christmas. I just remembered I have to clean my rifle as I was on guard duty yesterday. In the Army your rifle is your best friend, treat it well.

So long now Met look up the addresses to them guys & let me have them. Give my brother Val my regards in your next letter. Keep em flying kid. Give the gang my regards.

Your friend

Angelo

November 4, 1942

Hello Met,

It's been a long time since I last wrote to you but it couldn't be helped. Notice my new address Met & always include my serial number (32059032) when you write

I am stationed at Guadalcanal & that's just about all I'm allowed to say. But you'll get the news flashes over the radio & in newspapers.

I sent a shell with "Regards from Met" in it across the lines. I hope it hit some Japs. Since I've been here I met some guys from Jersey & boy they're from all over Jersey.

I am feeling fine these days & really feel good that I'm in it at last. We haven't much time to ourselves anymore and I find little time to write.

Well before this reaches you, you may be in uniform also. Well anyone can read this letter in your family & then send it on to you wherever your stationed. Tell Charlie Milsreski where I am, will you?

How's Bruno, wife & baby coming along. I hope to see more than one when I come back Bruno or I'll think you're slipping. Has Eugene joined the Navy? I hear Tiny is in the Air Corp. What's happened to Charlie (Julius) I haven't heard about him except he got a new job and questionnaire. Tell Mike Liluk to write & to expect a letter one of these days.

I can just picture that street in a deserted condition. Well our street put a lot of guys in the Service. That's what I like to hear.

I'll close now with Regards to everybody in your family & the gang. (What's left of them).

So long Met

Your friend Butch

Ange

November 28, 1942

Hello Meltaski,

I just received your letter of Oct. 25th I was glad to hear the dope. Yes I guess this letter will be forwarded to you wherever your stationed. I wrote to you a few days ago Met but just had to write again & answer your letter.

So my brother got married eh, well I wish him luck. Let me know your address as soon as possible Tiny, Eugene & Charley too.

Met I have moved from that other place & I can't reveal my new location anymore. Ask your sister to get any letters I wrote to her my mother in November and you'll know where I am. Were in action at last Met & I wrote your name on shells and sent them over the lines into Japs laps. I'd like to write about a lot of things Met but I just can't.

I have a few souvenirs socked away – Jap money, dope & parts of Zero fighters. I made a bracelet for my girl from the fuselage of a Zero that was shot down near here.

I just came back from a swim in the water & I feel like a million bucks. I washed some clothes too. I took a picture of myself naked & I will show it to you if it comes out. You'll have to wait until I get home though. (By next Christmas I hope!) Well it's ten months overseas for this boy. I'm used to this heat & everything I've found in the tropics. It's much hotter here being we're near the equator.

I met some Marines from Kearny & Newark, so it's a small world after all.

So Belleville hasn't been defeated in football, let me know if they remained undefeated. It seems they always outplay their opponents but always end up in a tie or lose. At least that's the way it was when I was going to high school anyway.

I guess Helen was tickled pink when you placed that ring on her finger, eh? I keep telling my girl I'm not going to buy her any engagement ring, but I am. Of course all this is subject to change without notice. But so far those Japs haven't drawn a bead on this boy.

So you were to Radio City, well I never was there myself but am I going to make up for lost time when I get back. You never know how lucky you were where there was everything until you land in a place like this where there isn't anything. I often say to myself how foolish I was for not seeing more of life while I was able. But being back home you figure heck there's plenty of time.

Heck its about time the Yankees lost for the interest of baseball itself. I don't think anyone wants to see any one team win year after year. It gets monotonous eh kid.

You were more fortunate than I am having your girlfriend beside you & having her (censor) it. Oh boy would I like to have been in your shoes but with my girlfriend. No offense Met. You understand & besides I wouldn't try cutting in on you.

I guess I'll close stations now Metalski. I'm feeling fine & glad to hear your niece is coming around. Let me have Bruno's address

Your friend, Ange

I wish you a Merry Christmas And A Happy New Year.

Please forward this to Met if he's in the Army or Navy. Regards to all

December 19, 1942

Hello Met,

It's been a long time since I wrote or heard from you. My last letter to you was in November I believe. Well I'm feeling as fine as can be expected. Nothing has hit this boy "yet."

I received a bushel of mail a few weeks ago, cards, packages & letters. I've been trying to answer them as soon as possible but I still have four to answer. Stationery is scarce as hell here, I borrow some from this guy & some from that guy, so I'm getting buy until I receive some through the mail.

The heat of 120 degrees isn't bad but these large mosquitoes are a real pain in the neck. They are the largest I've seen & when they bite they draw plenty of blood, then leave a welt the size of a quarter. You kill on e& fifty take its place. Aside from that & losing some weight, I'm alright, I guess. Oh, yes, a few heat rashes too.

This letter will probably reach you in the Army someplace but I do hope you get it. I hope you like Army life Met because if you don't it will be that much harder for you. How's the girlfriend Met? Did Julius go yet?

Yesterday I did two weeks laundry of mine & what a job. Generally I wash a few pieces every time I go for a dip but we've been some other place & what water we got was for drinking only. Now we're back in a rest area & have a little time to do things.

Well Metlaski we're doing alright for ourselves & it won't be long well have this place lock, stock & barrel. I'll see you in 1943 sometime, I hope. Well so long kid & take care of yourself.

We are using our old APO again.

Your friend,

Butch

March 21, 1943

Hello Met,

I received your letter of Feb. 23, glad to hear you're doing okay by yourself. Your still in the City You ain't lying you struck it rich. Living in a hotel – eating in a restaurant – maids taking care of your quarters. Well, well, that beats all hell. You lucky stiff. (period.)

I certainly hope you'll be more than a Corporal before your 20 weeks schooling is over. Well don't forget for a John you've done alright. Maybe I'll even have to address your letters Corporal as the next time I hear from you, you may get

<??> Could be, you know. Congratulations on our Corporal. That's the stuff kid.

I got a letter from Mike Siluk today & he's still chasing the women around as usual. It was good hearing from him. He was made bread man in Wrights.

Met, many a truth has been spoken in jest. Yes we could meet there someday. Nothing's impossible. But we should meet!

Met there's dam little I can write about from this end. But I'm okay & still kicking that's the main thing.

I saw some native women today. They're nothing to write home about. They just wear skirts & are black as coal. Ugly to boot! Their breast is very long. I'll take a white girl.

The team won one & lost in today in soft ball. I didn't play as I was too tired after that hike I took.

I'll close now Met & wish you all the best in the world. Give my regards to your brother and girlfriend.

Your Friend,

Ange.

April 6, 1943

Hello Met,

Just a few lines to let you know I'm well & still kicking. I've received a few V mail letters from you but I think I've mentioned them before.

A few days ago I received 14 letters & I heard from just about everybody. Stiffie Siluk even wrote. Top that. She said she owns a horse. I got one from Johnny Siluk too.

I'm enclosing a clipping out of the Newark Evening News & hope you recognize him.

I've had a cold for a week & it's really knocking me for a loop.

One of the fellows here gets the Newark Evening News & I get seconds on them. It's good to read about the old home town. I see Belleville is doing okay in basketball. They won 9 out of 10 games and tipped Bloomfield by a large margin. Boy I'll bet Foley pulled his hair out. They had to stop the game for 5 minutes because there was too much noise.

How's tricks with you Met, still attending classes? I am too but it's all old stuff. I'm really surprised that I had forgotten a lot of it too.

Well Metaloski, I think it's time to close stations now. I hope this letter finds you okay.

Adios Amigo

Your friend Butch

CLIPPING

Lt. William A. Heike Jr. (photo)

Flying Officers Get Commissions

LAKE CHARLES FLYING FIELD, La. – 2nd Lt. William A. Heike, Jr., 150 Coeyman avenue, Nutley, Army pilot.

May 7, 1943 – envelope

May 5, 1943

Hello Met,

I just received your letter of April 13th & I'm sure glad to hear from you Pollack. So they're "Indian Givers" eh, give you your rating and if you don't pass they break you. Well Met I don't think that will happen to you as your going to pass. Or I'll give you a hard boot in the ass when I get you. Do I make myself clear?

Glad to hear your captain of your class soft ball team Out her we haven't played in about two months. Shows are scarce also. The one that used to be near us moved & now you have to go up the line if you want to see it. Well rules state you can go so far from your camp at night. Too many accidents can happen when you travel at night. It may be an enemy & it may be a guard. So I "stood" in bed & the hell with all the shows.

Yes Met what you read about matches being scarce here is true. Your wrong about my not smoking too. I practically eat them. 1 ½ a day, well when there's excitement its 2 packs or so. I wrote to my girlfriend for a watch and cigarette lighter but later cancelled it because I heard they are hard to get. All you hear is "gimme a light," "let me know when you light up so I can light mine up to" etc. One way & another we manage. The boys who do have lighters are using "white gasoline" as lighter fluid ain't around. They get flint through letters as they're small & universal - so they fit every lighter.

Well I don' know if you have to be a Nation – "Savage as you expressed it" – to live here but I'll never come back here for love or money. The Nation's helped out a lot Met. Several have received medals for bravery etc. They attend church & seem to content with life now that the "other half" is gone. They've come down out of the hills & trade with the soldiers. I sent my niece a grass skirt which I got for two packs of cigarettes. They like to be photographed. I took two rolls in one of them villages once. There's nothing beautiful about the women either. Don't worry about this guy Met, I'll get along without it before I have any affairs with them.

You ask how I am receiving the mail, well its like the weather when it rains it pours. When mail comes in, it comes in by the sack or bushel. You get it usually in lump sums.

Well Met its ten minutes to two & I go on the switch board at two. I'll continue this later. Okay Metalski?

Well I'm back again, boy those two hours flew. Well my daily routine is changed around now. I'm not on the guns, instead in the Ranger Section. Its altogether different.

Say Met did I read right in one of your letters about you guys having maids to clean up? If it's true, man that's rich. Yeah, we don't see a white woman even, let alone clean up for us. Ha ha.

I wrote to Charlie & Tiny not long ago as I got a letter from each of them. Old Charlie is on the ball. He's on a machine gun. (Racket job during peace time) well during war it aint worth two cents. Life isn't long behind a "typewriter." Gee I think he'd go for mechanics being he knows a lot about motors.

I'll close for now, "Mitchell 2000", hoping this letter finds you in the best of health.

Above all Pass that exam. Give my regards to Helen also

Your friend,

Ange

Envelope dated May 17, 1943

May 15, 1943

(Includes letter from Ruth Robertson)

Hello Met,

Just received your letter of April 24th & I was glad to hear from you Pal. Yes we had another Field Day the other day but that's everyday stuff here.

Yeah Met I guess your girlfriend is right. The minute you boast of something, it goes sour. I do wish you luck in getting a transfer nearer to home so you can get married. Hope the Fortune Teller is right in her predictions.

Oh my cold is gone now & it was the worst one I ever had. Where the hell did you get the idea there were WACs here? But you ain't lying when you say I'd like to have one in a fox hole with me. So you guys had to move into another hotel eh?

Yes I'm getting my share of mail these days. Man I really like to hear from people.

Oh yes, Miss Robertson told me to tell you, you weren't pulling the wool over the teacher's eyes. Margaret Frost has a baby boy 2 years old. My kid brother wrote to her also. If you want to drop her a line her address is Ruth Robertson 1 Essex Street Belleville N.J.

Say Met I saw a show the other night & the picture was "Pride of the Yankees" & it was very good. I've tried to see that picture for a long time. Well we'll be seeing shows again as the show is near by again.

Arnold Thiting is on this island too but I've been here a helluva a long time & I haven't bumped in to him yet. Miss Robertson told me he was here.

I am sitting beside the radio man & I showed him your letter. He took a two months course & can now send out 19 words per minute. He said you're going good & should hit 30 words by the end of your class.

Well Met I'm feeling find & hope to hear the same from you. Let me know how that transfer works out. Give my regards to your brothers & Helen.

Your friend

Ange

PS I just got a letter from Phil – he weighs 250 pounds. Can you imagine. He has two kids too.

Miss Robertson letter

Written April 23 & 24th

Dear Angelo,

Your letters arrived on consecutive days. I was most disappointed when I thought the censor was keeping your pictures as well as a paragraph, but the second letter made me think better of him. I know they will be much appreciated by others at school tomorrow.

Is food, lack of exercise, or much exercise and much food which has given you the extra pounds? Looks as if the govt would have to let out a few seams and buttons on your uniform.

No one has told me exactly where you are, but my knowledge of the geography in that part of the world has improved greatly in the past year or so, due to my natural curiosity – also my favorite crossword puzzle in the N.Y. Times makes me go over that area with a microscope, so I am guessing – maybe incorrectly.

Arnold Thiting is resting and fighting malaria on Guadalcanal – and true Marine hoping for Round II.

Salvatore Pedalino has had 3 months in a Navy uniform, but hasn't yet been fired with the enthusiasm of the other fellows. Gus Vaccaro also is blues is loving a gunner's training and itching to be at sea.

Tell Mitchell M. that we teachers could usually read the stuff our people wrote, even tho' we may pretend we can't. Maybe that is where I got my love for puzzles.

Carmen Petti was in – on furlough from Carolina in photography training for the air corps. Your kid brother wrote a very nice letter, too, with no particular news for you I guess. He told me he loved mail "no matter who it's from." I know he didn't mean it the way it sounded, but we all got a laugh just the same.

Margaret Frost is married and has a nice little boy – 2 or 3 yrs. Old. Marie Frost takes more care of him than his mother but I guess he knows to whom he belongs when he gets into things as all boys do.

Miss Nelson gets to see us during rationing days. The H.S. teachers are sent out to the grade schools so we get a chance to catch up on news of old friends.

Don't let the idea of the boys form England and Africa getting furlough bother you too much. The only ones I know of who are back came for medical treatment. The others are still needed over there to finish a job we've begun. Bernard Ingo was in the hospital in Africa for shrapnel wounds a time back. A sailor friend he made on his way over on the troop ship brought back the story on one of his layovers in N.Y.

Out usual vacation at Easter is omitted since we had time out in Feb. to conserve fuel. But I fooled them. I took the week to spend in bed to get rid of the cold I have had all winter. Right now I've had enough of staying "put" and am ready to go to school a new person tomorrow. I guess I shan't start my evening job until about Wed.

On Tuesday we have a shower for Phyl Calicchio who is to be married to her attorney next Sunday.

I think I've told you every thing I know.

Keep smiling. Your teeth shine as they always did!! You see I remember your Tony Schiagvo's Carmen Macaluso's and a few others.

Sincerely

Ruth Robertson

Envelope dated: June 6, 1943

June 3, 1943

Hello Met,

I received two letters of yours yesterday – May 7 & 16th, Pretty good if you ask me. Say Met did you ever the story of the "Gold & Silver Shield"? Well it seems that two knights approached a mounted shield from opposite sides. One knight said – my what a gold shield, the other said: It's a Silver Shield, well one word lead to another & they had a duel. One was killed. The victor looks up & sees that the shield was gold on one side & silver on the other. So they had been both right. I forget what the lesson of that story was.

That brings us to that debate of ours Met, we could both argue from now to doomsday & we'd both be right, so let's park it.

It was news to me about Val visiting the Woodbridges, etc. Small world ain't it. Yeah I remember the old man Pal. I remember Joyce more though. Remember the dance she put on down in camp near the pond. She sure wiggled around plenty. Not saying what we used to do to her. All in all I don't think anybody got into the "ball park", a lot of guys got on bases and stuck out though. Ha ha.

So you asked your ole man to move the pigeon coop if he heard a bomb coming, eh? Some joke I'll say. Met [CONTENT CUT OUT] big ass into the nearest hole & shit with thinking about personal belongings etc. My hide is what interests me most. I aint shittin you either.

I'm glad about Joe being able to get out too Met but I burn up knowing no defense plant will take him because he isn't a citizen. He has his half papers etc. but the best he could do was get his old job back. He's married & can't afford to be choosy. Yeah kid when your married you have to put your pride in your back pocket & just take it. Now when you're single & don't like your job you just leave, & rely on your Mother. Joe is no slouch when it comes to working met. I know. I only wish he could land a decent job somewhere.

Glad to hear your coming along okay in radio school. Passed 26 words per minute eh & eight weeks to go. Well I think you ought to fit thru the 30 mark before school is over.

For the past few months I've been losing weight right along but as long as I feel good & stay in one piece, I've got no kicks coming.

Met I put in for O.C.S. & in the near future I go before the Board. That is if things go along accordingly. I've attended trig classes for the past month & that helps a lot in the long run. I look upon this golden opportunity & I'm hoping for the best.

Well Met ol boy I'll so say so long until next time. Hope this letter finds you well. Give Helen my regards & don't forget.

So long Pal

Your friend

Ange

Envelope dated July 5, 1943

July 3, 1943

Hello Met,

I received two letters of yours dated June 14 & 119th. That's something. The mail is sure coming in pretty regular these days.

So somebody told Miss Robertson about you eh. Well it's a good thing its all good or you'd have plenty of explaining to do.

I got a letter from Tiny and there was four pictures in it. Yes I was surprised to see how he filled out too. I have that on him in the trunks too. He looks like he can lick the whole family now.

I never saw that Wave that was supposed to be here so I wouldn't know what she looks like. Your right in saying what you did though. Just as long as it was a white woman, she'd be an Angel.

You ain't kidding about the Field Days Pal. It's every day stuff now. Pat was wounded but he's okay now. He'd better be! He's my "best man".

Thanks for getting me the lighter Met. Boy I can sue use one. I'll let you know when I receive it.

By the time this reaches you your classes will be over. Let me know your new address as soon as possible.

Say Met your wrong in saying shoot anything that doesn't speak English. Hell haven't you heard that some of them were educated in the States & can talk better than you or I. There' other tell tale signs though. Some habits – just like the rats I used to trap.

You ask what is the first thing I'm going to do when I get back. Well I had tried to get married but Marie don't see things that way. She's waited this long she may as well wait till it's over.

But if you meant coming back after the war – yea it would be marriage. I hope I'm not stuck out here till it ends because the end ain't near! If this mess is over by 1944, the drinks are on me.

Its true we're getting into high gear met but there's a lot of places to be taken that will take time. You can disagree with me as that's only my opinion. We shall see ole timer.

I'm feeling the best ever Met – no kidding. I hope I stay that way too. I saw a few good pictures this week. Andy Hardy's Double Life & They All Kissed the Bride. You ought to hear the guys yell when she (the bride) said: "If I want a sneak I'll hire a Jap."

By the way Met (going back to your love affair for a minute) what makes you say enough time has been lost already. You're wrong soldier. There's plenty of time, you or her isn't 30 years old you know.

Adios Amigo

Butch

PS Here's a few jokes Met

[BOTTOM OF LETTER PAGE CUT]

In Memorandum

At the close of existence when we've climbed life's golden stair

And the chilly winds of Autumn toss our silver hair

When we feel our manhood ebbing & were up to Life's Last Ditch

When we find the faithful Peter, sleeping soundly at the switch

God All mighty ain't it awful? For it makes a fellow sick

When the painful fact confronts us, that we've got a lifeless Dick

That he never will bristle on wet & windy days

When some maiden shows her stocking, in that naughty – funny way.

Oh my poor loyal king pin, how my heart goes out to you

For I cannot remember all the Stunts you used to do.

How you charmed the maidens & the matrons, & the dashing widows too

How you had the whole bunch begging for just a little piece of you

Think you now that I'll forget you, just because you seem so dead

And because when I command you, you cannot lift your sloppy head

No indeed valiant comrade, naught shall rob you from your fame

Henceforth you shall be my pisser & I'll love you just the same.

August 2, 1943

Hello Met,

Received two letters of yours dated June 28 and July 19th. Sorry to hear you bought the cigarette lighter for me and couldn't send it. I can't help with the mail rules as they change faster than the weather. At the time I asked you for it all that was needed – it be censored. I don't know what it is now Met. But present this letter to the Postal Clerk. I need a cigarette lighter out here & I'm sure its okay.

Met I just went and asked my Lieutenant about it & he said just show this letter of request for the lighter to the clerk. I thought it'd be that way but I just wanted to make sure. Don't forget envelope and letter. That's that!

I'll say you never got to first base, I'll even go further than that – you never got into the ball park. Ha ha. Yes Yes times have changed. Good causes too. Wish you all the luck in the world Pal.

Met I'm sorry I mentioned my trying out for O.C.S. to my friends as they all wished me luck. Well as luck would have it I never went up before the Board. I'm pretty far from that Board & Saturday I heard I was supposed to appear Friday. So you can see where I stand. You can't give me that boot in the tail Met yet anyway. If anything comes of it I'll let you know.

Ah, so you're out in Sunny California! Sunny my eye, as George Raft said, we only have 2 foot of dew there. (Picture: Stage Door Canteen)

Boy you sound as though you really need that rugged training. Pal you take my advice and don't miss a minute of it. And I ain't lying!

Met if you do go over, I too wish we could run across each other. Got a letter from Joe (Chris) Giron & he's been out this way. Seen plenty too. Action of course. Here's his address Joseph J. Giron Jr. USS Brooklyn – c/o PM NY NY (correction last page) He'll keel overboard with surprise.

I see you're a rolling stone. Well Pal you won't gather any moss anyway. I hope I can make that cross country trip some day.

Boy that Miss Robertson is a "shrewd particle" with her jig saw puzzles. She mentioned hearing from you & that's was at the bottom of it. Yes. Yes.

Met as you can see I'm still at large. Hope that's one number I don't draw. No how! I was sick in bed for a week but I'm okay now. God Bless them Pills.

I don't see any shows anymore as there ain't any in our area. Boy I miss them plenty. I did make the best of it while it lasted though – now I'll just have to make up my mind I must get along without it. That ain't hard. Eh, Met?

Met one of these days you'll get a little token from me. I won't tell you as I want it to be a surprise – to the both of you. You'd never guess in a million tries. So don't rack your brain.

In case you're overseas would you want me to still send it to you, Helen or your home? I'll try to get it off within two weeks. But this is just in case I can't. So Met answer as soon as possible.

I don't think of that "day" Met as it's a long way off. Just wait & see. Well there's nothing like wishing.

I'm feeling fine & hope this letter finds you well & in the best of health.

Your friend Ange

P.S. (Robertson received a letter in 6 days from me.)

PS # 2, I wonder if I should call you Jersey Met or California. Why? Well you wish you were back in Jersey but your in California. I'll toss a coin. You win California!

Adios Amigo

If you had wished for California you would have probably ended up in Jersey. Could be?

Met on Chris' address that I gave use U.S.S. Brooklyn. Chris wrote & its U.S.S. Jersey c/o Fleet Post Office. I play it save & put both. (New York)

Probably 080843 (page seems missing)

PS I just received your letter of March 23 which wasn't bad time at all. I bet you ain't lying when you say your writing is difficult to read. V-Mail is hard to read but Met two sheets of V-Mail typewritten can't be beat. That way you have a long letter & its easy to read.

Well Met somewhere I saw this saying, "Why Worry, when you can pray," I seen that a long time ago. Something I live up to. Your right in saying if you know what war was like you wouldn't make that wish about wanting to join me here. I wouldn't wish this place on a dog or even my worst enemy.

So when you do go, just go over and take your time at bat. Go down slugging if you do go down.

Yesterday I watched a good "field Day" Boy it was the (mets?). I started to write this a few days ago but forgot to mail it. Today's the eighth. Once before you mentioned a "field day" we had. Well I saw this one but couldn't see the other.

Met remember how Tslinskis's (old man Bra Has) tumblers used to tumble. Likewise!

Last night I thought I'd cough my brains out boy I got it bad. I take pills but they don't seem to do any good.

I got a letter from Andy Bello & he's in the guard house. He went home for 41 days when his kid brother was in that "jam". Can't say I blame him. He was in the Army 18 months & that was an Emergency but they turned him down. Well he furloughed himself home. I'd do that myself if I was in his shoes. He'll be out sometime this month. He got 3 months. Met he blames it all on his brother Nick.

Well Met it is going to be a long time before I meet you and your girlfriend. That's on the level. Well soldier again. I'll close hoping you the best of everything.

Ange

Hello California,

I received you letter of August 26th and it was good hearing from you again. I really hit the jackpot this week – in mail I mean. I also got your package. Thanks a lot Met. You don' have to send me Flint & fluid as the boys here have plenty of flint & we use a few drops of white gas & it's just as good & more abundant.

You're right about Val not liking his outfit. If he'd a kept it to himself he'd still be a Corporal. I should talk, eh Pollack!

Met that training your getting you'll never regret. I can't tell you what kind of terrain you be fighting in but you've seen pictures & should have a fair idea. I can't ask you about your guns Met but I see your getting variety. That's the best way of learning

Well Fella I sure wish you luck in getting your furlough. I might add that if I were in your shoes & anxious to get married Pal I wouldn't wait for a furlough, I'd make my own. But stick it out till you're settled. That isn't far off. I may sound nuts to you fella, but I'm not. I'm giving you a piece of advice. Whether its good or bad depends on how you look at it.

Maybe your mother will get her wish at that. This world's full of surprises. Or should I say disappointments?

Met, those drinks you mentioned will have to wait a year, maybe more. There's no outlook in my getting home for quite sometime. It's been a long time Mitchell since I last saw my folks and girlfriend. But I'm still hanging on. A break may come through all of those dark clouds yet.

Going back to that bit of advice a minute. Out here we say "If I knew then, what I know now." I for one can kick myself in the ass for not getting married first. Things happened to fast & before I woke up I was somewhere in the Pacific. Well, now I'll just have to grin and bear it.

I seen a white woman last week for the first time in one year. She was a Nurse and worked on the Air Transports. It was short lived but nice to know those creatures are still in existence.

Met I got a boot in the tail coming as I went up for O.C.S. but didn't pass. I'm thinking of trying again in a few months. Your one up on me Pal & I'll pay off. Ha Ha.

I seen some good pictures lately such as Random Harvest, Yankee Doodle Dandy – Mrs Miniver & also a few others.

Well I won't see any for a few weeks as the projector went to another Battery for a week or so. We alternate.

I lost my shirt this month in Crap. The dice changed faster than the wind. I'm due Met as I've lost steady the past four months. (Four pays, I should say.) That's eight months to you.

Well Pollack I guess I'll sign off till next time. Give my regards to the boys & let me have Donkeys address as soon as possible.

I received your package & now I'm waiting to hear you received mine. Then everything will be all right!

So long Pollack

Regards to Helen

Ange.

May 21, 1945

Hello Helen,

Just a note to let you know I received your letter the other day. I was glad to hear from you & I was wondering why no answer. But your forgiven as I'm beginning to see the light (as the song goes.)

I'm busy driving a truck around Camp & last week I went on a Convoy that took me away from camp for two days. Boy the bed sure fits good after that trip.

I'm busy driving a truck around Camp & last week I went on a Convoy that took me away from camp for two days. Boy the bed sure fits good after that trip.

I've done quite a bit of skating at the rink they have here. I go about 3 or 4 nights a week. Did you ever roller skate? Haven't taken in the sights around town yet but eventually I'll get around to it.

No doubt you've heard of the Point System, etc. Well I just barely cleared the fence with 88 points. I don't know when I'll get out but just knowing I'm slated makes me drool. How I'd love to get back to my wife and be a civilian again. Well I can dream can't I? I was thinking of having her out here with me but I priced the rooms & its highway robbery $40 for 1 room - $60 for two if you can find an opening. Well that will never do for me.

I'll wait another month and put in for a furlough. The reason I'm waiting is to see how large the next quota will be as I wish my next trip Ease is permanent. Period! So why throw $100 into the winds.

I'm glad you like the set up there – it makes things easier for you. Now if Met was a sailor – his ship may put into port every so often but since he's not – well – Your guess is as good as mine. Liking where you're staying helps a great deal too.

Well how long it will last now who can say? I hope its short & sweet So we all can go home & back to our normal ways of living.

Glad to hear Met made you a bracelet Helen out there you can't buy gifts etc. So you try a hand at making something in your spare time. If & when Met does send you more gifts you'll find what I said is true.

Between you and I Helen – I like California better than Jersey. This place is a paradise. Down here the weather is fine – plenty of jobs. Well its having your relatives back East etc. that makes you want to go back. My parents are old and nearly helpless as far as speech & legal matters are concerned & somebody's got to take care of them. But California is nice.

Helen I'll make that trip after pay day as I'll feel safe to travel. I have another wife to see in Alameda also. She's staying there & waiting for her sailor husband to return. She's my wife's best girlfriend. I'll write & let you know & I'll keep your telephone number handy too.

Are there nights you go out? I don't want to miss you when I come up. It will probably be over a week end most likely. Sat. night or Sunday. I'll let you know ahead of time for sure.

I just hope I can live up to the build up Met gave me. Ha ha. In case Bruno didn't tell you when we were up to their place we saw your room – wedding pictures etc. You were adorable Helen & Met was handsome. I know you have a fine man for a hubby & vice versa. Someday you'll drop in on us & we'll show you our pictures etc. too. Okay.

Say if you want to send Met something the 1st thing I'd say he'd like is pictures of you. If you can – get some film & send it to him as somebody may have camera in his outfit. Write first & ask if he'd like some film & to state the size. Pictures will live on & on. Don't you forget that.

Well Helen I'll close for now- hoping to see you in the near future.

Your friend

Ange

June 19, 1945

Hello Fatstuff,

Just a few lines to let you know I was safe and sound in Bakersfield 7:15 p.m. & I could have made it sooner if I wanted to I went straight to the U.S.O. took a shower & shave & went skating. The rink opened at 8 p.m. It was hotter coming back than going up. Yes indeedy!!!

Monday morning I picked up my two day pass (which wasn't necessary) & went to the potato shed. While waiting for things to get started I changed my mind & worked for a carpenter for $1 an hour. I worked yesterday and today.

I received three letters from my wife today & she asked if I paid you a visit. She'll learn in due time. I'm enclosing her address in case you like to write to her. I'm going to phone her tomorrow & I may take my furlough July 3rd.. Here's hoping.

I'll probably see Bruno & your in laws while I'm home & I'll tell them what a darling angel you are. (Pat yourself on the back.)

I'll tell them you're getting along fine & for them not to worry any. I'll tell my wife what happened while I was there as I didn't write much about it in my letter as I told her I'd tell here when I get home. I did mention a few things.

I'll write to Met in a day or so as I sent my last letter "free" & I never got an answer to it. I'll splurge and send it air mail. Ha ha. Oh wait til I tell him a few things. Am I going to pour it on thick. Your ears are going to burn plenty. Ha ha. You can take it out on me next time I come up. I'm going to wear a suit of armor, it will be your elbows that will hurt not my ribs. You'll be sorry now!

Say Helen I think I did forget to tell you your sweet, well you are & I think I know why Met fell like a ton of bricks. You're everything a guy could possibly ask for. I'm not kidding this time or I'd say take a bow.

Well tomorrow nite I'll indulge in skating 7 have some clean fun. Remember at the table I said I hadn't cheated on my wife – well every word of that is the gospel Helen. I haven't met a girl who could make me forget my marriage vows. I love my wife – that's why I married her. Guess you understand. A marriage without faith in each other will never last.

Well Helen I'm going to close now asking you to give everybody up there my regards & love. Tell them I said thanks for the swell time. I enjoyed myself. I hope I lived up to the build up Met gave me.

I'll close now hoping to hear from you in the near future.

Always

Your friend

Ange

Sept. 24, 1945

Hello Helen,

Just a line to let you know I was discharged sat. I am now one happy civilian.

I'm running around like a chicken who's just had his head chopped off. Going to take things easy for a week or so then land a job.

Honest Helen I'm sorry I've delayed paying that debt but my mind is here & there – mostly there. At last I sat myself down & dood it. Enclosed you'll find five dollars.

I'll stop in and see Bruno as I'm going to live in my mother's house – ahem as soon as we can get those people out.

What's the latest from Met? Hope he's well. Better yet hope he comes home son. Before Xmas I hope!! Don't be scared to drop me a line once in awhile Fatstuff or when Met gets home I'll have to start all over & greet you as a stranger.

How's things up there in Dexter? How's your mother? Better I hope.

Well Helen I'm running out of gab so I'll close trusting this letter finds you in the best of health. Give my regards to Met – by all means. Or else!!!

So long Fatstuff

Your friend

Ange

Korean War

Robert G. Bliss

(Feb. 26, 1953) – Robert G. Bliss died Feb. 4, during Army maneuvers in Germany. He is the son of Mr. and Mrs. Albert M. Bliss, of Belleville.

Bliss, 22, died of asphyxiation in his sleep in an army mess truck to which he was attached as a cook with Battery C, 517th Armored Field Artillery battalion.

The accident occurred near Zallenlmuse during field maneuvers. It was an unusually cold night in the German mountains. Bliss and several other soldiers rolled themselves into their blankets on the floor of the mess truck near lit cooking stoves.

Bliss, who formerly lived on Centre Street, Nutley, was a strong six-footer. He had attended Central High School in Newark and worked as a salesman after graduation. He married a Hillside girl shortly before entering the Army in October 1951. His tour of service about to end, his family had their home redecorated and were making elaborate plans for his welcome. Bliss is survived by his wife, Arline; his parents, and a brother, Walter.

Services were scheduled for Brown funeral home and the Mt. Pleasant Baptist Church, Newark, where the youth's father is a deacon.

Sources: The Belleville Times, The Nutley Sun

Rene J. Flory Jr.

(June 22, 1951) – "Mother, I know you have been plenty worried since I've been over here, but believe me, now the worst is over," wrote Rene Joseph Flory to his parents, Mr. and Mrs. Rene J. Flory of Center Street, in a letter they received last week from Korea.

Yesterday afternoon, the Florys received a telegram from the War Department which said, in part, "Deeply regret to inform you that your son, Corporal Rene Joseph Flory Jr., USMC was killed in action June 9 in the Korean Area in performance of his duty and service of his country."

The letter received before the telegram was dated Korea, June 6 and was from a rest camp area. In the letter he described conditions in the camp and his chief concern was whether his pants would dry.

The youthful soldier was born in Newark but had resided in Belleville for 11 years. He attended Belleville Schools and before graduation from Belleville High

School three years ago was president of the Student Council and a member of the National Honor Society.

He also served as an altar boy at the Holy Family Church, Nutley, for ten years before he was called into service.

Flory likely received a field or posthumous promotion.

Sgt. Flory was a member of Company C, First Battalion, Seventh Regiment, First Marine Division. He served with other youths from this area who were members of the Marine Reserves training at Dover.

He was sworn into Federal service on Sept. 7, last year, came home on furlough and reached Korea in April.

At one period, when the United States forces were having a rough time in Korea, he saw 56 days of continuous action in the front lines.

Sgt. Flory was awarded the Purple Heart, the Combat Service Ribbon, the Korean Service Medal, the United Nations Service Medal, the National Defense Service Medal and the Korean War Service Medal.

He was born on Feb. 27, 1930

A monument honoring Flory was rededicated during a Veterans Day ceremony at School 7 on Nov. 11, 1999.

Erected in 1952, the plaque and stone on the Joralemon Street side of the school had become over grown with shrubbery. The growth was cut down and the area was cleaned up recently on the recommendation of Schools Superintendent Joseph Ciccone.

The Belleville-Nutley Chapter 22 Disabled American Veterans and the board of education took part in the rededication ceremony, which was open to the public.

Source: The Belleville Times, The Newark Star-Ledger.

John R. Gorman

(April 25, 1952) – Corporal John R. Gorman, 24, was declared killed in action in Korea a year ago, the Defense Department said.

His parents Mr. and Mrs. Francis H. Gorman, who moved to Nutley only a month ago from Belleville, were informed of the casualty by a telegram from Washington. He had been listed as missing in action since May 18, 1951.

Drafted in September 1950, Gorman arrived at the front in Korea late last summer. He was a member of the 38th Infantry Regiment, Second Infantry Division.

Cpl. Gorman was awarded the Purple Heart, the Combat Infantryman's Badge, the Korean Service Medal, the United Nations Service Medal, the National Defense Service Medal and the Korean War Service Medal.

Born in Scranton, Pa., Gorman was graduated from Good Counsel High School in Newark and Seton Hall University.

Source: The Nutley Sun

Brendan Hyland

(Jan. 4, 1951) – Private Brendan Hyland of Chestnut Street was killed in action in Korea last July.

Private Hyland was killed in action while fighting the enemy along the Kum River, South Korea on July 20, 1950. The 19-year-old soldier had previously been listed as missing in action. A veteran of two years' service, Pvt. Hyland was attached to the 11th Field Artillery Battalion, 24th Infantry Division.

Hyland was awarded the Purple Heart posthumously.

Born in Newark, Hyland was educated in St. Patrick's and St. Michael's schools. His family has resided here since May of last year. A brother, Donald, served in Germany with the Army.

Source: The Belleville Times

Henry Svehla

Essex, New Jersey, Born 1932, Private First Class, U.S. Army, Service Number 21748254

Killed in Action, Died June 12, 1952 in Korea.

Private First Class Svehla was a member of Company F, 2nd Battalion, 32nd Infantry Regiment, 7th Infantry Division. He was Killed in Action while fighting the enemy in North Korea on June 12, 1952. His remains were not recovered. His name is inscribed on the Courts of the Missing at the Honolulu Memorial. For his leadership and valor, Private First Class Svehla was awarded the Distinguished Service Cross, the Purple Heart, the Combat Infantryman's Badge, the Korean Service Medal, the United Nations Service Medal, the National Defense Service Medal, the Korean Presidential Unit Citation and the Republic of Korea War Service Medal.

Source: American Battle Monuments Commission

Belleville High School memorial to Medal of Honor awardee PFC Henry Svehla.

Distinguished Service Cross

Awarded posthumously for actions during the Korean War

The President of the United States of America, under the provisions of the Act of Congress approved July 9, 1918, takes pride in presenting the Distinguished Service Cross (Posthumously) to Private First Class Henry Svehla (ASN: RA-21748254), United States Army, for extraordinary heroism in connection with military operations against an armed enemy of the United Nations while serving with Company F, 2d Battalion, 32d Infantry Regiment, 7th Infantry Division. Private First Class Svehla distinguished himself by extraordinary heroism in action against enemy aggressor forces at Pyongony, Korea, on 12 June 1952. Committed to determine enemy strength and capabilities on key terrain, Private Svehla's platoon forged up the rocky slope. Coming under heavy automatic-weapons and small-arms fire, the troops began to falter. Realizing the success of the mission was imperiled, Private Svehla charge forward, firing his weapon and throwing grenades. The men, rallying to the challenge, joined in the assault against a numerically superior foe and inflicted numerous casualties. Although wounded by a mortar burst, Private Svehla refused medical treatment and continued to lead the attack. During the ensuing conflict, an enemy grenade fell in the midst of the group. While attempting to dispose of the grenade to protect his comrades from injury which might result from the explosion of the grenade, Private Svehla lost his life.

General Orders: Department of the Army: General Orders No. 18 (February 18, 1953), Action Date: 12-Jun-52

Medal Of Honor

Henry Svehla (circa 1932 – June 12, 1952) was a United States Army soldier who on May 2nd 2011 was posthumously awarded the United States military's highest decoration, the Medal of Honor, for his actions in the Korean War. Previously he had been awarded the Distinguished Service Cross.

By June 12, 1952, Svehla was a private first class serving in Korea as a rifleman with Company F, 32nd Infantry Regiment, 7th Infantry Division. On that day, his platoon came under heavy fire and he charged forward to attack the enemy. When a grenade landed amidst his group, he smothered the blast with his body in order to protect those around him. He was killed in the explosion.[1] His remains have never been recovered.

For these actions, Svehla was awarded the Medal of Honor by President Barack Obama on May 2 during a White House ceremony. His sisters Dorothy Mathews and Sylvia Svehla accepted the medal on his behalf. Also receiving a Medal of Honor at the ceremony was the family of Private First Class Anthony T. Kaho'ohanohano, a fellow 7th Infantry Division soldier killed in the Korean War.

Source: http://en.wikipedia.org/wiki/Henry_Svehla

President Obama to Award Medals of Honor

On May 2, President Barack Obama will award Private First Class Anthony T. Kaho'ohanohano, U.S. Army, and Private First Class Henry Svehla, U.S. Army, the Medal of Honor for conspicuous gallantry.

Private First Class Kaho'ohanohano will receive the Medal of Honor posthumously for his heroic actions in combat on September 1, 1951, while in charge of a machine-gun squad with Company H, 17th Infantry Regiment, 7th Infantry Division in the Republic of Korea.

When faced by an enemy with overwhelming numbers, Private First Class Kaho'ohanohano ordered his squad to take up more defensible positions and provide covering fire for the withdrawing friendly force. He then gathered a supply of grenades and ammunition and returned to his original position to face the enemy alone - delivering deadly accurate fire into the ranks of the onrushing enemy. When his ammunition was depleted, he engaged the enemy in hand-to-hand combat until he was killed. His heroic stand so inspired his comrades that they launched a counterattack that completely repulsed the enemy.

Private First Class Kaho'ohanohano's sister, Elaine Kaho'ohanohano, and brother, Eugene Kaho'ohanohano, will join the President at the White House to commemorate their brother's example of selfless service and sacrifice.

Private First Class Henry Svehla will receive the Medal of Honor posthumously for his heroic actions in combat on June 12, 1952, while serving as a rifleman with Company F, 32d Infantry Regiment, 7th Infantry Division in the Republic of Korea.

Coming under heavy fire and with his platoon's attack beginning to falter, Private First Class Svehla leapt to his feet and charged the enemy positions, firing his weapon and throwing grenades as he advanced. Disregarding his own safety, he destroyed enemy positions and inflicted heavy casualties. When an enemy grenade landed among a group of his comrades, without hesitation and undoubtedly aware of the extreme danger, he threw himself on the grenade. During this action, Private First Class Svehla was mortally wounded.

Private First Class Henry Svehla's sisters, Dorothy Mathews and Sylvia Svehla will join the President at the White House to commemorate their brother's example of selfless service and sacrifice.

Source: The White House, Office of the Press Secretary, April 13, 2011

Vietnam War

Lt. Col. Alfred Barnes

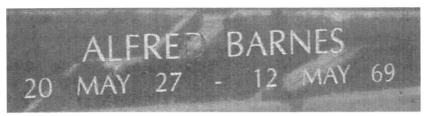

(May 22, 1969) – Lt. Col. Alfred Barnes of Ralph Street, Belleville, a 20-year career Army office, was killed during an enemy rocket and mortar attack in Quang Ngai, South Vietnam, on May 12.

Mrs. Sadie R. Barnes, his wife, was notified by telegram of the overseas tragedy.

Lt. Col. Barnes had a personal dream fulfilled when he assumed command of a battalion two months ago.

On March 15, Lt. Col. Barnes had taken command of the Fifth Battalion, 46th Infantry, a position of which he was very proud, his wife said.

"This is something that he had trained for all the years that he had been in the service," she said. "He had always been a commander, and he felt that battalion commander was the complement to the rank of lieutenant colonel."

Mrs. Barnes added that her husband was very dedicated to the Army and felt very strongly that it was necessary to be in Vietnam.

"I know that my husband was happy in his job and that he died happy in that sense," she said. "He believed that what he was doing was right."

Barnes began his service career at Ft. Benning, Ga., in 1949, after receiving his commission as a second lieutenant upon graduating in 1948 from Howard University in Washington, where he had been a member of the Army ROTC.

In June 1950, he accompanied the first contingent of American troops into Korea and in the ensuing year participated in five major campaigns as platoon leader and rifle company commander. During the conflict he received seven citations which included the Silver Star with oak leaf cluster, the Bronze Star with two oak leaf clusters, the Purple Heart and the Korean Presidential Citation. A decoration of bronze or silver oak leaves and acorns is given to holders of various U.S. military medals in recognition of acts entitling them to another award of the same medal.

Upon returning to the United States in June 1951, Lt. Col. Barnes spent two years with the 82nd Airborne Division at Ft. Bragg, N.C., and two years in the First Army area, which includes New York and the New England states.

After completion of the infantry officers' advanced course in 1955, Lt. Col. Barnes was attached to the 10th Mountain Division at Ft. Riley, Kan., where he was a rifle company commander.

The unit was sent to Europe for a three-year tour of duty that was cut short for Lt. Col. Barnes when he was injured in an auto accident in 1956.

He was brought back to the United States and spent the next nine months in an Army hospital in Valley Forge, Pa.

The 42-year-old soldier was station commander in the Army Personnel Center at Ft. Dix for three years before returning to Europe for a four-year tour of duty during which he was promoted to major in 1962.

In 1964, he became an assistant professor of military science at Virginia State College, Petersburg, Va., and headed that department at Norfolk State College, Norfolk, Va., in 1965.

Alfred Barnes was born May 20, 1927. His hometown is listed as Montclair, N.J. His tour of duty began on July 15, 1968.

The Wall: Panel 25W – Line 60

Sources: The Belleville Times, The Wall-USA.com

William Anderson Branch

Captain William Anderson Branch, 28, was killed in action on June 6, 1970, when the helicopter in which he was a passenger crashed on landing due to hostile enemy action in Binh Duong, South Vietnam.

Capt. Branch served with the 25th Infantry Division. His tour of duty began July 24, 1969.

Born on Friday, July 11, 1941, Capt. Branch was married.

A Note from The Virtual Wall

Two men from Headquarters Company, 2/14 Infantry, were killed when OH-6A tail number 68-17366 was shot down 10 kilometers southeast of the Dau Tieng base camp - Captain William A. Branch and Captain William L. Byrd of Rossville, Georgia.

Captain Branch was on his second tour of duty in Vietnam; his first was in 1966-67 when he served as a MACV Advisor with the 2nd Bn, 46th ARVN Infantry in Long An Province.

North Georgia College is "The Military College of Georgia," a Senior Military College.

Neither as large nor as well-known as some of the Senior Military Colleges (The Citadel, VMI, Virginia Tech, Texas A&M, and Norwich) The Military College of Georgia has provided commissioned officers to the Armed Forces since the 1870s.

The twenty-seven members of North Georgia's Corps of Cadets who died in Vietnam are remembered by a memorial stone on the campus. Captain Branch is the third name engraved on the memorial. Similar stones remember the men who died in the World Wars, Korea, and more recently in the Middle East.

- *Courtesy Virtual Wall*

The Wall: Panel 09W - Row 018

Sources: Georgia Military College; Photo courtesy The Wall-USA.com; http://www.virtualwall.org/db/BranchWA01a.htm; Jennifer Branch Denard.

Frank A. Cancelliere

Corporal Frank Anthony Cancelliere of Sanford Avenue, was killed March 15, 1969, near Quang Tri Province in Vietnam. According to the official report, he died as a result of fragmentation wounds to the head and body from a friendly grenade that was accidentally detonated in the chow line at the mess hall.

Born on June 27, 1948, he enlisted in the Marines and began active duty on Sept. 13, 1967.

He served with the Company B, First Battalion, Third Marine Division.

Cpl. Cancelliere, 20, son of Mrs. Fannie Albano of N. 7th Street, Newark, and Frank Cancelliere of Florence Avenue, Belleville, was ordered to Vietnam for a 13-month tour on March 17, 1968.

A lifelong resident of Belleville, Cancelliere was a graduate of Belleville High School and worked for the Belleville Tool Corp., before joining the Marines.

He leaves also two brothers, Joseph of Belleville, and Robert of Newark. He is buried in the Belleville Avenue Cemetery, Bloomfield.

The Wall: Panel 29W - Row 044

Sources: The Belleville Times, The Wall-USA.com; Remembrance - George Sbarra

Roger Brian Crowell

ROGER B CROWELL
16 AUG 47 - 31 JAN 68

(Feb. 15, 1968) – A military guard snapped to a salute as pallbearers removed the body of 20-year-old Roger Bryan Crowell from Holy Family Church in the bitter cold last Sunday morning following funeral services there.

Young Crowell is another Belleville victim of the Vietnam conflict.

The telegram of regret from the Army states that he died of gunshot wounds suffered during an engagement with the enemy Vietcong forces in Binh Duong, South Vietnam, on Jan. 31. The body was flown home to Belleville.

Crowell served in the 25th Infantry Division.

He was a product of the Belleville school system and his parents have been long-time residents of Tiona Avenue. He was an outstanding Little Leaguer and winner of many trophies for athletics.

He attended School 5 on Greylock Parkway, and went on to Belleville High School where he was especially active in football, baseball and basketball. He graduated from BHS in 1965.

Crowell was engaged for several years to Gail Corino, his high school sweetheart. A draft notice precipitated the marriage but because their marriage was kept secret, the ceremony was held at three different times in as many different churches – in June, September, and December 1966.

The young couple had only four days plus Roger's leave time, to be together in all their married life. Their son, Roger Jr. is now 10-months old; he was born in Clara Maass Memorial Hospital. Roger Sr. was able to obtain leave and arrive to be with his wife and new baby the day after the birth.

In his letters home from Vietnam, Crowell shows that he still had the same hopes and interests in his family's activities that he had before he became a soldier.

Letters From Vietnam

"Hello Brother, How's things going back home? Good, I hope. I hear you put the engine in Vinnie's car (a racing motor). How does it go? Mom said you were over to get my address about a week ago so maybe I'll be hearing from you soon. We just got back from a big operation last night and boy did it feel good to sleep on a cot and have a shower. I guess Mom told you that they finally made me a Specialist 4th Class. It's about time, especially after 11 months of Pfc. What have you been doing lately? Are you still working in the schools? Well, there isn't much more to write about ..."

"Hello Mom and Dad. I guess it's been quite a while since the last letter I wrote you. Everything is okay here. I came back to Cu Chi just in time to see Bob Hope. They had a pretty good show and it really gave the guys a good time so it kinda made up for not bein' in on Christmas..."

Father Robert Cassini officiated at the services Sunday at Holy Family. Burial was at Holy Cross Cemetery, North Arlington.

He is survived by one brother, Winfield, of Newark, who recently returned from active duty in Vietnam; and by a sister Mrs. Della Dranow of Verona. Services were conducted from Landolfi Funeral Home, Union Avenue, where the body was on view.

The Wall: Panel 36E - Row 004

Sources: The Belleville Times, The Wall-USA.com

Helder Arthur C. Da Silva

> HELDER A C DA SILVA
> 28 JAN 42 - 07 FEB 66

Army Spec. 4 Helder Arthur C. Da Silva, 24, was killed in action on Feb. 7, 1966 in South Vietnam. Da Silva began his tour of duty on Sept. 12, 1965. His service number is 036285328. Da Silva was married.

The Wall: Panel 05E - Row 016

Sources: The Vietnam War Memorial Wall, The Wall-USA.com

Raymond DeLuca

> RAYMOND P DE LUCA
> 12 FEB 48 - 27 JUN 68

(July 11, 1968) – Army Spec. 4 Raymond P. DeLuca, 20, of Meacham Street, died as a result of wounds in a firefight in Long An, South Vietnam on June 27. His tour of duty began on Dec 11.

A lifelong resident of Belleville, De Luca, who was born Feb. 12, 1948, attended Essex Catholic High School, Newark, where he graduated as an honor student in 1966.

He was a member of the National Honor Society, a National Merit Scholarship finalist, and served as editor-in-chief of the school's yearbook Talon. He also was a member of Boy Scout Troup 152, Nutley.

De Luca had begun college at William and Mary in Williamsburg, Va., but decided to enlist and serve with his brother Gerard who was aboard the USS Barney off the coast of Vietnam.

After training as an engineer at Ft. Leonard Wood, Mo., and as a medic at Ft. Sam Houston in Texas, he was attached to Company C, Ninth Medical Battalion, Ninth Infantry.

He is survived by his parents, Charles and Sophia Musko De Luca; and his brother, Gerard.

A High Mass was offered at Holy Family Church, Nutley, with burial at Glendale Cemetery, Bloomfield.

In lieu of flowers, the family would appreciate contributions for a special scholarship fund in honor of their son.

The Wall: Panel 54W – Line 5

Sources: The Belleville Times, The Wall-USA.com

Jerry Richard Donatiello

(Nov. 30, 1967) – Marine Lance Corporal Richard Donatiello, 22, of Frederick Street, was killed in action near Quang Namn, Vietnam on Nov. 20.

Cpl. Donatiello died after sustaining a gunshot wound.

He had been in Vietnam since Oct. 5. His tour of duty began Oct. 7. He enlisted in the Marines on March 3, 1965. He served with Company F, Second Battalion, Seventh Marine, First Division.

Born in Newark on June 27, 1945, Richie, as he was known at home, attended South Eighth Street School and graduated from Bloomfield Technical School class of 1963 before moving his family to Belleville two years ago.

He was attending Fairleigh Dickenson University, Rutherford at nights for two years when he was drafted into the Marine Corps in 1965, and sent to Vietnam in 1967.

While attending college, Richie had been very active with a CYO organization in Clifton, the town from which his girlfriend for three years, Roberta 'Cookie' DeMolli, comes.

At that same time he held two jobs to meet school expenses, a full-time job with Wilson Imperial, Newark and a part-time job at a local Acme Food Market.

Cpl. Donatiello is survived by his mother, Rose, and four brothers: Patrick, Anthony, Angelo Jr. and Robert.

Funeral services were held at Murray's Funeral Home, Belleville Avenue, Bloomfield. A High Mass was held at St. Anthony's Church, and interment was at Holy Cross Cemetery, North Arlington.

The Wall: Panel 30E - Row 040

Sources: The Belleville Times, The Wall-USA.com; Remembrance - George Sbarra

John Michael Hoar

JOHN M HOAR
17 SEP 45 — 13 FEB 66

(Feb. 24, 1966) – Pfc. John M. Hoar, 20, of Cleveland Street, was killed in action February 13, in Bongson, Vietnam.

Pfc. Hoar left for Vietnam on Christmas Day 1965. He became the second Belleville serviceman killed in Vietnam.

His gray, flag-draped coffin arrived at 9:30 p.m. Sunday aboard a sleek military transport plane which landed at Newark Airport accompanied by Sp. 5 Bob White, a military escort provided by the Army for its fallen warriors.

Hoar died of a head wound "incurred by small arms fire while on a combat operation" at Bongson, 265 miles northeast of Saigon on the South China Sea.

"When we came up here," he wrote before the fight, "we had 15 guys in the squad. Now we have nine. One was taken sick, another broke his leg, and three others were wounded."

He is survived by his parents, Mr. and Mrs. Robert J. Hoar, a brother Robert Jr., and a sister, Mrs. Mary Beth Weber of Bloomfield.

Pfc. Hoar was born on Sept. 17, 1945, in Kearny. He attended Queen of Peace School, St. Peter's and Belleville High School before leaving at the age of 16 while in his junior year.

He took a job with Eastern Tool and Manufacturing Co., here, and had been scheduled for the draft sometime in October.

"But that wasn't good enough for him," said his mother, Mae, "he wanted to serve right away." And with the youthful optimism of all boys, her son managed to have his induction date advanced to Aug. 6.

After basic training camp at Fort Dix, Pfc. Hoar and the rest of Company B, who were part of the First Calvary Division (Airborne) left for California.

Then, on Christmas Day, the company was marched aboard a military transport and sent to Vietnam. There he took part in the fierce fighting near An Khe Now.

"We went through Hell," he wrote his mother. "Yesterday," he wrote, "we sat down upon a mountain and looked out at the Pacific and thought of home – even more than usual."

He was killed in action the day after writing his last letter.

He had been overseas less than two months.

A High Mass was held in St. Peter's Church.

Six Belleville servicemen served as casket-bearers for Pfc. Hoar. "We had to turn others down," said Mrs. Mae Hoar, who added that many other friends had offered to serve. All six servicemen were given special leaves. A six-man honor guard from Fort Dix shattered the air over his grave with the crack of rifle fire, followed by the sound of Taps which carried far across the crisp February air.

The Wall: Panel 05E - Row 029

Sources: *The Belleville Times, The Wall-USA.com*

Dean Knox
CO, B/2/12 Cav, John's Unit
Mesa, AZ 85206 USA

I was the company commander of B Co, 2/12 Cav, 1st Cav Div on the day John M. Hoar died and I remember that day and him so very well even though it has now been 36 years since his death.

Our company was given the mission to conduct a helicopter assault at last light on 12 February and we did just that.

Although not officially recognized as such, it was the first night assault conducted by this new Division of the Army and the assault was conducted by the soldiers of the unit perfectly. We put down in the middle of Vietnamese Cemetery and were immediately taken under intense fire by an estimated battalion of the enemy.

The battle was fierce but we did not budge. Sometime during the night John was wounded but it was impossible to get him med-evacted because of hostile fire.

He died of his wounds early in the morning of 13 February as did a number of his friends and comrades.

I can say that after all these years, my emotions are still uncontrolled when I recall the fine young men who gave their lives doing their duty.

Like those killed on 9/11, all were heroes in their own right and live in my heart.

Rest in Peace John. We will meet again.

Sunday, February 24, 2002
Dean Knox
dandeknox@cox.net
Unit Commander

Carl L. Mickens

**CARL L MICKENS
09 APR 44 - 04 JUL 70**

(July 16-21, 1970) – Private Carl Lawrence Mickens, 26, son of Mr. and Mrs. Carl D. Mickens of Wilber Street, was killed in action on July 4 in Thua Thien, South Vietnam.

Pfc. Mickens, lost his life in a booby trap explosion while he was on a military mission, according to a telegram received by his parents.

His tour of duty started April 22.

A lifelong Belleville resident, Mickens had planned to be a vocational high school teacher. Before entering the service, Mickens had completed three years toward a teaching degree at Montclair State College.

Earlier he attended night school at Fairleigh Dickinson University. Mickens had also completed four years of apprenticeship as a tool and die maker at Western Electric Co., Kearny.

"He planned to finish college after his discharge from the service next year," his father said. "He hoped to put his experience as a tool and die maker, and his teaching degree, to use as a vocational high school teacher."

He was drafted into the army in July 1969. After completing basic training at Ft. Dix, he took advanced training at Ft. Lewis, Wash., and Ft. Benning, Ga. Last April, Pfc. Mickens was assigned to Vietnam and became a member of the 101st Airborne Division.

"He was a good soldier and took the problems of war in stride," his father said. "He really did not want to go to Vietnam, but when the word came through, he went cheerfully."

While at Montclair State, Mickens was a member of the Kappa Sigma Chi fraternity. He was also a member of the choir at Grace Episcopal Church, Newark.

Pfc. Mickens leaves two sisters, Linda Gail, and Shirley Jean, both at home.

The funeral was from the S. W. Brown and Son funeral home, Nutley. Mass was offered in Grace Episcopal Church in Newark. The Wall: Panel 09W - Row 119

Sources: The Belleville Times The Belleville Telegram, The Wall-USA.com

Paul V. Nelson

PAUL V NELSON
05 SEP 48 - 31 MAY 69

(June 17, 1969) – Corporal Paul Vincent Nelson, 20, of Williams Street, was killed in action on May 31, in Quang Ngai, South Vietnam, according to the Army.

Nelson joined the Army last June and had been in Vietnam for the last six months. His tour of duty started Dec. 8.

Born in Newark, he had lived in East Orange 13 years before moving to Belleville two years ago.

Nelson, who was born Sept. 5, 1948, was a 1967 graduate of East Orange High School, where he won a varsity letter on the school bowling team. He leaves two brothers, Edward Jr., with whom he lived, and Lawrence of Circleville, Ohio.

Paul Nelson Awarded Silver Star

Corp. Paul V. Nelson was awarded the Silver Star "for gallantry in action against an armed hostile force in the Republic of Vietnam."

PFC. Nelson "distinguished himself by intrepid actions," on May 31, 1969, while serving as a radio telephone operator with Company B, 1st Battalion, 52nd Infantry.

On that date, the company was on a search and clear mission near Landing Zone Stinson when the point element came under intense enemy fire.

Observing one of his comrades fall seriously wounded, Private Nelson, disregarding the danger involved, braved the enemy fire to assist in evacuating the wounded soldier.

Returning to the area of contact, Private Nelson remained exposed to locate the enemy position. Despite the hostile barrage impacting all around him, Private Nelson located the insurgents' position and then directed gunship fire on the enemy targets.

At this point, Private Nelson was mortally wounded from the hostile fire. His timely and courageous actions were responsible for saving the life of his comrade and the defeat of the enemy force.

Private Nelson's personal heroism, professional competence, and devotion to duty were in keeping with the highest traditions of military service, and reflected great credit upon himself, the Americal Division, and the United States Army.

According to Buddy R. Sadler, Cpl. Nelson was assigned to Bravo Company 1st Battalion 52nd Infantry of the 198th Light Infantry Brigade of the Americal Division.

Sadler reports that the Daily Staff Journals of the 1st Battalion 52nd Infantry for May 31, 1969, listed the incident in which Cpl. Nelson was killed as taking place at 10:15 a.m. when Bravo Company received small arms fire. Leon Edward Barnard and Cpl. Paul Vincent Nelson KHA (Killed, hostile action). Two others were wounded. The company was pinned down until final dust-off (helicopter) at 1:05 p.m. All casualties were taken to the 27th Surgical Unit at Chu Lai.

Glendale Cemetery, Laurel section: Cpl. Paul Vincent Nelson, Co. B. 5th Infantry, 198th Lt. Inf., Sept. 5, 1948 - May 31, 1969.

The Wall: Panel 23W - Row 029

Sources: The Belleville Telegram, The Wall-USA.com; Buddy R. Sadler

Donald B. Saunders

(March 14, 1968) – "Since he had to leave this world, I'm glad he left it the way he did, with courage and fighting for his country."

There was little else for William D. Saunders of High Street, Belleville, to say. He is the father of Pfc. Donald Baron Saunders who was killed in action in Vietnam recently.

Saunders, 20, died of wounds on his head and body from enemy mortar fire in Quang Tri last week. His tour of duty began July 26, 1967. He was killed March 4, 1968. Saunders enlisted in the Marines two years ago on Sept. 28. It was a day that William Saunders will never forget as it was the elder Saunders' birthday. Donald completed his basic training at Parris Island, S.C., and advanced infantry training at Camp Lejeune, N.C. He volunteered for duty in Vietnam.

When asked why, Mrs. Maisie Saunders, his mother, said, "Donald was never too talkative. He made his own decisions. I think he felt the boys were doing a good job and he should back them up."

"It was just a job that had to be done, for him," added Saunders, and he never complained. In all his letters there was never a word of complaint. He tried to reassure us, in fact."

Mrs. Saunders states that Donald did mention in one letter that he did not know whether it was the last letter or not, and that they were surrounded by the enemy.

According to his mother, the difficulties of the people of Vietnam particularly affected him. He wrote home about the villagers who had to scramble for food and were so starved that they were eating garbage.

Donald did manage to telephone home just two weeks ago at 3 a.m. to talk to his parents. This is how Mrs. Saunders remembers the call:

"We were surprised and so happy to hear his voice. The first thing he said was 'don't talk about anything military, Mom.' There was so much confusion because of the relay through Hawaii that we could not say very much. I said something and then had to wait for it to be relayed.

"He did say though 'What's happening, Mom' which was his favorite expression. It was so good to hear that. I only wish we could have talked much longer, it was over so quickly, so very quickly."

Pfc. Saunders served in the First Battalion of the 13th Marines.

Saunders attended Belleville High School. He was a member of the cross-country team that won the Big Ten Conference Championship in 1965. He was a member of Little Zion U AME Church, Belleville.

Of the military conditions in Vietnam, Saunders never said a great deal, according to his family.

"Of course," Mrs. Saunders said, "he sometimes wrote that he gave candy and food to the Vietnamese children. The only thing he really asked for was undershirts. It seems that you could not purchase them over there because of the climate."

"When he enlisted," the senior Saunders adds, "we hoped for the best, we did not want anything to happen. But we knew he was on a machine gun and the first thought of any enemy is to knock the machine gun out.

"At least he wasn't like those doves or slobs, who try to find any excuse to get out of going. That's the one thing I remember, he never, even after he was in combat, said he was sorry or complained."

Pfc. Saunders leaves besides his parents, a brother Kenneth, and a sister, Miss Kathleen, both at home. The funeral will be from the William V. Irvine and Son Memorial Home.

Craig W. Tourte of Khe Sanh Veterans writes:

The mention of Quang Tri as the site of his death is like naming a county or state, as Quang Tri is both a city and providence. More important is that Donald was killed during the horrific and deadly 77 day Siege of the United State Marine Corps Combat Base of Khe Sanh - which was sited in our Presidents inaugural address - while he was assisting other Marines in fortifying their bunkers from an incoming attack of artillery, rockets and mortar fire. I just wanted to make that fact clear as it personalizes his death a little more. I knew Donald at Khe Sanh and talked to him just before he was killed. One little additional point I wanted to make, and that was that Donald did this while unselfishly exposing himself to the intense incoming fire of the enemy - a fact one does not always hear from the government.

The Wall: Panel 42E - Row 071

Source: The Belleville Times, The Wall-USA.com

PFC Donald Saunders Way Memorializes Sacrifice of Marine, Family

The following is adapted from a brief talk by Anthony Buccino at the street sign memorial dedication at Van Houten Place and High Street, Belleville, N.J., on Saturday, September 19, 2015.

In 2006, seven streets at Essex Park were renamed to honor veterans and four of the Belleville heroes who died while in service. Streets were named for a soldier killed in Vietnam, Raymond De Luca, and soldiers killed in Worldl War II, Carmine Olivo, Clatie Cunningham Jr. and William Hamilton.

In February 2015, the Belleville Township Council approved a resolution to dedicate High Street in honor of former Belleville resident Donald Baron Saunders, who was killed in action on March 4, 1968 while serving in the US Marines in the Vietnam War. Council members Kevin Kennedy and Vincent Cozzarelli are here today. Thank you for undertaking this effort to honor on the streets where they lived all 159 Belleville sons who died while in service.

Pfc. Donald Baron Saunders was the fifth of eleven young Belleville men who died in the Vietnam War.

Behind you, the Belleville Middle School was the high school where most of these men learned the value of life and community. They walked the halls, sat in those classrooms, played music in the auditorium, danced in the gym and marched to Clearman Field to play football.

My wife retired last year after teaching English for 38 years at Belleville Middle School, which was formerly Belleville High School. Through the years I spoke to several eighth grade classes in a full auditorium. I told half of the students in the auditorium to stand and told them that about that many young men from Belleville died in service to their country. After my talk, I read the street names where the soldiers lived. One student came up to me afterwards and said I announced his street name three times. I said, that's because three men from your street died in service.

For her last few years in the building, my wife, Mrs. Dawn Buccino, and her Social Studies partner did a Belleville Sons project with their 8th graders. She assigned one of the 11 men killed in Vietnam to each student. Then the student would research that man, and make a poster honoring our Belleville Sons.

Her goal was to not only inform the students of the toll the Vietnam took on our little town, but to also help them understand the sacrifices of these young men, who were students right in her building back when it was BHS. The students quickly made those personal connections and would soon begin referring to the man they were honoring as "my guy".

My wife was quick to point out the house where Donald Saunders lived (since you could see it from her classroom window) and the students would "pay their respects" every time they went out to High Street for a fire drill. The posters the students created were amazing - each one was touching and helped to be sure that Belleville students Never Forget!

Thanks to Mike Lamberti in *The Belleville Times*, who wrote on the 45th anniversary of Saunders's death. The mini biography under Donald Saunders' photo in his Belleville High School yearbook read:

Donald plans to become president. Watching television occupies much of his time. He admires Peter Snell, Olympic gold medal winner.

Lamberti wrote: A short but concise description of a Belleville original who was a fantastic athlete. *A 1967 graduate of Belleville High, Donald would go on to join the Marine Corps after graduation. Less than a year later, he lost his life in Vietnam, on March 4, 1968. He had turned 20 years old a little over two weeks earlier....*

Saunders was remembered by friends on the 45th anniversary as a humble young man who had a smile as wide as his athletic talents. He also held one of the most prestigious athletic records at Belleville High.

Donald broke the school record in the half mile in '67 with a time of 2:00.08. His record stood for 11 years. In addition to being a tremendous track runner, Saunders was also on the 1965 Belleville cross country team, which won the Big 10 championship.

Donald Saunders is not forgotten by the men he served with. Craig W. Tourte, a veteran of Khe Sanh Veterans writes: "...I just wanted you to know that March 4th is the date Donald B. Saunders was Killed In Action while defending the Marine Corps Combat Base of Khe Sanh in what was then the country of South Vietnam.

"I thought it important that you know I continue to mourn his loss and remember what a fine brave Marine his was.

"We who survived that horrific siege are all some of them have left who remember their sacrifice."

"The mention of Quang Tri as the site of his death is like naming a county or state, as Quang Tri is both a city and providence. More important is that Donald was killed during the horrific and deadly 77 day Siege of the United State Marine Corps Combat Base of Khe Sanh -- while he was assisting other Marines in fortifying their bunkers from an incoming attack of artillery, rockets and mortar fire.

"I just wanted to make that fact clear as it personalizes his death a little more. I knew Donald at Khe Sanh and talked to him just before he was killed. One little additional point I wanted to make, and that was that Donald did this while unselfishly exposing himself to the intense incoming fire of the enemy - a fact one does not always hear from the government."

We need to remember the sacrifice Donald Saunders' family made. It surfaces in *The Belleville Times* article on March 14, 1968, at the report of his death, Pfc. Saunders left his parents William and Maisie, a brother Kenneth, 16 at the time, and a sister, Kathleen, both at home, 27-29 High Street.

We are here today to honor Pfc. Donald Saunders, a young man from this town, Belleville, from this street, High Street, from that green house a few doors away, who answered his country's call in a difficult time.

Pfc. Saunders volunteered to go to South Vietnam with the Marines. He was killed in action while unselfishly exposing himself to the intense incoming fire of the enemy.

He loved his family. He loved his hometown. He loved his fellow Marines. He loved his country.

Here, today, we post this marker, this memorial to one of Belleville's best, Belleville's bravest.

We salute you, Pfc. Donald Baron Saunders. We will not forget you or the 158 other Belleville sons who paid for our freedom with your lives. Semper fi.

POW Martin S. Frank Returned Safely

1967-1973

On July 12, 1967, Sgt. Cordine McMurray, then Sgt. Martin S. Frank, SP4 James L. Van Bendegom; SP4 James F. Schiele, SP4 Nathan B. Henry, SP4 Stanley A. Newell, and SP4 Richard R. Perricone were riflemen assigned to a search and destroy patrol operating in the Ia Drang Valley, Pleiku Province, South Vietnam.

The area in which the patrol was operating was covered in jungle with scattered grass covered clearings approximately 4 miles east of the South Vietnamese/Cambodian border, 6 miles south of QL19, the primary east/west road in this region, 10 miles south-southwest of Duc Co and 68 miles from the tri-border region where South Vietnam, Laos and Cambodia meet.

In the early morning hours, the company came in contact with a VC force of unknown size. In the ensuing battle, several members were wounded, including Sgt. McMurray, SP4 Van Bendegom and SP4 Schiele.

In the case of James Schiele, other members of the patrol saw him hit several times in the legs and chest by automatic weapons fire. The medic treated their wounds before moving on to treat others.

Shortly thereafter the American position was overrun. As some members of the patrol successfully evaded, the VC captured Sgt. McMurray, Sgt. Frank, SP4 Van Bendegom, SP4 Henry, SP4 Newell and SP4 Perricone. They also captured SP4 Schiele who reportedly died of his wounds just before or shortly after capture.

James Van Bendegom and Cordine McMurray were taken to the V211 Front Field Hospital where their wounds were treated.

A week later, Sgt. McMurray joined the other four Americans in the B-3 Front Camp. He reported to the others that when he last saw James Van Bendegom before leaving the field hospital, SP4 Van Bendegom was alive.

While still being incarcerated in the B-3 camp, the camp commander told the others captured with SP4 Schiele and SP4 Van Bendegom that "James Van Bendegom died about two weeks after entering the hospital" and "James Schiele was buried near the battlefield."

The V211 Hospital and B-3 Front POW Camp compound were described in the following manner: The camp and hospital were a complex of buildings in several separate locations, all within close proximity of each other inside the territorial boundary of Cambodia.

The camp's graveyard was associated with the hospital. The hospital itself was located just inside the treeline on the north side of the Tonle San River and the Stoeng Ta Pok tributary bordered the hospital on the east side of it.

Sgt. McMurray, Sgt. Frank, SP4 Henry, SP4 Newell and SP4 Perricone were moved to a POW camp they called "Camp 101," which was located just inside Cambodia in the tri-border area due west of the city of Kontum, South Vietnam.

Two other POWs, PFC Joe L. Delong and WO1 David W. Sooter who were captured in the same general area months earlier, were eventually moved to a larger compound, Named "Camp102," located nearby that could house additional captives.

In November 6, 1967, Stanley Newell, Cordine McMurray, Richard Perricone, David Sooter and Joe Delong attempted to escape from Camp 101 when PFC Delong clubbed a guard and took his rifle way from him.

The POWs moved through to jungle in an east to southeasterly direction. Several hours after they escaped, other prisoners heard shots in the distance. Within a short period of time, all but Joe Delong were captured and returned to the prison camp.

On November 8, VC officers showed the prisoners clothing that was positively identified as belonging to Joe Delong. The VC told them that he was dead and if they tried to escape again, they would end up the same way. The pants had several bullet holes in them and were covered in blood.

The other prisoners were never shown a body, and while some believed the officers' report that Joe Delong died while escaping, others did not. The men who escaped with Joe Delong believed he only got 2 to 3 kilometers away from the camp before the VC guards caught up with him.

For Americans captured in South Vietnam, daily life could be brutally difficult. Some of these camps were actually way stations the VC used for a variety of reasons. Others were regular POW camps. Regardless of size and primary function, conditions in the VC run camps frequently included the prisoners' being tied at night to their bamboo bunks anchored by rope to a post in their small bamboo shelters.

In others, they were held in bamboo cages, commonly referred to as tiger cages, and in yet other camps the dense jungle itself provided the bars to their cage.

There was rarely enough food and water to sustain them, and as a result, the Americans suffered from a wide variety of illnesses in addition to their injuries and wounds.

Likewise, the primitive lifestyle imposed on these men by their guards was particularly barbaric. Prisoners were reduced to animals, relying on the basic instinct of survival as their guide.

After months in this psychological conditioning, many prisoners lucky enough to survive the early adjustment period of captivity, discovered that they were considerably better treated if they became docile prisoners who did not resist their captors.

In November 1969, the surviving POWs were moved north up the Ho Chi Minh Trail by foot to North Vietnam. The two groups arrived in Hanoi in April 1970.

In 1970 a VC rallier said he interrogated two Americans in the V211 Field Hospital, one of whom was black and the other was white. The black soldier has been identified as Cordine McMurray and James Van Bendegom was identified as the white American.

The rallier said he heard the white American died in the hospital. He also heard that a third American who was captured at the same time who "committed suicide shortly after he was captured and was buried near the battlefield."

US intelligence personnel correlated that hearsay information to James Schiele and included a copy of the report in his casualty file.

Cordine McMurray, Nathan Henry, Stanley Newell, Martin Frank, Richard Perricone and David Sooter returned to US control on 5 March 1973 during Operation Homecoming. The six returnees provided their debriefers with detailed information about their capture, incarceration and missing comrades.

Source: Task Force Omega, Inc.; http://www.taskforceomegainc.org/f033.html

NOTE: Thomas VanHouten who died Jan. 23, 1967, of Nutley was listed in earlier editions as his brother lived in Belleville.

Peacetime Casualties

Charles Marsh

(July 31, 1958) – A military funeral was held on Monday for Staff Sgt. Charles A. Marsh, 45, of Belleville, a former Nutley resident, who died July 23 of injuries suffered two days earlier in a highway accident in Burlington, Vermont.

Sgt. Marsh was attached to the Ethan Allen Air Force Base in Burlington.

An Air Force veteran with 16 year's service, Sgt. Marsh suffered a fractured skull and multiple injuries when the car in which he was a passenger plunged off the road in South Burlington.

Sgt. Marsh was born in Nutley and attended Nutley schools. He entered the service from Nutley in March 1942. He was a flight engineer and his service included duty in the Burma - China - India theater in World War II, and the Korean War.

Sgt. Marsh held the Air Medal with oak leaf cluster, the Korean Service Medal and a Silver Medallion from the Costa Rica Minister of Health for his part in rushing medical supplies to the country during a yellow fever epidemic.

Sgt. Marsh was a member of the Veterans of Foreign Wars and the American Legion.

He leaves his mother, now of Belleville, and his two sisters, Mrs. Howard L. Montgomery of Edgar Place, and Mrs. Archibald M. Stone of Chestnut Street.

Source: The Belleville Times; Brian Lindner, Burlington Free Press; Mary Ann Fitton.

Lt. Edward J. Zuczek

(October 23, 1958) –Hope has grown dim in the search for a Navy photo reconnaissance plane which went down Saturday with four men, among whom was Nutley-born Lt. (jg) Edward Joseph Zuczek of Gless Avenue.

The plane went down at sea off Guam. Four surface vessels and 15 airplanes have continued the search which began Saturday night after radio direction finders picked up signals on a frequency used by emergency equipment carried by the plane.

The hunt was hampered at times by stormy weather. A Navy spokesman said he doubted that a life raft that was glimpsed through rain squalls Sunday with possibly three men aboard would ever be seen again.

The lost plane was an AJ5P en route from Guam to Manila.

Zuczek, 22, enlisted in the Navy in 1954 and took his flight training at Pensacola Naval Air Training Station in Florida. He was a pilot in a heavy photographic squadron.

Sixteen years ago he moved from Nutley to Belleville with his family. He has two brothers, Benjamin and Theodore. His father is employed at Federal Telephone & Radio Corp. in Clifton.

Nutley, New Jersey-born Edward J. Zuczek enlisted in the U.S. Navy in the summer of 1955, one year after graduating high school.

He was selected very shortly thereafter for the rare opportunity of attending Aviation Officer Candidate School in Pensacola, Fla., without holding a college degree. Edward Zuczek was commissioned as an ensign in 1956 and earned his Naval Pilot Wings in 1957. Zuczek was assigned to Aviation Photographic Squadron (VAP-61) at Naval Air Station, Agana, Guam. Ed was serving as navigator aboard Navy AJ-2P Photo Reconnaissance Plane 9194 on a routine flight from NAS, Cubi Point, Philippines to NAS Agana, on Oct. 18, 1958.

After taking off at 8:45 a.m., local time, all was normal until 2:20 p.m. when 9194 lost power in its left engine. Combined with a strong headwind, fuel ran short forcing the crew to ditch the plane at 5:41 p.m. about 140 miles northwest of Guam.

In one of the most extensive search and rescue efforts in the Navy's history, from Oct. 18 to Oct. 24, the only sign of the plane crew was the right wing tip tank. Being that this tank was undamaged the most logical theory is that the ditching was unsuccessful and when the plane broke up, the tank was released due to a broken wing.

An eight-day search involving 217 aircraft flights and 10 ships covered 192,000 square miles of ocean. It was virtually impossible for them not to spot swimmers since a life raft would have been much easier to spot than the recovered tank. On Oct. 25, the search was terminated and the crew was listed as presumed dead. The lost crew of four included: Lt. Leroy E. Souders, pilot; Lt. j.g. Edward Zuczek, navigator; Robert D. McDuffie AD1, plane captain; and Clarence E. Luster, PHAAN, photographic technician.

Sources: The Belleville Times, The Nutley Sun; Clifford E. Fanning, Commander. U.S. Navy; Angelo Scalo; Steve Rogers.

Donald S. Murray

CW3 Donald Murray Apr 1996

Chief Warrant Officer Donald S. Murray, 37, was killed in a mid-air helicopter crash on April 14, 1996, during live Hellfire Missile drill.

A 14-year veteran, paratrooper Murray grew up on Moore Place in Belleville and attended Holy Family School.

Murray was born on April 26, 1958, in Montclair, N.J., and died as a result of injuries sustained in a helicopter accident at McGregor Range Complex near Fort Bliss, Texas.

Murray enlisted in 1982 and was stationed at Camp Humphreys, Korea as a UH-1 Crewchief. Following Initial Entry Rotary Wing Training at Fort Rucker, Alabama, CW3 Murray was appointed as a Warrant Officer One in November 1987.

Murray was initially assigned to the 3rd Squadron, 17th Cavalry at Fort Drum, NY in March 1988 as an OH-58 pilot. In May 1990, following the AH-1 qualification course, CW3 Murray was assigned to B Company, 4th Battalion, 501st Aviation Brigade in Camp Page, Korea as an AH-1 pilot.

In July 1990, he was reassigned to C Company, 4th Battalion, 501st Aviation Brigade where he eventually served as an OH-58 Instructor Pilot.

In June 1993, CW3 Murray was assigned to B Company, 1st Battalion, 82nd Aviation Brigade where he continued to perform duties as an OH-58 Instructor Pilot. In March 1995, he was certified as an Instructor Pilot in the OH-58D and served in that capacity until present.

Murray earned a Bachelor of Science degree in Agriculture and Forestry from the University of Maine and a Master of Arts degree in Aerospace Management from Embry-Riddle Aeronautical University.

Murray's awards include the Meritorious Service Medal, the Army Commendation Medal with three Oak Leaf Clusters, the Overseas Service Ribbon, the Army Achievement Medal with six Oak Leaf Clusters, the Army Good Conduct Medal, the National Defense Service Medal, The Army Service Ribbon, and the Senior Army Aviator Badge.

As a youth, Murray was a member of Boy scouts - Troop 152 Nutley, where he attained Eagle Scout with 2 gold palms. He was a summer camp counselor from

1973 to 1975 at Camp Tamarack, Oakland, N.J. While attending Belleville High School, class of 1976, he was a Key Club member, senior class play, JV wrestling, freshman football. He was a Theta Chi fraternity brother.

Murray is survived by his wife Song Cha, their two children Donald and Erin, his father Donald, his mother Irene, and brothers and sisters Neal, Scott, Mary, Patricia, Suzanne and Allison.

Sources: U.S. Army memorial service booklet; Neal Murray; Albuquerque Journal, N.M., April 16, 19, 1996; Photo courtesy of Neal Murray. Memorial Plaque in the Kiowa Warrior Training Command at Ft. Rucker, Alabama.

Streets Named For Local Heroes

In mid-2006, seven street names in the new residential development at City Homes at Essex Park were renamed to honor veterans and four of the Belleville, N.J., heroes who died while in service.

Streets were named for Raymond De Luca, Carmine Olivo, Clatie Cunningham Jr. and William Hamilton.

Army Spec. 4 Raymond P. De Luca, of Meacham Street, died June 27, 1968, as a result of wounds in a firefight in Vietnam. De Luca attended Essex Catholic High School, Newark, where he graduated as an honor student in 1966. He was trained as a medic at Ft. Sam Houston, Texas, he was attached to Company C, Ninth Medical Battalion, 9th Infantry.

Sgt. Carmen Olivo, 29, of Magnolia Street, was killed when his ship was sunk in the English Channel during the invasion of Normandy, France. He is listed as killed in action on June 9, 1944.

Three Belleville sons, Sgt. Edward Henris, Staff Sgt. Arthur Burke and Sgt. Olivo were likely to have perished on the same ship as all three served in 3422nd Ordnance Automotive Maintenance Company. The families were notified in July, November and December 1944, respectively.

Staff Sergeant Clatie Ray Cunningham Jr., was killed in action on a mission over the Mekong River in French Indo-China, or Vietnam, on July 23, 1945. Cunningham Jr., 23, was survived by his wife Alice Sylvia, of Stephens Street, Belleville, and twin sons Clatie III and John W, born June 5, 1945, in Glen Ridge, N.J., whom he never saw.

Sgt. William Hamilton was killed in action in Germany on April 2, 1945. He served with the 7th Army.

Hamilton grew up in Newark but lived on Arthur Street for years before he entered the service in 1942.

Belleville Sons Honor Roll co-editor Anthony Buccino, a classmate of council members Lou Pallante and Steve Rovell, had suggested to Pallante that the housing development across from where the two grew up on Carpenter Street be named for the town's fallen soldiers. Buccino submitted a list and the mayor and council took the project from there.

Former Belleville Mayor Gerald DiGori, former Councilman Pallante and former Township Manager Mauro G. Tucci worked with Centex, the developer of the site on Franklin Avenue near the former Essex County Isolation Hospital.

The street name changes, which also include Memorial Drive, Hero Way and Freedom Lane, went into effect in 2006.

Names Added to Memorial

To The Memory Of Those Who Served

Lest We Forget

Veterans Council dedicated the Union Avenue memorial which now bears the names of more than 150 Belleville sons who died in service to our country.

The memorial bearing the newly engraved names of all the Belleville Sons who lost their lives for our freedom in World War I, World War II, Korea and Vietnam.

The engraving of the more than 50-year-old monument was sponsored by American Legion - AMVETS - Disabled American Veterans - VFW, and a grant from the Township of Belleville.

Belleville Boy Scout G. Daniel Lukowiak renovated the areas around the monuments, polished the old brass plates and continues to care for the grounds.

Let the people of Belleville forget none of the 20 sons who died in WWI, the 117 who died in WWII, the 4 who died in Korea, the 12 who died in Vietnam, or those Belleville Sons who died in service during peace time.

Previously, the names of the fallen were painted on a wooden billboard alongside the monument which read: TO THE MEMORY OF THOSE WHO SERVED - LEST WE FORGET

This improvement was made after Joe Fornarotto, adjutant of the Disabled Veterans Chapter 22, approached the Belleville Township Council about remodeling the area.

Fornarotto initially proposed that the veterans committee would do all of the fund-raising but the council agreed to pay for this.

Engraving the names costs $5,000. "It is a small price for something that is so great," said Belleville Councilman John Notari.

"These are our local veterans and I really believe we should honor our veterans," Notari told The Belleville Post.

Sources: Joseph Fornarotto, Worrall Community Newspapers, Leslie Scott, Belleville Post.

American Revolution Roll Call

NAMES OF SOLDIERS, SERVICES,
MILITARY REFERENCES

John Bayley – Private, Essex Militia, Stryker, p 502, Shaw p 33

Dutch Reformed Church, Belleville, N.J., family records in Church Register

Henry Brown – Private, Essex Militia, Stryker p 521, Shaw p 33

Isaac Brown – Private, Essex Militia, Stryker p 521, Shaw p 33

John Brown – Private, Essex Militia, Stryker p 521, Shaw p 33, family records in Church Register

Henry Cadmus – Private, Essex Militia, Stryker p 528, Shaw p33

Died 1809, age 58. Family records in Church Register. Grave stone still standing in churchyard, also one to his wife, Letty Keene

Isaac Cadmus – Private, Essex Militia, Stryker p 528, Shaw p33, family records in Church Register

John P. Cadmus – Private, Essex Militia, Stryker p 528, Shaw p33, family records in Church Register; "Daughters of the American Revolution" Numbers 15617-164701. Buried in churchyard. Verified by his granddaughter, Mrs. Sarah Cox King - living (1927); some of the Cadmus plots were covered by the chapel.

John H. Cadmus - Family traditions verified by his great-granddaughter, Mrs. Harriet Cadmus Wilde.

Peter Cadmus - "Minute Man", also Essex Militia, Stryker p 528, Shaw p 33; Family records in Church Register. DAR numbers 164701-156117, 180000-208995-77220; Gravestone in churchyard. Removed from plot, over which the chapel stands by Henry L. Cadmus of East Orange, N.J.

Lt. Col. Thomas Cadmus - Lt. Col., Essex Militia, Stryker p 358, family records in Church Register; an original deed is still in possession of the church dated 1795 when land was given to the church by Col. Thomas Cadmus and his wife Pietershe Cadmus

James Campbell – Private, Essex Militia, Stryker p 528, Shaw p 33, family records in Church Register

Minard Curen - Private in Capt. Squire's Co., Essex Militia, Stryker, Shaw p 34, Family records in Church Register

Amos Dodd – Captain, Essex Militia, Commissioned May 28, 1777, Shaw p 32, Family records in Church Register

Thomas Doremus – Private, Capt. Scudder's Co. 2nd Essex Militia, Shaw, p 34, family records in Church Register

Anthony Francisco – Private, Essex Militia, Stryker p 528, Shaw p 34, family records in Church Register

John Francisco – Private, Essex Militia, Stryker p 528, Shaw p 34, family records in Church Register

Jacob Freeland – Private, Essex Militia, Stryker p 528, Shaw p 34, family records in Church Register; Died July 5, 1816, age 60; gravestone in Dutch Reformed Church yard

John Garland – Private, Capt. Van Blarcum's Co. 2nd Reg. Also State Troops, family records in Church Register. Stryker, p 602, Shaw p 34

Garrabrant Garrabrants – Private, Capt. Speer's Co. 2nd Reg. Essex Militia; Metross Artillery, Continental Army; Stryker p 603, Shaw p 34, family records in Church Register

John Gilliland – Private, Capt. Craig's Co., State Troops, Shaw p 34, family records in Church Register

John Harrison – Private, Essex Militia, Stryker p 528, Shaw p34, family records in Church Register

James Hornblower – Private, Essex Militia, Stryker p 528, Shaw p34, family records in Church Register; gravestone standing in 1847; age 77

Josiah Hornblower

James Jacobus – Private, Capt. Joralemon's Co. 2nd Reg. Essex Militia, State Troops; Stryker p 643; Family records in Church Register

John Jacobus – Private, Essex Militia, Stryker p 528, Shaw p35

Henry Jacobus – Private, in Capt. Speer's Co of State Troops; Stryker p 643; Shaw p 35; Family records in Church Register

Richard Jacobus – Private, Essex Militia, Stryker p 528, Shaw p33, family records in Church Register

Henry Joralemon - Captain 2nd Reg. Stryker p 336; Shaw p 32, family records in Church Register

Helmich Joralemon – Private, Essex Militia; also is Capt. Kidney's Exploit; Stryker p 644; Family records in Church Register

James Joralemon - Lt. Captain 2nd Reg. Essex Militia. Wounded near Springfield, N.J. June ?, 1780. Stryker p 296, Shaw 32; Family records in Church

Register; "Bloomfield Old and New"; stone still standing, 1927, Died 1809, age 60 years.

John Kidney – Captain, Essex Militia. Hero of Capt. Kidney's Exploit; "Bloomfield Old and New"; Stryker p 397, Shaw p 32

Abram King – Private, Essex Militia; also Capt. Van Blarcum's State Troop, Stryker p 654, Shaw p35; Family records in Church Register

Aurey King – Private, Capt. Henry Speer's Co., 2nd Reg. Essex Militia; Shaw p 35; Family records in Church Register

John King – Private, Essex Militia, Stryker p 528, Shaw p 33, family records in Church Register; died 1816, age 72 years

William King – Private, Essex Militia, Stryker p 655, Shaw p 35, family records in Church Register

Isaac Kingsland – Private, Essex Militia, Capt. Speer's Co. 2nd Reg.; Stryker p 655, Shaw p 35; Family records in Church Register

John Kingsland - Private in Capt. Henry's Co. 2nd Reg. Essex Militia; Stryker P 655, Shaw p 35; Family records in Church Register

John Luker – Private, Essex Militia, Stryker p 528, Shaw p33; Spelled "Luke" in Church Register.

Joseph Miller – Private, 1st Batt. 2nd Essex Militia, Stryker p 251, Family records in Church Register

William Nixon- Private, Essex Militia Capt. Craig's Co. State Troops; "Nexon" family records in Church Register; Stryker p 704

John Peer – Ensign, Capt. Cornelius Speer's Co., 2nd Reg. Essex Militia, Commissioned May 25, 1777, Church Register, Shaw p 32.

Jacob Pier – Private, Capt. Lyon's Co. 2nd Reg. Essex Militia; Baptism record states he was son of Johannis. Stryker p 719, Shaw p 36.

Jacob Riker – Private, Essex Militia, Stryker p 734, Shaw p 36, family records in Church Register

Daniel Rutan – Private, Essex Militia, Stryker p 742, Shaw p 3, family records in Church Register

Thomas Seigler – Captain, 2nd Reg. Essex Militia, Stryker p 408, Shaw 32; Family records in Church Register

Abraham Speer – Captain, 2nd Reg. Essex Militia; Stryker p 411, Shaw p 32; Family records in Church Register

Cornelius Speer – Captain, 2nd Reg. Essex Militia, Stryker p 411 - Shaw p 32; Family records in Church Register, also State Troops

Henry Speer – Captain, 2nd Reg. Essex Militia; Stryker p 411 Shaw p 32; Family records in Church Register

Francis Speer – Private, Essex Militia, Stryker p 764, Shaw p 35, Family records in Church Register

Lt. Herman Speer – Private, Essex "Light Horse"; Stryker P 764, Shaw P 32; Lieutenant in Artillery and Militia

James Speer – Private, 1st Reg. Essex Militia; Stryker p 289, family records in Church Register

John Speer – Private, 1st Reg. Essex Militia; Lt. Capt. Craig's Co; Stryker p 289; Family records in Church Register; DAR numbers 117039-3242

John Spier – Private, Essex Militia, Stryker p 528, Shaw p33, family records in Church Register

John Spier Jr. – Lieutenant, Essex Militia; Stryker P 764, Shaw p 36; Family records in Church Register

Christian Stimets - Private in Continental Army, Stryker, p 769; Shaw p 36; Family records in Church Register

Daniel Teurs (Tours) - State Troops, Continental Army, Stryker, p 791, Shaw p 36; Family records in Church Register

Thomas Van Riper – Private, 2nd Essex, Also Capt. Craig's Co., Shaw p 31, family records in Church Register

Simeon Van Winkle – Private, Capt. Joralemon's Co., 2nd Reg. Essex Militia, Shaw p 37; Family records in Church Register

Michael Vreeland - Private in Continental Army, Shaw p 37, family records in Church Register

Ezekial Wade - "Captain" on stone in church-yard, family buried there. Died 1817, age 77.

Samuel Ward – Private, "Spencer's Regiment", Stryker p 314 Shaw p 37, family records in Church Register

John Winne – Private, "Spencer's Regiment", Stryker p 314, family records in Church Register

A LIST OF MEN OF TRENTON AND VICINITY WHO SERVED IN THE WAR OF THE AMERICAN REVOLUTION

(1) - New Jersey Official Register - Stryker

(2) - Newspaper Extracts

(3) - The Battles of Trenton and Princeton - Stryker

(4) - Monographs of the Revolution - Stryker

(5) - History of the Presbyterian Church - Hall

(6) - History of Burlington & Mercer Counties - Woodward

(7) - The Mechanics Bank - Dr. Godfrey

(8) - Burial Records - Mrs. Murray

(9) - Nelson's Biographical Encyclopedia

(10) - History of Trenton - Raum

(11) - Historical Collections - Barber & Howe

Mabel W. Howell

Historian - The General David Forman Chapter, Soldiers and Heroes of the War of the American Revolution, from the Dutch Reformed Church - Belleville, New Jersey, (formerly Second River).

REFERENCES

Jersey-men in the Revolutionary War - William Stryker

History of Essex and Hudson Counties - William H. Shaw

Proceedings of the New Jersey Historical Society - Vol. I 3rd Series

New Jersey Archives Marriage Records from 1665-1800, 1st Series, Vol.22

Bloomfield Old and New - Joseph F. Folsom

Church-Yard Records - taken in 1847-1901 & in 1926-27

Manuscript Copies of 1847-1901 Church-Yard records in possession of New Jersey Historical Society, Room 16, West Park St. Newark, N.J.

Family Traditions

Daughters of the American Revolution National Numbers.

– Compiled by Grace Louise Ward (Mrs. Henry C.)

ALPHABETICAL BY WAR

American Revolution Soldiers

John Bayley
Henry Brown
Isaac Brown
John Brown
Henry Cadmus
Isaac Cadmus
John P. Cadmus
John H. Cadmus
Peter Cadmus
Lt. Col. Thomas Cadmus
James Campbell
Minard Curen
Capt. Amos Dodd
Thomas Doremus
Anthony Francisco
John Francisco
Jacob Freeland
John Garland
Garrabrant Garrabrants
John Gilliland
John Harrison
James Hornblower
Josiah Hornblower
James Jacobus
John Jacobus
Henry Jacobus
Richard Jacobus
Capt. Henry Joralemon

Helmich Joralemon
Lt. Capt. James Joralemon
Capt. John Kidney
Abram King
Aurey King
William King
John King
Isaac Kingsland
John Kingsland
John Luker
Joseph Miller
William Nixon
Ensign John Peer
Jacob Pier
Jacob Riker
Daniel Rutan
Capt. Robert Rutgers
Capt. Gerard Rutgers
Capt. Thomas Seigler
Capt. Abraham Speer
Capt. Cornelius Speer
Capt. Henry Speer
Francis Speer
Lt. Herman Speer
James Speer
John Speer
John Spier
Lt. John Spier Jr.
Christian Stimets
Daniel Teurs
Col. Van Courtland

Thomas Van Riper
Simeon Van Winkle
Michael Vreeland
Capt. Ezekial Wade
Samuel Ward
John Winne
Civil War
Captain Henry Benson
John J. Rogers (Rodgers)
Thomas Stevens

World War I
William C. Bain Jr. – 55 Dewitt Ave.
Harry B. Blekicki
Carmine Corviccio
Edward J. Crowell – 19 Factory St.
Gregory M. Davey
George Eyre
Michael A. Flynn – 11 Washington St.
Harry M. Garside
Henry C. Hoag
George J. Kalvio – 10 Oak St.
Edward J. Kane
Charles McGinty
Thomas J. Mooney – 3 Cedar Hill Ave.
Charles E. Morgan – 492 Joralemon St.
Michael J. Murray
Charles A. Schaffer – 10 Smith Street
George S. Smith – 34 Isaac St.
William T. Smith – 41 Harrison St.
Fred W. Stockham

George A. Younginger – 44 Wilson Place

World War II

Eugene Adams – 18 May St.
Ernest H. Alden Jr. – 58 Prospect St.
Peter Andrusyn
Joseph Antonik – Ralph St.
Walter Antonik – 133 Ralph St.
Patrick Barbone – 16 Eugene Place
Joseph Bengivengo
Giavanni Bocchino – Lake St.
Charles Braun
Alvin Brown
John Brown – 262 Hornblower Ave.
Victor Bruegman – 101 Malone Ave.
Arthur Burke – 577 Washington Ave.
Joseph Burlazzi – 16 Mt. Pleasant Ave.
Morris C. Catalano – 14 Belleville Ave.
Kenneth Chewey – 178 Malone Ave.
Joseph J. Cifrodella – 16 Magnolia St. / 282 No. Belmont Ave.
Clatie Cunningham Jr. – Stephens St.
Joseph J. Curran
John J. Daly Jr.
Edward DiCarlo
John Del Grosso – Cleveland St.
Nicholas Del Grosso – 56 Mt. Prospect St.
Herman M. Doell – 169 Linden Ave.
George Fredericks – Montgomery St.
Harry Fredericks Jr. – 33 Montgomery Place
William Fredericks – 33 Montgomery Place
Michael Froehlich – 369 DeWitt Ave.

Gerald J. Fuselle – 138 Belmont Ave.

William Gaydos – 189 Cortlandt St.

Angelo Guarino – 19 Carmer Ave.

Stanley Guzik – 64 Cortlandt St.

William Hamilton – 15 Arthur St.

Donald Hartley – 51 Mertz Ave.

Richard Hayes – 176 Washington Ave.

Edward Henris – 306 Washington Ave.

Patrick J. Hoey – 18 Prospect St.

William Hourigan – 97 Tiona Ave.

Louis Jannarone – 225 Passaic Ave.

John Johnson – 66 Greylock Parkway

William B. Jones

Warren Jordan – Belleville Ave.

John Kant Jr. – DeWitt Ave.

John Kirwin – 90 Forest St.

Joseph Klimchock – 34 Clinton St.

Thomas Lamb – 511 Union Ave.

Joseph M. LaPenta – 68 Eugene Place

Albert H. Lariviere – 92 Tappan Ave.

Ralph E. Ledogar – 17 Floyd St.

Arthur Leithauser – 659 Belleville Ave.

Emil M. Liloia

Benjamin Lucas – 30 Newark Place

Arthur H. Lundgren – 50 Smith St.

George Malizia Jr. –107 Conover Ave.

John Marshall – 80 Ralph St.

Joseph Masi – 54 Lake St.

Ronald Mc Cormack – Overlook Ave.

Joseph Mc Dermott

Francis C. Mc Enery – 34 Fairway Ave.

Edgar H. Mc Ginty – 50 New St.

Hector Mc Neill – 42 Cedar Hill Ave.

William J. Mears – 21 Jefferson St.

Roger J. Mellion – 70 Overlook Ave.

Frank H. Metzler – 10 Reservoir Place

John Miller Jr. – 18 Elmwood Ave.

Emanuel J. Montalbano

Mario Morano/Maorano – 102 Dow St.

Stevano Julio Mosco – Honiss St.

Glenn Nelson – 511 Washington Ave.

Anthony Noto – 40 Frederick St.

Vincent Nucci – 62 Cedar Hill Ave.

Walter Nusbaum – 589 Union Ave.

Harry W. Nyegaard – 329 Main St.

Carmine Olivo – 44 Magnolia St.

Emil Ostrowski – 540 Union Ave.

Stephen Rocalo Otozky

John Paterno – 15 King St.

Angelo Patrizio – 13 Watchung Ave.

Thomas A. Peacock – 20 Harrison St.

Frank Pepitone

Albert E. Pole – 380 Washington Ave.

Wilfred Potis – 64 Hornblower Ave.

Frank Rankin – 18 Hornblower Ave.

Joseph A. Razes – 133 Brighton Ave.

Wallace Reed – 25 Van Houten Place

Stanley Reynolds – 207 Malone Ave.

Joseph Rizzo – Frederick St.

John F. Rogers – 150 Birchwood Drive

Frank J. Rosania

Edmund Sadlock –25 Adelaide St.

William Salmon – 36 DeWitt Ave.

Harry Salz

Theodore Sanok – 16 Montgomery St.

George Schemm – 45 Division Ave.

Salvatore Sena – Heckel St.

George Skeen – 75 Van Houten Ave.

John J. Smith – 115 New St.

Robert A. Stecker – 76 Beech St.

Gerald Strigari

Joseph C. Taibi – 67 Frederick St.

Robert C. Taylor – 15 Bremond St.

Robert S. Taylor – 209 Joralemon St.

William Thetford Jr. – 180 Linden Ave.

Gus Vaccaro – 172 Holmes St.

John Verian – 128 Washington Ave.

John Volinski – 29 Ralph St.

Louis J. Wagner – 385 Stephens St.

Harry Ward Jr. – 70 DeWitt Ave.

John N. Waters

James T. White – 75 Holmes St.

Lee O. White – 235 Ralph St.

William R. White – 63 Holmes St.

Leonard R. Willette – 137 Stephens St.

Edward P. Wood – 55 Berkeley Ave.

Fred R. Wyckoff – 481 Union Ave.

Joseph Zecca – 197 Fairway Ave.

Korean War

Robert G. Bliss

Rene Flory Jr. – 40 Center St.

John R. Gorman

Brendan Hyland - 129 Chestnut St.

Vietnam War

Alfred Barnes – 53 Ralph St.

William A. Branch

Frank A. Cancelliere – 23 Florence Ave.; Sanford Ave.

Roger B. Crowell – 100 Tiona Ave.

Helder A. C. DaSilva

Raymond DeLuca – 30 Meacham St.

Jerry R. Donatiello –14 Frederick St.

John M. Hoar – 80 Cleveland St.

Carl L. Mickens – 61 Wilber St.

Paul V. Nelson – 132 Williams St.

Donald B. Saunders – 127-129 High St.

Peacetime

Charles A. Marsh

Donald P. Murray, Moore Place

Edward J. Zuczek, Gless Avenue

CHRONOLOGY

1862
Thomas Stephens, June 27.
Henry Benson, August 11.
1865
John Rogers (Rodgers), April 8.
1941
Stanley Reynolds, May 3.
1942
John Volinski, March 28.
Harry Fredericks, May 19.
Arthur Lundgren, September.
Louis Wagner, Oct. 2.
1943
Stephen R. Otozky, Feb. 2.
John Paterno, February.
Joseph Burlazzi, March.
Joseph Taibi, April.
Mario Morano, May.
Charles R. Braun, June 5.
Michael Froehlich, June 11.
Gerald Fuselle, July 10.
Harry Salz, July 25.
Donald Hartley, Aug. 18.
Fred R. Wyckoff died in August.
Thomas Peacock, Sept. 11.
William White, Sept. 11.
William Gaydos, Oct. 9.
Vincent F. Nucci, Oct. 21.
John Del Grosso, Nov. 8.
Joseph Klimchock, Dec. 2.
1944
Francis C. Mc Enery, Jan. 4.
Edward P. Wood, Jan. 10.
Joseph LaPenta, Jan. 21.
John Rogers MIA February.
Robert S. Taylor KIA February.
Nicholas Del Grosso, Feb. 20.
Salvatore Sena, April 8.
Morris Catalano, May 14.
William B. Jones, May 27.
Ralph Ledogar, May 30.
Hector Mc Neill, June 1.
Patrick J. Barbone, June 2.
Joseph Razes, June 2.
Herman M. Doell, June 6.
Albert Lariviere, June 6.
Carmen Olivo, June 6.
Lee White, June 8.
Arthur Burke, June 9.
Edward R. Henris, June 9.
Ronald McCormack, June 9.
Harry Nyegaard, June 19.
Emil Ostrowski, in June.
Steveno Mosco, July 27.
Victor R. Bruegman, July 2.
John J. Daly, July 4.
Angelo Guarino, July 18.
Wallace Reed, Aug. 6.

Albert E. Pole, Aug. 7
Gerald Strigari, Aug. 10.
Robert Stecker, Aug. 15.
James T. White, Aug. 16.
Robert C. Taylor, Aug. 20.
John Kirwin, Sept. 5.
Glen C. Nelson, Sept. 12.
William Mears, Sept. 15.
John Verian, Sept. 18.
William Salmon, Sept. 23.
George Skeen, Oct. 19.
Giavanni Bocchino, Oct. 25.
Joseph A. Masi, Oct. 25.
Joseph Zecca, Oct. 29.
Louis Jannarone, Oct. 31.
Arthur Leithauser, Nov. 2.
Joseph Cifrodella, Nov. 4.
William Hourigan, Nov. 5.
Harry Ward Jr., Dec. 12.
Patrick J. Hoey, Dec. 14.
John J. Miller Jr., in 1944.
William Deighan, Dec. 30.

1945

Walter Antonik, Jan. 3.
John J. Smith, Jan. 5.
Roger J. Mellion, Jan. 13.
Edmund Sadlock, Feb. 19.
Peter Andrusyn, Feb. 26.
Gus F. Vaccaro, Feb. 26.
Emil M. Liloia, March 1.
John McDermott, March 1.

Frank Rankin, March 6.
Warren C. Jordan, March 7.
Theodore Sanok
William Hamilton, April 2.
Alvin C. Brown, April 6.
George Malizia, April 7.
William Thetford, April 20.
Walter Nusbaum, April 25.
Wilfred Potis, April 26.
Richard T. Hayes, April 27.
Gilmer Adams, April 28.
Anthony Noto, April 28.
Angelo Patrizio, May 16
John Brown, May 28.
Joseph Bengivengo died in May.
Stanley Guzik died in May.
Edward DiCarlo, June 26.
John Marshall, July 8.
Kenneth Chewey, July 23.
Clatie Cunningham, July 23.
John Johnson, Aug. 4.
Frank Metzler, Sept. 10.
Leonard Willette, Sept. 22.
Benjamin Lucas, Sept. 28.
Ernest Alden, in November.
Edgar H. Mc Ginty, Dec. 15.
Thomas Lamb died in 1945.

1946

John Waters, Feb. 13.
Joseph Curran, March 1.
Joseph Antonik

George R. Fredericks
Emanual J. Montalbano
Frank Pepitone
Joseph Rizzo
1950
Brendan Hyland, July 20.
1951
John R. Gorman, April 1951
Rene Flory Jr., June 9, 1951
1952
Henry Svehla
1953
Robert Bliss, Feb. 4.
1958
Charles A. Marsh, July.
Edward J. Zuczek, October.
1966

Helder DaSilva, Feb. 7.
John Hoar, Feb. 13.
1967
Jerry Donatiello, Nov. 20.
1968
Roger Crowell, Jan. 31.
Donald Saunders, March 4.
Raymond DeLuca, June 27.
1969
Frank Cancelliere died March 15.
Alfred Barnes, May 12.
Paul Nelson, May 31.
1970
William Branch, June 6.
Carl Mickens, July 4
1996
Donald P. Murray, April 14.

ACKNOWLEDGEMENTS

Angelo Buccino, Dawn Buccino. Harry and Nancy Vincenti. Russell Roemmele

Gary Peter Formica, the soldier named above the street sign, Bloomfield

George Sbarra, Angela Immersi, Mildred Miele, Mary Tritto

Thanks to all the writers who first penned these profiles.

Kathleen M. Hivish, publisher, The Belleville Times, The Nutley Sun

Belleville Public Library: Joan Taub, director; Reference desk: Fred Lewis and Cindy LaRue;, Nutley Public Library: JoAnne Tropiano, Director; Senior Reference Librarian Kiran Patel; and reference librarians Deborah D'Ambrosio and Jeanne Sylvester; The Belleville Historical Society. The Nutley Historical Society. Newark Public Library, Charles F. Cummings, Andy Andriola, Mary Ann Fitton; Brian Lindner, Clatie Cunningham III, Ed Stecewicz, Joseph T. Fornarotto, Lee & Alice W. White, Norman Price, Michael Perrone, Thomas Francisco, Jean Lupo, Kenneth J. Potis; Peter Strumolo; John Esposito; Russell Baker, Linda Peaver; Steve DeVries; Jack Kane, Lucille and Rodger Gustafson; Peter and Donna Gustafson, Salvatore and Sharon Buttaci; Dr. Manny Alfano; Kevin Kennedy.

American Battle Monuments Commission, National Archives and Records Administration; National D-Day Museum, New Orleans

Newspapers

The Belleville Post, Worrall Community Newspapers

The Belleville Times; The Nutley Sun, Nutley, N.J.

The Belleville Telegram

The Newark News, Newark, N.J.

-Newark Evening News Index to New Jersey Servicemen 1941-1945; 1950-1953

-The Newark Evening News 1883-1972. Microfilm.

-The Newark Evening News Indexes, 1914-1972.

The Star-Ledger, Newark, N.J.

Books

Ambrose, Stephen E. http://www.stephenambrose.com/

-Americans At War, Berkley Books, New York 1998

-Band of Brothers, Touchstone, New York, 1992

-Comrades, Simon & Schuster, New York, 1999

-Citizen Soldiers, Touchstone, New York, 1997

-D-Day June 6, 1944: The Climactic Battle of World War II, Touchstone, Simon & Schuster, New York 1994

-Pegasus Bridge Touchstone, New York, 1985

-The Victors, Eisenhower And His Boys: The Men of World War II Touchstone, New York, 1998

-The Wild Blue Simon & Schuster, New York, 2001

-To America, Personal Reflections of an Historian Simon & Schuster, New York, 2002

-Undaunted Courage, Meriwether Lewis, Thomas Jefferson, and the Opening of the American West Simon & Schuster Paperbacks, New York, 1996

Baker, Russell, Growing Up

Belmonte, Peter Louis Italian Americans in World War II (Voices of America) Arcadia, Chicago, 2001

Binns, Stewart & Wood, Adrian America At War In Color Carlton, London, 2001

Boyington, Gregory "Pappy" Baa Baa Black Sheep, Bantam Books, New York, 1977

Bradley, James Flyboys, A true story of courage Back Bay Books, Little, Brown & Co. New York 2003

Brady, James

- The Marines of Autumn, a novel of the Korean War Thomas Dunne Books, New York, 2000

- The Coldest War, A Memoir of Korea Thomas Dunne Books, New York, 1990

Buccino, Anthony and Andrea, Nutley Sons Honor Roll – remembering the men who paid for our freedom Cherry Blossom Press, 2004

Buccino, Anthony, Belleville and Nutley in the Civil War – a brief history, 2011

Burnett, Robert B., and the Belleville 150th-Anniversary Committee Belleville, Belleville: 150th-Anniversary Historical Highlights 1839-1989 Belleville, New Jersey. 1991

Canfora, Nicole T. Images of America – Belleville, Arcadia, Charleston, S.C., 2002

Caruso, Patrick F. Nightmare on Iwo Naval Institute Press, Annapolis, Md., 2001

Christman, Calvin L. Lost in the Victory Reflections of American War Orphans of World War II, North Texas Press, 1998

Collier, Peter; Del Calzo, Nick Medal of Honor, Portraits of Valor Beyond the Call of Duty Congressional Medal of Honor Foundations 2003, 2006

Collins, Max Allan

-Saving Private Ryan, Based on the screenplay by Robert Rodat, Signet, NY 1998

-Windtalkers Based on a screenplay by Joe Rice and Joe Batteer, Harper Entertainment, New York, 2001

Cox, Hank H. Lincoln and the Sioux Uprising of 1862 Cumberland House Publishing, Nashville, Tenn. 2005

Davis, Burke The Civil War Strange & Fascinating Facts Wings Books, New York, 1960

Di Ionno, Mark A Guide to New Jersey's Revolutionary War Trail for Families and History Buffs Rutgers University Press 2006

DiStasi, Lawrence Una Storia Segreta, The Secret History of Italian-American Evacuation and Internment during World War II Heyday Books, Berkeley, Calif., 2001

Enyedy, Patricia Farawell A Redcatcher's Letters from Nam, Reflections of Family and Friends 1st Books Library 2002

Fecarotta, Diana F. and Eichler Thomas J. Khe Sanh Veterans The Khe Sanh Veterans Book of Poetry 2005

Flagel, Thomas R. The History Buff's Guide to World War II Cumberland House, Nashville, Tenn. 2005

Fletcher, Charles J. Quest for Survival Glenbridge Publishing Ltd., Aurora, Colo. 2002

Goldstein, Donald M.; Dillon, Katherine V.; Wenger, J. Michael The Story and the Photographs D-Day Normandy Brassey's, Herndon Va., 1999

Greene, Bob Duty: A Father, His Son, and the Man Who Won the War Perennial, 2001

Hackworth, Col. David H. Steel My Soldiers' Hearts Rugged Land, New York, 2002

Hagedorn, Jane There'll Come A Day Xlibris Corp., 2001

Hammel, Eric Chosin: Heroic Ordeal of the Korean War Presidio Press, 1990

Haydu, Bernice "Bee" Falk Letters Home 1944-1945 Topline Printing 2003

Holden, Henry M. Women in Aviation, Leaders and Role Models for the 21st Century Black Hawk Publishing 2001

Irwin, John P. Another River, Another Town, Random House Trade Paperbacks, New York, 2002

Jones, James The Thin Red Line Delta Trade Paperbacks, Dell Publishing, New York, 1998

Kagan, Norman The War Film, Pyramid Illustrated History of the Movies Pyramid Communications, New York, 1974

Kindre, Tom The Boys From New Jersey, Trafford, 2004

Kornbluth, Jane and Sunshine, Linda, editors "Now You Know" Reactions after seeing Saving Private Ryan Newmarket Press 1999

Kotlowitz, Robert Before Their Time, Anchor Books, New York, 1998

Lamb, Richard WAR IN ITALY 1943-1945 A Brutal Story Da Capo Press, 1994

Leckie, Robert March To Glory, ibooks, New York, 1960, 2001

Mailer, Norman The Naked and the Dead Picador USA 1948, 1998

Mauldin, Bill Bill Mauldin's Army Presidio, Novato, Calif., 1995

Marshall, S.L.A. Pork Chop Hill, The American Fighting Man In Action, Korea, Spring, 1953 Berkley Books, 2000

Mays, Jeffery C. Belleville renews Korea vet memorial The Star Ledger, Nov. 11, 1999

McCrary, Lacy Armed Guard Veterans Finally Get Their Thanks The Philadelphia Enquirer, July 8, 1998

Miller, Lee G. An Ernie Pyle Album Indiana to Ie Shima William Sloane Associates, New York, 1946

Moore, Lt. Gen. Harold G. We Were Soldiers Once ...And Young Harper Torch, New York, 2002

Munn, David C. Battles and Skirmishes of the American Revolution in New Jersey New Jersey Geological Survey, 1976
http://www.nj.gov/dep/njgs/enviroed/oldpubs/battles.pdf

Nichols, David, editor ERNIE'S AMERICA The Best of Ernie Pyle's 1930s Travel Dispatches Random House, 1989

O'Brien, Tim The Things They Carried Penguin, New York, 1990

O'Donnell, Patrick K. Into the Rising Sun, The Free Press, Simon & Shuster, 2002

Offley, Ed Pen & Sword, A Journalist's Guide To Covering the Military, Marion Street Press, 2001

O'Nan, Stewart The Vietnam Reader Anchor Books, Doubleday, New York, 1998

Palmer, Laura Shrapnel in the Heart, Letters and Remembrances from the Vietnam Veterans Memorial Vintage Books, Random House, 1987

Paolicelli, Paul Dances With Luigi, A Grandson's Search for His Italian Roots Thomas Dunn Books, St. Martin's Griffin, New York, 2000

Penrose, Jane The D-DAY COMPANION Osprey Publishing, Oxford, England 2004

Perrone, Stephen M. World War II B-24 'Snoopers' Low Level Anti-Shipping Radar Night Bombers in the Pacific Theater NJSG Books, Somerdale, N.J., 2003

Proser, Jim with Cutter, Jerry "I'm Staying With My Boys..." The Heroic Life of Sgt. John Basilone, USMC Lightbearer Communications, 2004

Pyle, Ernie

-Brave Men Aeonian Press Mattituck, N.Y., republished 1978

-Here is Your War Ayer, North Stratford, N.H., Reprint edition 1998

-Typewriter Soldier Carter, Horace W., and Faircloth Rudy; Atlantic Publishing Co. Tabor City, N.C., 1982

Ray, John The Illustrated History of WWII Weidenfield & Nicolson, The Orion Publishing Group, Orion House, London 2003

Rooney, Andy My War Public Affairs, New York, 2003

Russ, Martin

-Breakout The Chosin Reservoir Campaign, Korea 1950 Penguin Books, New York, 1999

-The Last Parallel A Marine's War Journal Fromm International, New York, 1990

Ryan, Cornelius The Longest Day Touchstone, New York, 1994

Sears, Stephen W. The Battle of the Bulge, ibooks, Simon & Schuster, 1969

Sides, Hampton Ghost Soldiers, Anchor Books, New York, 2001

Simmons, Thomas E. Forgotten Heroes of World War II – Personal Accounts of Ordinary Soldiers Cumberland House Nashville House, 2002

State of New Jersey: World War II Honor List of Dead and Missing, State of New Jersey, War Dept. June 1946

Stavinsky, Samuel E. Marine Combat Correspondent, World War II in the Pacific Ivy Books, Ballantine Publishing Group, Random House, New York 1999

Steinman, Louise The Souvenir Plume, New York, 2002

Talese, Gay Unto The Sons Ivy Books, New York, 1992

Taylor, James C., Civil War Diary of James C. Taylor, Belleville, 1925

Tobin, James Ernie Pyle's War – America's Eyewitness to World War II University of Kansas Press, Lawrence, Kan., 1997

Terkel, Studs "The Good War" an oral history of World War II, The New Press, New York, 1984

Tregaskis, Richard Guadalcanal Diary The Modern Library, 1943

Turner, Brian Here, Bullet Alice James Books, Farmington, Maine 2005

Viglino, Camillo; Viglino Victor Memoirs of Lt. Camillo Viglino: Italian Air Force 1915-1916 Trafford, 2001

The World Almanac and Book of Facts for 1921, 1956, and 1963. Publisher: New York World-Telegram and Sun.

Wright, Mike What They Didn't Teach You About World War II, Ballantine Books, New York, 1998

Libraries

Belleville Public Library

Camden County Library, Jennifer Whelan

Newark Public Library New Jersey Information Center

Nutley Public Library

South Brunswick Public Library

Other Sources

Air Force Historical Research Agency www.au.af.mil/au/afhra

Allan Jackson, Esso Tanker http://members.tripod.com/esso4/id59.htm

American Battle Monuments Commission www.abmc.gov

American Civil War http://americancivilwar.com/statepic/va/va021.html

American Forces In Action book series www.army.mil/cmh-pg/collections/AFIA.htm

American Legion www.legion.org

American Visionaries Tuskegee Airmen, http://www.nps.gov/history/museum/exhibits/tuskegee/airoverview.htm

Amvets www.amvets.org

Army Specialized Training Program www.astpww2.org

B-17 Combat Crewmen and Wingmen www.b-17combatcrewmen.org/linkpage.htm

B-17 Combat Crewmen.org www.b-17combatcrewmen.org

Belleville-Nutley DAV Chapter 22, Joseph T. Fornarotto

Civil War 1861-1865
www.njstatelib.org/cyberdesk/DIGIDOX/Digidox20.htm

The Chosin Few http://home.hawaii.rr.com/chosin/Main.html

CSP Navy www.csp.navy.mil/othboats/593.htm

Department of Defense – MIAs
www.dtic.mil/dpmo/pmsea/files_full.htm#usaf

The Drop Zone www.thedropzone.org/

Ehistory http://www.ehistory.com/wwii/books/bulge2/0239.cfm

Final Crossing of the Leopoldville, Battle of the Bulge: December 24, 1944, Disaster for the 66th Infantry Division
http://members.aol.com/troopship/leopoldv.htm

First World War.com www.firstworldwar.com/index.htm

Fitzgerald's Legislative Manual for the State of New Jersey, 1923, pg. 239, Nutley Population, 1920, QandANJ.org www.qandanj.org

Fleet Submarine

45th Division, 157th Infantry Regiment
http://www.45thdivision.org/157thCombat.htm

Hazardous Duty Nuclear Submarine Accidents
www.naval.ca/article/young/nuclearsubmarineaccidents_bymichaelyoung.html

Homecoming II Project, March 15, 1991; POW Network 1998

Marine Heritage Foundation www.marineheritage.org

Marne salient www.spartacus.schoolnet.co.uk/FWWmarne2.htm

Maritime Organization Subs Lost

NARA US National Archives & Records Administrator
www.archives.gov/index.html

National D-Day Museum www.ddaymuseum.org

National Museum of the Marine Corps http://www.usmcmuseum.org

National Park Service Tuskegee Airmen, http://www.nps.gov/tuai/

New Jersey Almanac 1964-1965 (QandANJ.org)

New Jersey Historical Society www.jerseyhistory.org

New Jersey Korean War Memorial www.state.nj.us/military/korea/main.html

New Jerseyans who served (Korea) www.state.nj.us/military/korea/serve.html

New Jersey State Library www.njstatelib.org/

New Jersey Dept. of State Div. of Archives & Records Management: World War I Casualties: Descriptive Cards and Photographs.

New Jersey State Library Cyberdesk www.njstatelib.org/cyberdesk

New Jersey Vietnam Veterans' Memorial

The New York Times

No-Quarter www.no-quarter.org

Nutley Historical Society

Official Register of the Officers and Men of New Jersey in the Revolutionary War www.njstatelib.org/cyberdesk/DIGIDOX/Jerseymen.htm

QandANJ.org

Rutgers University Oral History http://fas-history.rutgers.edu/oralhistory/memorial.htm

Saving Private Ryan online encyclopedia www.sproe.com

Ships Sunk or Damaged – January to June 1942 www.usmm.org/sunk42a.html

Subnet Memorial http://www.subnet.com/memorial/mf294.htm

Third Marine Aircraft Wing http://www.3maw.usmc.mil/

U.S. Army Air Forces
- 91st Bomb Group http://www.91stbombgroup.com/323rdground.html
- 91st Bomb Group 323rd Ground Crew

- 94th Infantry Division http://www.94thinfdiv.com/94th376stCasualtyH-K.html

- 846th Bomber Squadron, 490th Bomber Group, Large http://www.us8thaaf.com/history.htm

- History of the 490th Bomber Group

U. S. Army Total Personnel Command

U. S. Korean War Memorial www.nps.gov/kwvm

U. S. Marine Corps www.usmc.mil

U. S. Maritime Service Veterans; www.USMM.org

U.S. Merchant Marines

–Armed Guards; U.S. Merchant Marines - Armed Guards

–Casualties – Listing; U.S. Merchant Marine Casualties - Listing

–Casualties During WWII; U.S. Merchant Marine Casualties during World War II

–U.S. Merchant Marines – Ships Sunk 1942; U.S. Merchant Marines Ships Sunk 1942

U.S. Navy WW2 Boats Escolar

The Vietnam War Memorial Wall http://thewall-usa.com

Veterans Council, Nutley

Veterans of Foreign Wars, Nutley

Virtual Wall www.virtualwall.org

World War II Honor List of Dead and Missing, State of N.J., War Dept. June 1946

World War II National Monument http://www.wwiimemorial.com/

World War II Orphans Network www.awon.org

World War II U.S. Veterans Web site ww2.vet.org

Links are subject to change without notice.

About the Editors

Anthony Buccino

New Jersey author Anthony Buccino published eighteen books including five essay collections, three military history books and seven full-length poetry collections. He has been published in New Jersey Monthly, The Wall Street Journal, the Passaic Herald News and other publications.

The Belleville Sons project is serious writing about a serious subject. He was struck by the movie Saving Private Ryan, and later by the personal account of veteran Anthony "Andy" Andriola of Nutley – since recounted in Nutley Sons.

At that point the Belleville native realized he knew nothing of the men behind the names on the plaques. Buccino and his daughter Andrea began researching the lives behind the names on the memorial plaques for the Belleville Sons commemorative project.

Born 10 years after D-Day, Mr. Buccino grew up on Gless Avenue, across the street from the Zuczek family, and down the hill from the cousin he never knew, Raymond DeLuca on Meacham Street.

Buccino attended Holy Family School in Nutley, School 10 in Belleville and both the junior and high schools in Belleville. He attended Montclair State College where he majored in English and minored in journalism.

In 1990 he edited The Belleville Times. In the mid-90s, he was managing editor at Worrall Community Newspapers, Bloomfield. Buccino also worked on national, state and regional trade magazine publications and business news.

Visit AnthonyBuccino.com

Andrea Buccino, DC

Dr. Buccino is a Certified Chiropractic Sports Physician. She graduated Magna Cum Laude from the University of Bridgeport College of Chiropractic in 2007. She received the 2007 Clinic Service Award. She received her Bachelor of Science degree with a major in biology from the University of Bridgeport in 2003, where she was class president. As part of her clinical training, she worked at the Veterans Administration Hospitals in New Haven and Newington, Conn., and interned at three private practices. She currently is an adjunct professor at William Paterson University where she teaches Anatomy and Physiology. Dr. Buccino and has a private practice in Cedar Grove, N.J.

Visit DrAndreaBuccino.com

Next of Kin?

Need More Information?

Individual Deceased Personnel Files are held by the U.S. National Archives and Records Administrator for every service man or women who lost their life during WWII. The IDPFs are at the National Archives but can only be accessed by U.S. Army personnel. Civilians are barred from viewing any of these files until they are screened under the FOIA. The IDPFs contain all known information about the death of a service man or women.

For information, contact:

US ARMY TOTAL PERSONNEL COMMAND

200 STOVALL ST RM 7N50

ALEXANDRIA VA 22332-0404

Phone: 703-325-5300

Fax: 703-325-5315

http://www.archives.gov/veterans/

Please share your results with us at

A Buccino – Belleville Sons

PO Box 110252

Nutley NJ 07110

Made in the USA
Middletown, DE
16 January 2016